Good Practice in the Law and Safeguarding Adults

Good Practice in Health, Social Care and Criminal Justice Series
Edited by Jacki Pritchard

This series explores topics of current concern to professionals working in social care, health care and the probation service. Contributors are drawn from a wide variety of settings, both in the voluntary and statutory sectors.

also in the series

Good Practice in Assessing Risk
Current Knowledge, Issues and Approaches
Edited by Hazel Kemshall and Bernadette Wilkinson
ISBN 978 1 84905 059 3

Good Practice in Safeguarding Children
Working Effectively in Child Protection
Edited by Liz Hughes and Hilary Owen
ISBN 978 1 84310 945 7

Good Practice in Safeguarding Adults
Working Effectively in Adult Protection
Edited by Jacki Pritchard
ISBN 978 1 84310 699 9

Good Practice in Brain Injury Case Management
Edited by Jackie Parker
ISBN 978 1 84310 315 8

Good Practice in Adult Mental Health
Edited by Tony Ryan and Jacki Pritchard
ISBN 978 1 84310 217 5

Good Practice with Vulnerable Adults
Edited by Jacki Pritchard
ISBN 978 1 85302 982 0

Good Practice in Working with Victims of Violence
Edited by Hazel Kemshall and Jacki Pritchard
ISBN 978 1 85302 768 0

Good Practice in Working with Violence
Edited by Hazel Kemshall and Jacki Pritchard
ISBN 978 1 85302 641 6

Good Practice in Health, Social
Care and Criminal Justice

GOOD PRACTICE in
the Law and
Safeguarding Adults

Criminal Justice and Adult Protection

Edited by Jacki Pritchard

Jessica Kingsley *Publishers*
London and Philadelphia

Crown copyright material is reproduced with the permission of the
Controller of HMSO and the Queen's Printer for Scotland.

First published in 2009
by Jessica Kingsley Publishers
116 Pentonville Road
London N1 9JB, UK
and
400 Market Street, Suite 400
Philadelphia, PA 19106, USA

www.jkp.com

Copyright © Jessica Kingsley Publishers 2009
Printed digitally since 2011

Library of Congress Cataloging in Publication Data
Good practice in the law and safeguarding adults : criminal justice and adult protection /
edited by Jacki Pritchard.
       p. cm.
    Includes bibliographical references and index.
    ISBN 978-1-84310-937-2 (pb : alk. paper) 1. Social workers--Legal status, laws,
etc.--England. 2. Social work with older people--Legal status, laws, etc.--England. 3. Social legis-
lation--England. I. Pritchard, Jacki.
    KD3302.G66 2009
    344.4203'288--dc22
                                                2008017379

British Library Cataloguing in Publication Data
A CIP catalogue record for this book is available from the British Library

ISBN 9781 84310 937 2

This book is dedicated to all the victims of abuse
who have been let down by the system
and are still waiting for justice

CONTENTS

INTRODUCTION

JACKI PRITCHARD

> It is not desirable to cultivate a respect for law,
> so much as a respect for right
>
> *Henry David Thoreau*

I believe I am very fortunate to have been trained as a social worker in an era when teaching on the law was an integral part of the social work training and was covered in depth. I acknowledge that workers still do receive training on some aspects of the law but it is very clear from the training I deliver myself on adult abuse that often workers' knowledge about the legal framework is sadly lacking. This was my main reason for wanting to put together a book which would provide essential information regarding the law for anyone who is working with adults and who may become involved in safeguarding issues.

In the past I have worked on child protection cases and it was absolutely essential for me to know the law relating to all aspects of child care. I feel very strongly there should be the same emphasis in adult protection work. There has been much debate over the years regarding elder and then adult abuse as to whether a criminal justice model should be followed or a welfare model. I do not see why the two models cannot be married up; following one should not automatically rule out the other. Some professionals have felt that when working with adult abuse cases it would be wrong to go down the same route as child abuse cases, that is, to use similar policies and procedures. I totally disagree with this as I believe we can all learn from mistakes which have been made during the past 30 years in child protection work but also we can learn from the good practices which have emerged.

Obviously there are differences between working with abused children and working with abused adults. We have to respect the fact that many adults will be able to make their own decisions – maybe unwise choices – but they have the right to do so. Practitioners have to be careful not to go into 'rescuing mode'. I am certainly not saying that the prime concern in working with abused adults is to secure a criminal conviction. Obviously the first objective must be to promote a person's safety and wherever possible uphold the principle of self-determination. However, it is important that an adult knows what options are available to them. Workers should never stereotype and perhaps make the assumption that an abused person is not going to want to do something about it. Many victims of abuse have no idea what options are open to them. It is also necessary to acknowledge that sometimes it can take years for a victim to decide to leave an abusive situation; this is why it is essential that we endeavour to promote long-term work with adults which offers them advice, support (maybe therapy) whilst they make their decisions. Ideally this should be done through a detailed and workable (that is realistic) protection plan.

What has come out clearly in my own research projects and current work with survivors is that very often the abused adult did want to do something about their situation but they said professionals had not asked them direct questions about the abuse or their wishes; for example whether they wanted the police involved (Pritchard 2000, 2001 and 2003). When asked in research interviews if they would want police involvement or to take some legal action the majority responded positively. A crucial finding of the project was that professionals who had been involved had rarely asked the adult's wishes regarding police involvement. Practitioners should remember that all adults who are abused have the right to justice. The introduction of *Achieving Best Evidence* (Home Office 2002; revised CJS 2007) under the *Action for Justice* implementation programme (1999 and 2002) has given us a positive and creative way forward in order to support a vulnerable witness through the criminal justice system; this guidance is discussed in detail through chapters of the book.

I totally support the premise that we should all be undertaking preventative work as promoted in the national framework of standards *Safeguarding Adults* (ADSS 2005). Nevertheless, adult abuse investigations do have to take place and therefore managers and workers across the sectors not only need to have a basic understanding of the legal framework within which they are required to function, but also to understand what constitutes a criminal offence and what options are available under civil law. All practitioners must have a sound knowledge of national and local guidance, policies and procedures related to adult protection work together with a basic understanding of the law. I find it frightening that I meet so many practitioners who do not have this fundamental knowledge and yet are undertaking abuse investigations. This is very dangerous practice indeed.

So my objective in editing this book was to put together all the essential legal information anyone working within the adult sector should have and present it in a format that can be accessed easily; that is, when a worker needs to refer to the law urgently (perhaps because of a crisis situation) they can locate it quickly using the book as an essential guide.

I personally find the law fascinating but I know many people find it 'boring'; so I was mindful of this fact when thinking about what should be in this book. Also I was clear that it had to be written in a way that is interesting and draws in the reader so they have a thirst for more legal knowledge. I feel very privileged that in my career I have had the opportunity to work with some very sound, dynamic, and committed police officers and solicitors. So it was only natural that I invited some of them to contribute. I have also been able to include chapters from other very motivated, practical and passionate people to address a wide range of law-related topics, which I think will stimulate and maintain the reader's interest.

The book is a resource which can be dipped into – when and as needed. It delivers the basic information regarding all aspects of the law – criminal and civil – for England, Wales and Scotland. Separate chapters address the key issues regarding the implementation of the *Mental Capacity Act 2005* and the use of Independent Mental Capacity Advocates (IMCAs). I felt it was also imperative to include chapters which look at the roles of particular profession-als and how they can play a part in abuse investigations but also in supporting vulnerable witnesses through the criminal justice system. I have also included a reflective chapter on practice and key issues we should be addressing in adult protection work, for example, forced marriage and honour-based violence.

The legal framework is a huge animal and I do not expect any reader to be a legal expert after reading this book. However, I do hope that this volume can provide a basic text regarding the law and adult protection work that will help workers to practise in the best way possible to safeguard adults.

REFERENCES

ADSS (Association of Directors of Social Services) (2005) *Safeguarding Adults. A National Framework of Standards for Good Practice and Outcomes in Adult Protection Work.* London: ADSS.

Criminal Justice System (2007) *Achieving Best Evidence in Criminal Proceedings: Guidance on Interviewing Victims and Witnesses, and Using Special Measures.* London: Home Office and Criminal Justice System.

Home Office (1999 and 2002) *Action for Justice.* London: Home Office Communication Directorate.

Home Office (2002) *Achieving Best Evidence in Criminal Proceedings: Guidance for Vulnerable or Intimidated Witnesses including Children.* London: Home Office Communication Directorate.

Pritchard, J. (2000) *The Needs of Older Women: Services for Victims of Elder Abuse and Other Abuse.* Bristol: The Policy Press.

Pritchard, J. (2001) *Male Victims of Elder Abuse: Their Experiences and Needs.* London: Jessica Kingsley Publishers.

Pritchard, J. (2003) *Support Groups for Older People Who Have Been Abused: Beyond Existing.* London: Jessica Kingsley Publishers.

CHAPTER 1

A REVIEW OF RELEVANT LEGISLATION IN ADULT PROTECTION

SIMON LESLIE AND JACKI PRITCHARD

Many practitioners feel frustrated by the fact that when dealing with adult abuse cases there is no statute equivalent to *The Children Act 1989*. However, criminal and civil law can provide remedies to protect vulnerable adults. It is important that any incident of abuse is placed within the relevant legal framework. The purpose of this chapter is to present a review of legislation[1] which is relevant to adult protection work, in a way that can be easily accessed by practitioners when they need to make reference to the law.

We believe it is imperative that anyone working with vulnerable adults should have some basic understanding of legislation; we obviously do not expect them to become legal experts. However, when following a criminal justice model it is necessary to have some knowledge about criminal offences, but in many cases of abuse it will be difficult to get enough evidence to prove a crime has been committed; nevertheless, a case conference must decide whether on the balance of probabilities abuse has occurred. It may then be possible to use common law or civil law.

HOW TO USE THIS CHAPTER

Finding the correct statute when you need it can be difficult; especially if you are not familiar with the law. Many safeguarding policies and procedures include sections on the legal framework but workers often complain that the information presented is not written in an easy or understandable way. We wanted this chapter to be written in an accessible way so that anyone needing information urgently can find it quickly. We gave a lot of thought as to how the chapter should be laid out and also we did not want to bombard the reader

---

1   This chapter will only refer to legislation in England and Wales. Scottish law is discussed in Chapter 2.

with too much information or legal jargon. Consequently, we have divided the chapter into sections. We begin by giving an overview of the different aspects of the law which can be used in adult protection work; the following sections then list the relevant statutes first by looking at key issues and then by the categories of abuse as defined in *No Secrets* (DH 2000).[2] To summarise, the sections are as follows:

Section 1: Human Rights

Section 2: Information Sharing

Section 3: Local Authority Powers and Duties in Cases of Suspected Abuse and Neglect

Section 4: Vulnerable Witnesses and Suspects

Section 5: Protection for People with Impaired Mental Capacity

Section 6: Powers to Protect People with Mental Disorder

Section 7: Protecting People from Physical Abuse

Section 8: Protecting People from Sexual Abuse

Section 9: Protecting People from Financial or Material Abuse

Section 10: Protecting People from Emotional Abuse

Section 11: Protecting People from Abuse by Neglect and Omission

Section 12: Protecting People from Discriminatory Abuse

Section 13: Protecting People from Institutional Abuse

Section 14: Recent Legislation relevant to Domestic Violence and Safeguarding Adults.

As this chapter is an overview of relevant legislation, we regularly cross-reference in footnotes to other chapters in the book which go into more detail.

A BRIEF INTRODUCTION TO SOME LEGAL ASPECTS

A useful starting point for any practitioner is to think about the different types of law which exist, but also how certain statutes can address specific problems which can arise when vulnerable adults are subjected to abuse.

2   Department of Health (2000) *No Secrets: Guidance on Developing and Implementing Multi-Agency Policies and Procedures to Protect Vulnerable Adults from Abuse*. London: DH.

Criminal law

Vulnerable adults are protected in the same way as any other person against criminal acts; thus if a person commits theft, rape or assault against a vulnerable adult they should be dealt with through the criminal justice system, in the same way as in cases involving any other victim. The Home Office guidance *Achieving Best Evidence*[3] promotes this principle and is discussed elsewhere in this book.[4]

Civil law

Civil law includes family law and property law and defines issues such as 'duty of care' and 'negligence'. Thus, for example, the Court of Protection makes arrangements for the supervision of property on behalf of people who are not deemed capable of managing their own financial affairs. Under the *Mental Capacity Act 2005* the Court of Protection can make orders determining what steps are in the best interests of someone who lacks the capacity to decide for themselves. Family law allows an individual to take out an injunction against a member of their household who is threatening their safety. Employment law is also relevant. The law of torts (legal wrongs) can apply in some situations, including negligence and nuisance.

Compensation law

This enables a private action to be taken against an individual in the civil courts for compensation, and the criminal injuries compensation scheme enables recompense for injury or damage caused by a crime of violence.

Specific laws relating to vulnerable adults

There are various statutes which acknowledge the needs of certain groups of vulnerable adults; these will be discussed in full below. For example, the *Mental Health Act 1983* (section 127) recognises that the ill-treatment or neglect of patients with a mental disorder by professional staff or unpaid carers is an offence; and the *Sexual Offences Act 2003* (sections 30–41) recognises that adults with severe learning disabilities may not able to consent to sexual acts or relationships and need special protection from exploitation, whether from paid staff in a hospital or care home or from carers (paid or unpaid) in their own home.

---

3   Home Office (2002) *Achieving Best Evidence in Criminal Proceedings: Guidance for Vulnerable or Intimidated Witnesses including Children.* London: Home Office Communication Directorate. Criminal Justice System (2007) *Achieving Best Evidence in Criminal Proceedings: Guidance on Interviewing Victims and Witnesses, and Using Special Measures.* London: Criminal Justice System.
4   See Chapters 3 and 4.

Law relating to bad practice

Bad practice by workers is a common problem in adult protection work and is covered by the *Care Standards Act 2000* and the *Care Homes Regulations 2001*[5] as well as the Codes of Conduct or Practice issued by the General Social Care Council, Nursing and Midwifery Council and other professional bodies.

Legal advice and the vulnerable adult

The local authority receives advice from its own lawyers about its powers and duties to protect vulnerable adults. In some cases it will be necessary for a vulnerable adult to obtain advice of their own. This will be important for example when the vulnerable adult may be able to apply to court for an injunction, and where allegations of abuse may lead to criminal proceedings. Independent legal advice for an individual also helps ensure that there is no conflict of interest between that individual and the authority's responsibility as commissioner or provider of services. There may also be a need to protect and assist vulnerable witnesses throughout the legal process and particularly at the investigation stage.

SECTION 1: HUMAN RIGHTS

It is important to consider the human rights both of the alleged victims of abuse and of alleged perpetrators. The key human rights to be aware of are:

- The right to respect for private and family life under Article 8 of the *European Convention on Human Rights* (ECHR). Investigating and responding to the risk of abuse will almost invariably involve or 'engage' Article 8. Interventions must be lawful, justified and proportionate given the risk.

- The right not to be subjected to torture or 'inhuman or degrading treatment' (Article 3 ECHR). Treatment is degrading if it 'humiliates or debases an individual showing a lack of respect for, or diminishing his or her human dignity or arouses feelings of fear, anguish or inferiority capable of breaking an individual's moral and physical resistance'.[6] The courts have held that local authorities are under a proactive duty to take reasonable steps to prevent ill-treatment of children or vulnerable adults which they knew about, or should have known about.[7]

- Article 6 of the Convention gives people a right to a 'fair hearing'. This includes the right to be consulted and to have one's views recorded and considered.

5   See Chapter 10.
6   *Pretty* v *UK*, European Court of Human Rights 2002.
7   *Z* v *United Kingdom*, European Court of Human Rights 2001 at para. 73.

Under the *Human Rights Act 1998* public authorities must not act incompatibly with people's human rights. This also applies to other bodies exercising public functions – though not to private care homes.[8]

Human Rights Act 1998

Article 2:   Right to life.

Article 3:   Prohibition of torture, and inhuman and degrading treatment.

Article 4:   Prohibition of slavery and forced labour.

Article 5:   Right to liberty and security.

Article 6:   Right to a fair trial.

Article 7:   No punishment without law.

Article 8:   Right to respect for one's home, private and family life.

Article 9:   Freedom of thought, conscience and religion.

Article 10:   Freedom of expression.

Article 11:   Freedom of assembly and association.

Article 12:   Right to marry.

Article 14:   Prohibition of discrimination.

Article 16:   Restrictions on political activity of aliens.

Article 17:   Prohibition of abuse of rights.

Article 18:   Limitation on use of restrictions on rights.

SECTION 2: INFORMATION SHARING

Practitioners need to be clear about when they have a power or duty to share information in the interests of safeguarding adults.[9]

---

8   *YL* v *Birmingham CC*, House of Lords 2007.
9   See Chapter 5.

Confidentiality

There is a common-law duty of confidence to keep information confidential either when the person supplying it says the information is confidential, or when it is clear from the circumstances that it should be treated as confidential (e.g. consultations between doctor and patient, and social worker and client). It is important for any worker to discuss in full with a service user what confidentiality actually means and the limitations within which the worker has to function. A worker always needs to be clear for what purpose the information is being given. It is also imperative that a service user is clear that information given to the worker belongs to the agency, not to the individual worker.

The duty of confidence is not absolute. The public interest in preserving confidences may be outweighed by a greater public interest in the information being disclosed. A professional who reasonably believes that people will be put at risk of danger if confidential information is not disclosed 'is entitled to take such steps as are reasonable in all the circumstances to communicate the grounds of [their] concern to the responsible authorities'.[10]

Data protection

Under the *Data Protection Act 1998*, all *personal data* must be recorded and shared lawfully. Personal data are any information from which an individual can be identified. Data should only be shared if:

either[11] the data subject (the person the information is about) agrees to disclosure

or there is some overriding legal reason to disclose.

Section 115 of the *Crime and Disorder Act 1998* enables anyone (but does not oblige them i.e. it is not a duty) to disclose information to a local authority, NHS (National Health Service) body or the police where disclosure is necessary to prevent or reduce crime.

GOOD PRACTICE POINTS

WHEN INFORMATION CAN BE DISCLOSED TO AVERT OR REDUCE RISK – SOME POINTERS

- Selective information-sharing can be an important element of a comprehensive adult protection plan.

- Disclose only if there is a 'pressing need', and if this is a proportionate response given the risk.

---

10   *W* v *Egdell* (Court of Appeal 1989).
11   See *Data Protection Act 1998* schedules 2 and 3.

- Give people causing concern the chance to comment on the information about them, and its proposed disclosure.

- Balance the protection of vulnerable adults against individuals' rights to a private life, and record this balancing exercise.

- Consider the role of the proposed recipient and how they are likely to respond if the information is disclosed to them.

- Disclose only if the person(s) affected have given informed consent, or there is an overriding reason to disclose without consent.

Capacity and consent

Throughout adult protection work it is important to ask whether the person has the capacity to make an informed decision themselves.[12] If they do, then that decision is for them to make. If they lack that capacity, then, under the *Mental Capacity Act 2005*, the decision needs to be made on their behalf by someone else according to their best interests.

Capacity is specific to the individual and to the decision at the time it has to be made. 'Capacity' means being able to:

- understand the information one needs in order to make a decision

- retain it while making a decision

- use and weigh it in coming to a decision and

- communicate one's decision.[13]

In particular, people should not be medically examined or interviewed without an assessment whether they have capacity to give informed consent to this.

Protecting service users from abusive carers – the Vetting and Barring Scheme

The POVA or Protection of Vulnerable Adults list[14] prevents people from working with vulnerable adults if in the past they have harmed such an adult or placed them at risk of harm.

---

12   See Chapter 6.
13   See section 3(1) *Mental Capacity Act 2005*.
14   Department of Health (2006) *Protection of Vulnerable Adults Scheme in England and Wales for Adult Placement Schemes, Domiciliary Care Agencies and Care Homes: A Practical Guide*. London: DH.

Starting in autumn 2008 the POVA scheme will gradually be replaced by the Vetting and Barring Scheme operated by the Independent Safeguarding Authority under the *Safeguarding Vulnerable Groups Act 2006*. The Vetting and Barring Scheme will in stages replace not only the POVA List, but also the POCA or Protection of Children Act List and List 99, operated by the DCSF[15] and containing the names of people unsuitable to work in teaching.

Everyone working in direct contact with children or vulnerable adults will be required to join the Vetting and Barring Scheme, which will eventually cover over ten million people. There will be two barred lists, of people unsuitable to work with children and vulnerable adults respectively.

Information about what may constitute risk will continue to be gathered and collated by the Criminal Records Bureau. Decisions to 'bar' someone will be taken by the Independent Safeguarding Authority. The authority will bar an individual if it is satisfied on all the information available that he or she presents a risk of harm to children or vulnerable adults.

Until the Vetting and Barring Scheme has been fully implemented, the POVA list will continue to operate in parallel.

SECTION 3: LOCAL AUTHORITY POWERS AND DUTIES IN CASES OF SUSPECTED ABUSE AND NEGLECT

It is important to bear in mind that all local authority work to assess and address possible risk to vulnerable adults is covered by the Department of Health guidance *No Secrets*.[16] Since *No Secrets* was issued under section 7 of the *Local Authority Social Services Act 1970*, local authority workers are expected to follow it unless there is exceptional reason not to. The following statutes are part of civil law:

National Assistance Act 1948

Section 21(1): Local authorities have a duty to provide or arrange residential accommodation, including private and voluntary, for 'people aged 18 or over who by reason of age, illness, disability or any other circumstances are in need of care and attention which is not otherwise available for them' and who are ordinarily resident in their area. Such accommodation is usually provided in a residential or nursing home.

Section 29: To promote the welfare of people with disabilities 'the local authority shall make arrangements for promoting the welfare of persons blind, deaf or dumb or who suffer from mental disorder of any description or who are substantially and permanently handicapped by illness, injury or congeni-

---

15   For further information see www.dcsf.gov.uk.
16   Department of Health (2000) *No Secrets: Guidance on Developing and Implementing Multi-Agency Policies and Procedures to Protect Vulnerable Adults from Abuse*. London: DH.

tal deformities or other disabilities'. These are mostly services provided in people's own homes.

Chronically Sick and Disabled Persons Act 1970

Sections 1 and 2: These sections place duties on the local authority to inform themselves of the number of persons to whom section 29 of the *National Assistance Act 1948* applies; and to make arrangements under that section for such persons.

Health Services and Public Health Act 1968

Section 45: This places a duty on local authorities to promote the welfare of old people in order to prevent or postpone personal or social deterioration or breakdown. Meals on Wheels and day centres are examples of services provided under this section. The approval of the Secretary of State must be sought (who can also direct the extent of the provision).

Disabled Persons (Services Consultation and Representation) Act 1986

This act entitles disabled people to a written assessment of need. It also gives people the right to have a representative present at the time of their assessment.

Care Standards Act 2000

The Act established what is now the Commission for Social Care Inspection (CSCI) and makes provision for the regulation of services. Part II of the Act covers the registration and inspection of the following adult services: independent health care; nurses agencies; domiciliary care agencies; and care homes. Note that from June 2009 the functions of the CSCI (and the Healthcare Commission) will be taken over by the new Care Quality Commission.

Public Health Act 1936

Section 83: This gives a local authority powers to enter and cleanse premises which constitute a public health risk.

Section 287: Authorised local officers have power to enter premises and inspect for possible breaches of the *Public Health Act*; no warrant is required.

NHS and Community Care Act 1990

Section 47: This act provides a framework for all assessments of vulnerable adults. It makes provision for multi-agency assessment of complex situations. The lead agency for the coordination of assessments is adult social care.

Section 48: The Secretary of State authorises persons to enter and inspect premises in which community care services are or are proposed to be provided by that local authority. The service user/resident of the premises may be interviewed in private for the purpose of investigating a complaint.

If the evidence available does not meet the criminal standard of proof, i.e. beyond all reasonable doubt, it may meet the less stringent civil standard, i.e. balance of probabilities. Compensation may be sought from the Criminal Injuries Compensation Authority (CICA)[17] or by suing in civil law for compensation.

Service users should always be advised of the right to discuss alleged mistreatment with the police and/or independent legal advisors.

In many cases the vulnerable person will not be able to give instructions to a lawyer, so before the case can proceed someone must be found to act on his/her behalf. They may have proceedings brought on their behalf by a 'litigation friend' under Part 21 of the Civil Procedure Rules.

Housing Acts 1985 and 1988

These include as grounds for the grant of a possession order on the application of the local authority/housing association the fact that a partner has left the dwelling because of violence or threats of violence by the other partner and the court is satisfied that the partner who has left is likely to return. A tenancy granted by a private landlord does not qualify.

Housing Act 1996

Section 177: This section provides that it is not reasonable for a person to continue to occupy accommodation if it is probable that this will lead to domestic violence or threats of violence from a person with whom they are associated.

Section 178: This provides that a person is associated with another if (i) they are or have been married to each other (ii) they are or have been cohabitants (iii) they live or have lived in the same household (iv) they are relatives – whether full blood, half blood or by affinity.

Housing Act 1996 Part VII

This places a duty on local authorities to provide accommodation for homeless people with a priority need, i.e. people who are vulnerable because of old age and homelessness, mental illness or disability or physical disability or other special reason. People in apparent priority need must be accommodated pending assessment and decision.

Family Law Act 1996

Section 33: Refers to the occupation of the dwelling house (occupation orders) in proceedings before the Magistrates Court, County Court or High Court. The applicant must be either a person with a legal right to occupy the house (normally because he/she is a freehold or beneficial owner or tenant), a spouse of such a person, or a former spouse whose matrimonial home rights have been extended by order of the Court. The Court may make orders to reg-

17   For further information see www.cica.gov.uk.

ulate the occupation of a dwelling house, particularly in cases where an adult (or child) has suffered – or is at risk of suffering – significant harm.

Section 42: Non-molestation orders. The class of potential applicants is wider than Section 33. An 'associated person' includes: father, mother, stepfather, stepmother, son, daughter, stepson, stepdaughter, grandfather, grandmother, grandson, granddaughter, brother, sister, uncle, aunt, niece, nephew of a person or of that person's spouse or former partner. Non-molestation injunctions are now also available to those in same sex relationships and to those who have never cohabited.

The Court is obliged to attach a power of arrest where violence has been proven, unless the Court is satisfied that the applicant will be protected without it. Where a power of arrest has not been attached, an order may still be enforced by the new procedure of the issue of a warrant for arrest.

Breach of a non-molestation order is now a criminal offence, with a maximum penalty of five years.

Declaratory relief

It is possible for a local authority to seek from the High Court a declaration that a person lacks capacity to make a particular decision; and that it is in that person's best interests for the local authority to take some action on the person's behalf or prevent a third party from taking an action.

Under sections 15 and 16 of the *Mental Capacity Act 2005* the High Court can make a declaration that someone lacks capacity to make a particular decision; and can then make orders concerning a wide range of aspects of the care of such a person, for example:

- where they should live

- their level of supervision

- arrangements for personal care

- restraint arrangements if necessary, and

- in extreme circumstances their short-term detention for their own safety if required or any emergency injunction.

SECTION 4: VULNERABLE WITNESSES AND SUSPECTS

A vulnerable adult may be required to give evidence in court as a victim or witness to a criminal offence. The *Youth Justice and Criminal Evidence Act 1999* recognises five categories of vulnerable witness. The first of these are young witnesses under the age of 17. The other four categories are:

- learning disabled witnesses

- physically disabled witnesses

- witnesses with mental disorder/illness

- witnesses suffering from fear and distress (intimidated witnesses).

A vulnerable adult may present with one or more of the above. Mental illness or disorder does not in itself preclude the giving of reliable evidence. The criminal justice system guidance *Achieving Best Evidence in Criminal Proceedings*[18] should be consulted as it contains information about the support and assistance which may be considered to help the witness to communicate and provide the best evidence. At Court Special Measures[19] may be available for the protection of eligible witnesses such as screens, evidence given by live videolink or in private, removal of wigs and gowns, examination of a witness through an intermediary, aids to communication and video-recorded evidence-in-chief. Note however that video-recorded cross-examination has not yet been implemented; section 28 of the *Youth Justice and Criminal Evidence Act* has not yet been brought into force. In addition, the witness can be protected from cross-examination by the accused in person.

Witnesses are eligible for Special Measures on one or more of the following grounds: they suffer from a mental disorder, or have a mental impairment or learning disability, that the Court considers significant enough to affect the quality of their evidence. This might cover for example, autistic spectrum disorders.

Police and Criminal Evidence Act 1984

Code C: Police have a duty to treat people with learning disabilities or mental health problems as vulnerable adults who should be supported by an 'appropriate adult' during police interviews. The role of the appropriate adult is to advise the person being interviewed, to observe whether the interview is being conducted properly and fairly and to facilitate communication with the person being interviewed.

SECTION 5: PROTECTION FOR PEOPLE WITH IMPAIRED MENTAL CAPACITY

The *Mental Capacity Act 2005* (MCA) brings together in a statute the rules about incapacity and best interests developed by the courts (under the common law) over a number of years. The key areas which are relevant to safeguarding adults work are:

- an essentially functional statutory definition of incapacity as the inability 'to make a decision for [her- or] himself in relation to the

---

18   Criminal Justice System (2007) *Achieving Best Evidence in Criminal Proceedings: Guidance on Interviewing Victims and Witnesses, and Using Special Measures.* London: CJS.

19   See Chapter 4.

matter because of an impairment of, or a disturbance in the functioning of, the mind or brain' (Section 2 of the MCA)

- the key elements of capacity to make a particular decision (see section 2 of this chapter for detail)

- selective criteria for assessing what is likely to be in the best interests of someone who lacks capacity to decide for themselves (section 4 of the MCA)

- acts which can lawfully be done in providing care and treatment to someone who is incapacitated (sections 5–8 of the MCA)

- the Court of Protection has been enlarged to include responsibilities for the care and welfare of incapacitated people as well as their property and affairs. The 'new' Court of Protection may make declarations and decisions, but may also appoint deputies to make decisions (sections 15–20 of the MCA)

- Lasting Powers of Attorney (sections 9–14 of the MCA), which can cover personal care and welfare of people who have become incapacitated as well as their property and affairs

- advocacy and the use of the Independent Mental Capacity Advocate (IMCA) Service (Sections 35–41 of the MCA) for incapacitated people facing possible serious medical treatment or a move to long-term care and who have no other relative to advocate for them[20]

- section 44 of the MCA – offence of neglect and ill-treatment of an incapacitated person (see Section 11 of this chapter for detail).

Many of these measures can be used in a positive way to improve outcomes for people with impaired capacity. However, practitioners should always be aware of the potential for abuse, including at the hands of people entrusted to look after a vulnerable person or their property and affairs.

Also, with effect from April 2009, it will be possible for people who lack capacity to decide about their care and treatment to be looked after in conditions amounting to detention in either a care home or hospital. The case of L v UK (the 'Bournewood' case, European Court of Human Rights 2004) established in effect that there are a number of incapacitated people who are being deprived of their liberty in breach of Article 5 of the European Convention on Human Rights. This so-called 'Bournewood gap' has been filled by a scheme of administrative authorisations given under the amended MCA by primary care trusts (PCTs) in relation to patients in hospitals and by local authorities in relation to people in care homes.

20   See Chapters 8 and 9.

SECTION 6: POWERS TO PROTECT PEOPLE WITH MENTAL DISORDERS

The *Mental Health Act 1983* is a complex piece of legislation and the following 'guide' should be regarded as an index. Approved Social Workers (ASWs) have detailed knowledge of this piece of legislation and should be able to advise if you feel any of these sections would be useful. ASWs are the only practitioners with the power to make applications for admission under this Act.

Mental Health Act 1983

Section 2: This provides for compulsory admission to hospital of a person with a mental disorder for assessment in the interests of the person's own health and safety or with a view to the protection of others. As amended by the *Mental Health Act 2007*, the definition of 'mental disorder' for purposes including compulsory admission takes in 'any disorder or disability of the mind'.

Section 3: Compulsory admission for treatment for up to six months in the first instance. This can be renewed.

Section 4: Emergency admission/observation. Unlike sections 2 and 3, needs only one doctor to recommend. This section lasts for up to three days.

Section 7: Guardianship. This lasts six months and can be renewed. The guardian – usually the local social services – can require access for doctors, social workers or other professionals. The person may also be required to reside at a particular place. It can require the person to attend places for purposes of medical treatment (no power to override refusal of consent to the treatment itself), occupation, education or training. As amended, the *Mental Health Act* now includes a power to convey patients under guardianship to the place where they are required to reside. The use of guardianship is intended to protect and enable a person to remain in the community.

Section 13(4): This places a duty on social services to direct an approved social worker to consider making an application under the Act if requested to do so by the nearest relative. (This duty would be relevant if, for example, the nearest relative of a mentally disordered person complains of mistreatment/abuse of that person by a third party.)

Section 115: If a mentally disordered person is not receiving proper care, this section allows the ASW entry and inspection. Entry by force is not permitted.

Section 117: This provides for after care responsibility by the local authority jointly with the health authority for persons previously detained under Section 3, persons admitted to hospital in pursuance of a Hospital Order made under Section 37 (by order of a criminal court) and persons transferred to hospital from prison. Section 117 also applies to people on leave from hospital detention under section 17 of the Act.

Section 127(1) and (2): Provide that it is an offence for any staff member of a hospital or mental nursing home to ill-treat or wilfully neglect an in- or out-patient. It is also an offence for a guardian – or other person – who has the care (paid or unpaid) of a mentally disordered person living in the community to ill-treat or wilfully neglect that person.

Section 129(1) and (2): Proceedings may be taken if a social worker acting under the *Mental Health Act* is obstructed without reasonable cause.

Section 135: After presenting the case to a magistrate, a warrant may be given which allows for the search and removal of a person to a place of safety for 72 hours. To be used in conjunction with the police (often accompanied by a doctor). Applies where someone is 'suffering from mental disorder [and] has been, or is being ill-treated, neglected or not kept under proper control or who is living alone and unable to care for [themselves]'.

Section 136: Gives the police the power to remove to a place of safety a person suffering from a mental disorder in a public place.

Independent Mental Health Advocates

The *Mental Health Act 2007* will also introduce new arrangements into the 1983 Act for providing Independent Mental Health Advocates (IMHAs) to people who are detained under the Act, or subject of guardianship or Supervised Community Treatment. The role of the IMHA will be to help the patient understand the treatment proposed for them and the legal framework, and to obtain legal representation if they wish. The IMHA will be expected to interview the patient and staff caring for them and to inspect relevant documents. Patients will be able to refuse IMHA assistance.

SECTION 7: PROTECTING PEOPLE FROM PHYSICAL ABUSE

Physical abuse may amount to offences which range from common assault through to murder depending on levels of seriousness, intent and injury. It must be remembered that even if an assault leaves no mark, scratch, bruise or worse an offence of assault has still been committed.

Offences Against the Persons Act 1861

Assault which leaves physical injury.

Section 39: (Common) assault: Any blow or other physical contact without consent can amount to an assault, as can any actual or threatened use of physical violence. Assaults which leave no visible injury, or leave only grazes, scratches, minor bruising or swelling, or even a black eye, will usually be prosecuted as common assault, though they will be treated as more serious if the victim is older, disabled or otherwise vulnerable. Assaults that leave no physical evidence are rarely prosecuted unless there are witnesses besides the alleged victim. There are separate and more serious offences if the assault leaves evidence of injury, as follows:

Section 47: Assault occasioning actual bodily harm (ABH): This is any assault which leaves a more serious physical injury. This might include extensive or multiple bruising, minor fractures and (where there is expert evidence) psychiatric injury.

Sections 18 and 20: Assault occasioning grievous bodily harm (GBH): This is an assault which leads to, for example, permanent disability, serious disfigurement, compound fractures or blood loss requiring transfusion.

If the assault – or other offence – was aggravated by hostility based on race or religion or disability, the Court will reflect this in an enhanced sentence.

The substantive offences of both murder and manslaughter are offences contrary to common law, that is, they are not under any statute.

Murder is unlawful killing with the intention of killing or causing grievous bodily harm ('really serious harm').

Manslaughter (by violence) comprises two categories: 'voluntary manslaughter' (a killing which would have been murder had the killer not been provoked or suffering from diminished responsibility) and 'involuntary manslaughter' (killing caused by an unlawful act done with the intention of causing physical harm to the victim but not intended to kill or to cause grievous bodily harm).

Criminal Law Act 1967

Section 4(1): This section makes it an offence to assist an offender. If one knows or believes someone (A) has committed an offence, it is an offence to do anything which is intended to prevent A being prosecuted or apprehended.

Section 17: This gives the police the power to search and enter premises to save life or limb or prevent serious damage to property.

Section 24: Police may arrest without warrant anyone suspected of having committed or being about to commit an arrestable offence.

Section 25: Allows the police to arrest someone to prevent them causing physical injury to another person or to protect a child or others.

Medicines Act 1968

Section 58: It is an offence to administer drugs which have been prescribed for someone else.

SECTION 8: PROTECTING PEOPLE FROM SEXUAL ABUSE

Most sexual offences committed since May 2004 will be prosecuted under the *Sexual Offences Act 2003*, though with older allegations, previous statutes, including the *Sexual Offences Act 1956* will still be relevant.

Sexual Offences Act 2003

Section 1: Rape: A person (A) commits an offence if:

(a)   he intentionally penetrates the vagina, anus or mouth of another person (B) with his penis

(b)   B does not consent to the penetration, and

(c)   A does not reasonably believe that B consents.

Section 2: Assault by penetration: A person (A) commits this offence if they intentionally penetrate the vagina or anus of another person (B) with a part of their body or anything else and

(a)   the penetration is sexual

(b)   B does not consent to the penetration, and

(c)   A does not reasonably believe that B consents.

Section 3: Sexual assault: The elements of the offence of sexual assault are:

(a)   a person (A) intentionally touches another person (B)

(b)   the touching is sexual

(c)   B does not consent to the touching, and

(d)   A does not reasonably believe that B consents.

Section 4: Causing sexual activity without consent: The elements of this offence are:

(a)   a person (A) intentionally causes (B) to engage in activity

(b)   the activity is sexual

(c)   B does not consent to engaging in the activity

(d)   A does not reasonably believe that B consents.

It is important to note:

- There are new offences against trafficking persons into, within and out of the country for the purposes of sexual exploitation.

- There are preparatory offences, such as drugging a person with intent to engage in sexual activity with that person; committing any offence with intent to commit a sexual offence; and trespassing on any premises with intent to commit a sexual offence.

- There is an offence of engaging in sexual activity in a public lavatory.

Sections 30–33: These relate to offences against people who cannot give a valid consent to sexual activity because of a mental disorder impeding choice. This Act uses the same definition of 'mental disorder' as the *Mental Health Act 1983*.

Sections 34–37: These relate to offences against people who may or may not legally be able to consent to sexual activity but who are vulnerable to inducements, threats or deceptions because of a mental disorder.

Sections 39–42: These relate to care workers and their involvement with people who have a mental disorder. New offences relate to 'touching' in a sexualised manner i.e. not all offences are about penetration; and causing adults to engage in sexual activity which does involve touching e.g. by threats, deception etc. It is important to note that these offences may be committed by care staff irrespective of whether the service user has capacity to consent and in fact does so.

Section 66: Exposure – it is an offence to expose one's genitals (male or female) intending that someone else will see them and be alarmed or distressed.

Section 67: Voyeurism – it is an offence to observe someone else doing a private act if one observes without consent and for sexual gratification.

SECTION 9: PROTECTING PEOPLE FROM FINANCIAL OR MATERIAL ABUSE

There are a number of possible offences which need to be borne in mind when working with vulnerable people who are at risk of financial abuse.

Theft Act 1968

Section 1: Theft is the dishonest appropriation of property belonging to another intending to deprive the owner permanently.

Section 4(1): 'Property' includes money and all other property, real or personal e.g. objects of value, money and title documents.

Section 8 Robbery: A person is guilty of robbery if they steal, and immediately before or at the time of doing it, use force or the threat of force.

Section 21 Blackmail: It is an offence for anyone to make an unwarranted demand with menaces with a view of gain to themself or with intent to cause loss to another. An 'unwarranted demand' is made unless the person making the demand has reasonable grounds for doing so and the use of menaces is a proper means of reinforcing the demand. Accordingly, money demanded may be properly due but there would still be an offence if improper menaces were used.

Fraud Act 2006

This Act came into force on the 15 January 2007. The Act repeals all the deception offences in the Theft Acts of 1968 and 1978 and replaces them with a single offence of fraud (section 1) which can be committed in three different ways by: false representation (section 2); failure to disclose information when there is a legal duty to do so (section 3); and abuse of position (section 4). The Act also creates new offences of possession (section 6) and making or supplying articles for use in frauds (section 7). The offence of fraudulent trading (section 458 of the Companies Act 1985) will apply to sole traders (section 9). Obtaining services by deception is replaced by a new offence of obtaining services dishonestly (section 11). There are also other minor provisions.

SECTION 10: PROTECTING PEOPLE FROM EMOTIONAL ABUSE

Emotional abuse can be extremely difficult to identify and then prove in a court of law. Some forms of discriminatory abuse could also be deemed to be emotional abuse and therefore the reader should also refer to section 9. Threats can be a part of other offences, including assault and robbery, also threats to kill, but threats per se are not an offence.

Protection from Harassment Act 1997

Section 2: This addresses offences of harassment and causing fear of violence. A person is liable to prosecution if their conduct causes another person to fear (on at least *two* occasions) that violence will be used against them. This includes verbal abuse. At sentencing a restraining order can be applied or an injunction – with a power of arrest. As well as these criminal remedies, the County Court can make injunctions (on sufficient evidence) to prevent harassment before it happens.

SECTION 11: PROTECTING PEOPLE FROM ABUSE BY NEGLECT AND OMISSION

There are a number of protections for vulnerable adults against the risk of abuse and neglect. Some are part of the criminal law, some are regulatory and preventative in intent.

Mental Capacity Act 2005

Section 44: This covers the offence of neglect and ill-treatment. Carers who ill-treat or wilfully neglect a person lacking mental capacity will be committing a crime under the *Mental Capacity Act 2005*. The new offence applies to anyone caring for a person who lacks capacity to make decisions for themselves, including family carers, healthcare and social care staff in hospital or care homes and those providing care in a person's home. Those protected by the new offence include people with learning disabilities, dementia, or brain injuries. Unfortunately, it seems the offence may only protect those completely lacking capacity, and not those who, despite their limitations and vulnerability are able to make informed decisions on some matters.

National Health Services Act 2006 Section 254 and Schedule 20

Place a duty on local authorities to make arrangements to prevent illness, care for people who are suffering from illness and provide aftercare for people suffering from illness, care of expectant and nursing mothers (other than the provision of residential accommodation) and home help and laundry facilities.

National Assistance Act 1948 Section 47

A local authority has power to seek an order from a Magistrates Court authorising a person who is at risk. The application must be supported by a community physician stating that the person is either: (i) suffering from a grave chronic disease or (ii) aged, infirm or physically incapacitated and living in insanitary conditions, unable to look after themselves and not receiving proper care and attention from others.

National Assistance (Amendment) Act 1951

Section 1: Similar to above but allows for an application without notice and is for three weeks only, after which time the section 47 procedure must be followed. A medical officer of health must certify with another medical practitioner for removal without delay.

SECTION 12: PROTECTING PEOPLE FROM DISCRIMINATORY ABUSE

Race Relations Act 1976

This Act makes it unlawful to discriminate directly or indirectly on the grounds of colour, race, nationality (including citizenship) or ethnic or national origin, or to apply requirements or conditions which have a disproportionately disadvantageous effect on people of a particular racial group, and which cannot be justified on non-racial grounds.

The *Sex Discrimination Act 1975* and *Disability Discrimination Act 1995* make it unlawful to discriminate on grounds of gender or disability.

Crime and Disorder Act 1998

There are many new offences under this Act, which promote the reduction of crime in every local area of the UK.

Sections 28–32 and 82: These sections introduce new assault, harassment and public order offences with significantly higher maximum penalties where it can be shown that the offence was racially aggravated. For each of these new offences, the maximum penalty is higher than the maximum for the basic offence without the element of racial aggravation. Where the maximum sentence is life imprisonment, there is no racially aggravated alternative.

An offence is racially aggravated if:

- at the time of committing the offence, immediately before or after doing so, the offender demonstrates towards the victim hostility based on the victim's membership (or presumed membership) of a racial group

or:

- the offence is motivated (wholly or partly) by hostility towards members of a racial group based on their membership of that group.

This term applies to the following offences under the Act:

- **Section 29:** Assaults
- **Section 30:** Criminal damage
- **Section 31:** Public order offence
- **Section 32:** Harassment.

Racial and Religious Hatred Act 2006

This Act amends the *Public Order Act 1986* so as to create the offence of stirring up religious hatred. The offence can be committed by using threatening words or behaviour or any publication or broadcast if the intention is to stir up religious hatred. The offence is not to be used in such a way as to prohibit or restrict discussion and criticism of particular religions or their adherents.

Forced Marriage (Civil Protection) Act 2007

This Act seeks to address the problem of people being forced into marriage either against their wishes or despite their incapacity to give valid consent. An application can be made in the High or County Court for a Forced Marriage Protection Order to prevent people being forced into marriage. The Court has very wide powers to make whatever orders it considers appropriate. A power of arrest can be attached to such an order. Crucially, it is possible for an application to be made on behalf of the victim by someone else who has sufficient connection with the victim and knowledge of their circumstances.

SECTION 13: PROTECTING PEOPLE FROM INSTITUTIONAL ABUSE

The Department of Health has set down National Minimum Standards under the *Care Standards Act 2000* for each of the social care settings they regulate, including residential, nursing and domiciliary care and nursing agencies. Depending on the setting, these standards are geared to achieving outcomes including the following:

- that service users' health care needs are fully met, and their health, safety and welfare are promoted
- that service users feel they are treated with respect and valued as a person, and that their right to privacy is upheld
- that service users are helped to exercise choice and control over their lives
- that service users are protected from abuse, neglect and self-harm and
- that service users have their rights protected and their complaints listened to, taken seriously and acted upon.

SECTION 14: RECENT LEGISLATION RELEVANT TO DOMESTIC VIOLENCE AND SAFEGUARDING ADULTS

Domestic violence is a form of adult abuse and is defined as:

> Any incident of threatening behaviour, violence or abuse between adults who are or have been in a relationship together, or between family members, regardless of gender or sexuality.

> (www.crimereduction.homeoffice.gov.uk/dv/dv03a.htm#4)

The Domestic Violence, Crime and Victims Act 2004

Everyone needs to be aware of the new Act which came into force in March 2005, especially section 5 regarding 'familial homicide' – new offence of causing or allowing the death of a child or vulnerable adult. All members of a household, aged 16 and over, may be liable for the offence. Therefore, if a 'member of a household' knows that a child or a vulnerable adult is a victim of domestic violence/abuse they must report it.

Section 5(4) defines a member of a household as: a 'member' of a particular household, even if they do not live in that household, if they visit so often and for such periods of time that it is reasonable to regard them as a member of it.

A person can be found guilty of familial homicide if:

- they were aware or ought to have been aware that at the time the victim was at significant risk of serious physical harm s5(c) and s5(d)(i)

- they failed to take reasonable steps to prevent the person coming to harm s5(d)(ii)

- the person subsequently died from the unlawful act of the member of the household in circumstances that the defendant foresaw or ought to have foreseen s5(d)(iii).

The provisions of the Act also include:

- statutory multi-agency domestic homicide reviews when anyone over 16 years dies of violence, abuse or neglect from a relative, intimate partner or member of the same household

- common assault as an arrestable offence

- extending availability of Restraining Orders (from the *Protection from Harassment Act 1997*) to any offence, on conviction; or acquittal where the court considers it necessary to protect the victim from harassment, based on 'balance of probability' evidence

- introducing a statutory Victims Code of Practice and Commissioner for Victims and Witnesses. Also allowing victims to take their case to the parliamentary ombudsman if they feel the code has not been adhered to by the criminal justice agencies.

CHAPTER 2

SCOTTISH LEGISLATIVE FRAMEWORK FOR SUPPORTING AND PROTECTING ADULTS

KATHRYN MACKAY

INTRODUCTION

Adult support and protection has lagged behind developments in child care. The advent of the Scottish Parliament in 1999 marked a watershed and rapid change has ensued. This chapter focuses on three subsequent civil statutes that form the legal framework for inquiry, assessment and intervention in the lives of adults. It will provide the background context for these changes and explains Scottish legal and administrative institutions. It explores the *Adult Support and Protection (Scotland) Act 2007* (hereafter referred to as the adult support and protection statute) in some depth. It then draws upon the *Adults with Incapacity (Scotland) Act 2000* (hereafter referred to as the adults with incapacity statute) and finally the *Mental Health (Care and Treatment) (Scotland) Act 2003* (hereafter referred to as the mental health statute) to complete the framework.[1] An effective adult support and protection strategy will need to address all the Acts, with practitioners assessing which Act is best to use in a given situation.

Some sections of legislation are recorded verbatim and these will be set in *italics*. Where the author summarises sections, these will be printed in plain text.

BACKGROUND

Prior to 1999 there was limited scope for imposed intervention into the lives of adults unless they had a mental disorder. Mental health law was based on treatment in hospital and only two remedies addressed wider welfare

---

1   The word 'statute' has been chosen to ensure that readers do not confuse the full title of the Acts with the abbreviated title.

concerns. Curator Bonis[2] was used to gain access and control of money and property where capacity to manage affairs had been lost. It was an all-or-nothing approach where you had control over your affairs or you did not. Guardianship had fixed limited powers of residence and attendance at a place for treatment. Some parents resorted to the legal remedy of Curator Dative,[3] from the fifteenth century, to make welfare decisions. The Scots Law Commission produced two reports, which included specimen bills, for incapable adults (1995) and vulnerable adults (1997), which would modernise legislation, but at the time there was no political will to act.

Political and public interest in this area of welfare increased due to pressure groups and high profile inquiries (Atkinson 2006; Ferguson 2005) into the neglect by services of people in dangerous and abusive situations. The mental health statute created community-based compulsory treatment orders, improved rights and representation, and the Mental Health Tribunal for Scotland took over from Sheriff Courts as the decision-making legal forum. The adult with incapacity statute introduced a range of measures to intervene in the finances and welfare of people who had lost decision-making capacity. The adult support and protection statute is seen as finally filling the gap with its measures of access, assessment, removal and exclusion where adults are at risk of harm.

In general these new statutes are viewed positively but there are also concerns. The tension between individual freedom and state-led control lie at the heart of these. The legal-making processes and resulting increased role of solicitors make the process more adversarial. Parts of the adults with incapacity statute are already subject to revision due to the increased use of guardianship in particular. A limited review of the mental health statute is due to be announced because the application and hearing process for compulsory treatment orders is seen as unduly complex and time consuming. Another concern is that these new powers are being used paternalistically.

A DISTINCTIVE SCOTTISH APPROACH?

Scotland had its own legal and governmental systems for certain policy areas prior to 1999. The community care legal framework had always been a mixture of UK and Scottish statutes. The Scottish Parliament brought

---

2   Curator Bonis is a legal term and dates from the nineteenth century. A person is appointed by the courts to look after the financial affairs of someone who is deemed not to have the capacity to do so themselves.

3   Curator Dative is a much older legal remedy than Curator Bonis and was revived in the last century to allow the applicant to make personal welfare decisions for someone who lacked capacity. Whilst curators could be appointed at the regional sheriff courts, application had to be submitted to the Court of Session, the highest court in Scotland.

devolved powers in areas including health, social work, housing and law. Reserved matters such as employment, social security and immigration remain with the Westminster Parliament.

There is a debate about whether the Scottish Parliament has promoted divergence in policies with England and Wales; also whether there is a 'New' Scotland with an increasing distinctive cultural and political identity (Mooney and Scott 2005; Paterson *et al.* 2001). Some argue that Scotland is diverging, and cite free personal care and a single National Health Service framework as evidence (Tannahill 2005). Others argue for convergence due to the ongoing influence of New Labour and the fiscal limitations imposed by Westminster (Mooney and Scott 2005). Mental health law will be used to explore this debate.

At the time of writing, the Westminster Government has not succeeded in getting a new statute whereas in Scotland the statute arrived in 2003 despite the similar timescales. The announcements of the review of mental health law had a very different tenor. In England the stance was that community care had failed and the public needed protection (Department of Health 1998). In Scotland the reasons were that mental health law required to be modernised because most people continued to live in the community with mental distress and that those who required compulsory intervention needed stronger safe-guards (Scottish Executive 1998). Whilst both reviews produced similar rec-ommendations Pilgrim (2007) notes that the government in Westminster ignored the proposed increased rights and focused on its wish to enforce community-based treatment and detention for people with a dangerous and severe personality disorder.

In Scotland, some service user organisations opposed the community-based compulsory treatment orders but were generally supportive of the bill (Ferguson 2005). Another factor in Scotland which made the bill more palatable was that it took place within a wider policy drive of improving Scotland's mental health including the public health campaign 'See Me' (Pilgrim 2007). In England a coalition of professional and user organisations was created to lobby against the bill. Some of the safeguards now in place in Scotland will be added to the revised bill. Imposed treatment in the community will also be a point of convergence. Whilst on the surface diver-gence may be 'largely a change of pace' (Poole and Mooney 2005, p.37), it remains to be seen whether the underlying political motivations affect practice in the long term.

The Scottish Parliament, like the three statutes, is still in its infancy. Time will determine whether there will be a 'Scottish' approach. In May 2007 a Scottish National Party and Green Party coalition formed an administration after 70 years of Labour domination. Scotland is once again in uncharted political territory. It will be interesting to see what impact this has on welfare in general and specifically adults in need of support and protection.

ADULT SUPPORT AND PROTECTION (SCOTLAND) ACT 2007

This statute received its royal assent in 2007 and will be implemented in 2008. To date no draft guidance has been produced so this section relies heavily upon the Act itself to explore its possibilities and challenges. The Act 'raises difficult ethical issues about the role of society to protect people who are vulnerable, even if they themselves deny their need for help' (Patrick 2007, p.11). Local authorities have the lead role and are required to work with other agencies through Area Adult Protection Committees. The Sheriff Court is the legal decision-making forum. Although the Act refers to council officers, it is envisaged that assessments and applications will be led by qualified social workers due to their expertise of working with courts.

Principles

Principles act as a guide to workers in how to intervene under the Act. Principles are as follows:

Section 1 *There can be no intervention into the life of an adult unless that intervention will:*

(a) *benefit the person and could not be achieved through voluntary means*

(b) *the means of intervention is the least restrictive option in terms of that person's freedom.*

Section 2

- persons working under Act should have regard for the general principle (2a)
- regard for the person's ascertainable wishes (past and present) (2b)
- the views of nearest relative, carer or any other relevant person (2c)
- maximising the participation of the person and providing support and information to facilitate this (2d)
- not being treated less favourably than any other adult (2e)
- regard for the uniqueness and diversity of the individual (2f).

Ward (2007, p.16) argues principle 2(a) is a 'watering down' of the 'mandatory nature' of the general principle in section 1. Indeed much of the Act will require careful interpretation. How much advice and support is acceptable? Whilst section 6 contains a *duty to consider the importance of advocacy,* overall the duty to provide advocacy is weaker than in the mental health statute (Scottish Association for Mental Health 2006). How will the importance of ensuring that the adult is not, without justification, treated less favourably than any other, be interpreted? The sexual behaviour for people with a learning disability has long been a cause of anxiety amongst care workers. This Act does not resolve the dilemma of what normal sexual activity is and what is abusive.

Definition of an adult at risk of harm

Establishing a definition was not an easy task (Age Concern 2006). The Analysis of Responses to the 3rd Consultation Paper on *Protecting Vulnerable Adults – Securing their Safety* (Scottish Executive 2005) reveals a diversity of opinion that led to significant revision. There were objections to the original phrase *'may be in need of community care services'* as a basis for vulnerability. The term 'vulnerable adult' was replaced by the less contentious phrase 'adult at risk of harm'. 'Age' as an indicator of vulnerability was replaced by 'mental and physical infirmity'. Age Concern (2006) stress the point that people do not become at risk due to age per se but that other factors place them at risk.

Also the consultation paper contained a highly prescriptive definition of abuse. It included the word 'significant', suggesting a certain level of impact. There was also a requirement that the abuse existed in a relationship in which there was an expectation of trust and second that there should be evidence of distress. This suggested a lack of understanding of the variety of situations in which adults could be at risk of harm and how they might respond to it.

Section 3 of the statute defines the term as follows:

(1) 'Adults at risk' are adults who:

   (a) are unable to safeguard their own well-being, property, rights or other interests

   (b) are at risk of harm and

   (c) because they are affected by disability, mental disorder, illness or physical or mental infirmity, are more vulnerable to being harmed than adults who are not so affected.

(2) An adult is at risk of harm for the purposes of the subsection (1) if:

   (a) another person's conduct is causing (or is likely to cause) the adult to be harmed, or

   (b) the adult is engaging (or is likely to engage) in conduct which causes (or is likely to cause) self-harm.

This legal definition widens the net of who might be subject to this Act even though all criteria in section 3(1) have to be met. It opens up possibilities of intervening in situations earlier due to the inclusion of the clauses 'is likely to cause harm' or 'likely to engage'. One area that will be contentious is the Act's potential use in domestic abuse situations. Some years ago I visited a 70-year-old woman whose husband was physically abusive towards her. The woman was only known to social work via occupational therapy and the supply of aids to daily living due to arthritis that limited her mobility. She depended on her husband for shopping and cooking. The woman would not discuss the domestic violence and she was adamant I should not visit again. At that time the best I could do was to ask the occupational therapist to 'drop by' as a way of monitoring the situation.

Under the new Act there is now a duty towards such a woman because she met all three criteria: she was unable to physically protect herself, she was at risk of harm and she had a physical disability. However at what point does an adult who makes a choice to stay in an abusive relationship become an adult at risk of harm? The simple answer is the fulfilment of the criteria; the complex answers lie in how one assesses the real life multi-faceted situations and takes account of past and present informed choices.

Clarke (2006) discusses the need for social workers to have moral character because of the position they hold between the state, society and the subcultures in which they work. This Act underlines how necessary it is to have professional and ethical judgement as well as technical skill and knowledge.

Interventions under the Act

The Act can be seen to have a tariff of increasingly mandated actions from minimal to maximum use of authority and powers. The lowest form of statutory intervention is the right to access a building where a person may be at risk of harm. There is a right to request a variation or recall of a removal or banning order from the sheriff who granted the order. However only banning orders have been given the right to appeal beyond the sheriff who made the order. As such the exercise of judgement by the agency and the sheriff is critical in ensuring that actions under this Act are taken only when necessary and to the correct procedure.

Inquiries

The local authority has a duty to make inquiries about a person's well-being, property or financial affairs if it knows or believes that a person is an adult at risk and that it might need to intervene. In order to undertake this duty the Act gives a council officer the right to enter any place and to interview the person in private (section 7). Where appropriate there is also the right for a health professional to undertake a medical examination in private. It is essential that the person is informed of their right to refuse to answer any questions and a medical examination. There are also powers to request and examine records, though only a health professional can view a health record.

Assessment orders

Where an adult does not agree to being seen or where someone else is preventing contact, a council official can apply for an assessment order which will allow them to take that person to another place for interview and also if necessary medical examination. Under section 12 the council has to show that it:

(a)   has reasonable cause to suspect that the person in respect of whom the order is sought is an adult at risk who is being, or is likely to be, seriously harmed, and

(b)   that the assessment order is required in order to establish whether the person is an adult at risk who is being, or is likely to be, seriously harmed, and

(c)   as to the availability and suitability of the place at which the person is to be interviewed and examined.

The person should only be removed for the purposes of assessment it if is not possible to conduct the assessment in the place they are currently residing. The Scottish Exceutive Implementation Group are looking at pre-existing risk assessment tools which might assist practitioners and will provide guidance on how the assessemnt is undertaken.

Removal orders

If an adult is at risk of serious harm by their own action/inaction or by the action of others they can be removed to another place for up to seven days. The criteria under section 15 (1) are as follows:

The sheriff may grant a removal order only if satisfied

(a)   that the person in respect of whom the order is sought is an adult at risk who is likely to be seriously harmed if not moved to another place, and

(b)   as to the availability and suitability of the place to which the adult at risk is to be moved.

The appropriateness of the place of safety and the ability to keep the person there merit further discussion. Where physical harm has taken place that person may be admitted to hospital but a non-hospital environment is usually envisaged. There is concern about the capacity of councils to arrange a suitable place. A range of adults with varying physical and pyschological needs may be subject to a removal order. Only within mental health has the idea of a place of safety acquired any kind of currency, even then they are few and far between. Women's refuges will only be approriate for a few. Independent care providers may be unwilling to take on such a short-term and difficult situation. Will care staff understand and be able to respond appropriately?

Powers only extend to placing a person and not keeping them there. The more unsuitable the environment, the more likely an adult will leave it. A better option, albeit one that would require advance planning and more expense, is a team of staff who can be mobilised at short notice to provide care within a furnished facility that is used only for that purpose. The advantage of a specialised team is that they could also be used to provide care and support in a person's own home, with the person's consent, whilst an assessment is underway. This would act as a protective measure and meet the principle of minimum intervention.

Banning orders

These replicate the orders that can be gained in domestic violence situations. The subject of the order can be banned from an address and its vicinity, ejected from that place and a power of arrest can be attached to the order. Banning orders can last up to six months. Section 20 sets out the criteria for granting a banning order:

(a)   *that an adult at risk is being, or is likely to be, seriously harmed by another person,*

(b)   *that the adult at risk's well-being or property would be better safeguarded by banning that other person from a place occupied by the adult than it would be by moving the adult from that place, and*

(c)   *that either*

   (i)   *the adult at risk is entitled, or permitted by a third party, or*

   (ii)   *neither the adult at risk nor the subject is entitled, or permitted by a third party, to occupy the place from which the subject is to be banned.*

Temporary banning orders are an option to keep a person safe whilst preparing an application for a full order. The adults, or another person on their behalf can apply for a banning as well as a council official.

Implications for practice and services

It is hoped that some situations are resolved by the instigation of contact between the adult at risk of harm and a skilled practitioner who can offer appropriate support and advice where previously no one had a right of access unless a crime was being committed. This may give the adult confidence to take action, or allow others to take action, that reduces the risk of harm.

These new limited powers are only one part of the process and much will depend on the skill of the assessors in engaging people in a way that promotes interaction and confidence. Age Concern (2006) and the Scottish Association for Mental Health (2006) have both raised a number of issues about services. Both of them identified the need for suitable accommodation to act as places of safety. Age Concern (2006) are equally concerned that other services need to increase, in particular they are keen for mediation services that might help the person to address issues of harm without recourse to the Act.

ADULTS WITH INCAPACITY (SCOTLAND) ACT 2000

Some adults at risk of harm may also require longer-term intervention and the adults with incapacity statute provides a range of options to plan for incapacity or take action where a person has already lost capacity in welfare and financial matters. It created the Office of the Public Guardian, at a national level, to keep a register and oversee the financial interventions that have been created under this Act. The Sheriff Courts determine guardianship and intervention orders as these are seen as more major forms of intervention.

Principles

The principles are similar to those of the adult and support and protection statute in terms of minimum intervention and gaining the view of relevant people. They have positively influenced practice (Killeen, Myers and MacDonald 2004). The requirement to ascertain the person's views by any means of communication (section 1 (4a)) has led assessors, mainly mental health officers, to seek assistance of speech therapists and spend more time in observing the person and how others communicate with them. This improves the quality of the assessment, in particular hearing the 'voice' of the person.

The specific principle, that the adult should be encouraged to exercise whatever skills they have concerning his financial or personal welfare, and to develop new skills (section 1 (5)), emphasises that capacity is not all or nothing. For example a person may not be able to access their pension but, once they have the cash, will buy food etc. Also some adults may become subject to the Act but there may be improvement over time and new skills developed.

Definition of an adult with incapacity

There is a presumption that a severe cognitive impairment must exist but people at later stages of an illness such as multiple sclerosis may meet the following definition. Section 1 (6) breaks down different aspects of incapacity:

'Incapable' means incapable of

(a) *acting; or*

(b) *making decisions; or*

(c) *communicating decisions; or*

(d) *understanding decisions; or*

(e) *retaining the memory of decisions,*

by reason of mental disorder or of inability to communicate because of physical disability…does not include people who may be able to communicate by other means.

Intervention

This was a wide-ranging Act from minimum interventions around freeing access to joint bank accounts to major interventions via guardianship orders. Powers of attorney can be set up prior to the loss of capacity allowing a nominated person to carry out welfare and financial matters on their behalf once capacity is lost. There are safeguards built into these through the role of the Public Guardian for financial matters and the local authority has a duty to monitor welfare guardianships and to investigate welfare concerns.

One function provided a simple way of accessing funds once capacity was lost: 'the authority to intermit with funds' (section 25). This allowed a third party, except a paid carer or professional, to apply to the Public Guardian, to gain access to the adult's bank account. The application required exact details of what the money was needed for. It was possible to establish a monthly budget that covered living costs and a specified fixed sum transferred to a new account managed by the third party. However, it was underused and administratively quite complicated. The processes have been simplified by amendments in the adult support and protection statute to encourage wider and easier use, including local authorities being able to use this function.

Intervention and guardianship orders are similar in terms of duration (up to three years). They can have powers specified by a sheriff which can later be altered. Intervention orders are seen as more discrete and limited in duration; for example to renovate a house to meet the needs of an adult with incapacity. Guardianship is for more complex, ongoing situations and particularly where there are matters of welfare. It also demonstrates how the principles and practices have diverged with concerns about its overuse, particularly in moving people into care homes, and the length and expense of legal procedures (Killeen *et al.* 2004). Mental Welfare Commission produced guidance that proposed a procedure which enabled moving people without recourse to guardianship, whilst upholding the principles (Patrick 2004). Guardianship places can take six months to be processed by the courts.

The overuse of guardianship orders relates to two particular court rulings. The Bournewood judgements[4] in the House of Lords and then European Court of Human Rights[5] concerned a man who was a voluntary patient in hospital but the courts ultimately ruled he was unlawfully deprived of his liberty because his limited mental capacity meant he could not make informed decisions or take action to secure his wishes. Sheriff Baird in a case before Glasgow Sheriff Court[6] took account of the Bournewood situation and ruled that where there was incapacity, a guardianship order should always be used to ensure the person's situation was considered within a legal process with due checks and balances. This led to a rise in the use of these orders and an allied increase on delayed hospital discharges. Hilary Patrick in association with the Mental Welfare Commission produced guidance in 2005 to assist practitioners in placing these particular rulings within the context of the principles of the adults with incapacity statute and provides a detailed review of the issues for readers who wish to look in depth at this difficult practice dilemma.

However, in 2007 the adult support and protection statute introduced amendments to address the overuse of guardianship. It amended the *Social Work (Scotland) Act 1968* (section 64) to allow a local authority to provide community care services (including moves to care homes), without recourse to guardianship orders, where they are needed to improve the welfare of an adult with incapacity. This supports the principle of minimum intervention but where the adult in question or an appropriate third person objects to the intervention then an application for guardianship is made to allow the courts to decide what is necessary in the interests of the person. Also consideration has to be given to whether the environment is restrictive in such way that would also warrant legal safeguards (Ward 2007). The second change (section 55) requires of the sheriff, hearing any application, a new principle of taking account of the adults wishes and feelings *as expressed by a person providing independent advocacy service*. This further increases representation for the adult.

Even then some guardianship orders may not be compliant with Articles 5 (right to liberty and security) and 6 (right to a fair trial) of the European Convention of European Rights due to the limit of legal protection in this statute (Patrick 2005). Patrick argues that if there is authorised restriction of liberty which amounts to the use of regular force and detention, then community-based Compulsory Treatment Orders under the mental health statute affords greater legal protection and could be used in care home placements.

---

4   *R* v *Bournewood Community and Mental Health NHS Trust*, ex parte L [1998] 2 WLR 764; *R* v *Bournewood Community and Mental Health NHS Trust*, ex parte L [1999] AC 458.
5   *HL* v *UK* European Court of Human Rights October 2004.
6   Glasgow Sheriff Court, W 37/04.

MENTAL HEALTH (CARE AND TREATMENT) (SCOTLAND) ACT 2003

This section explores the new community-based compulsory treatment orders that can impose greater control than guardianship orders on people with a mental disorder. It also details the new rights to representation that should safeguard people against unnecessary or excessive intervention, and therefore limit the number of people on these new orders. The principles in this Act are similar to the above two statutes but with one important difference: the inclusion of reciprocity. The Scottish Association for Mental Health (2006) also lobbied for its inclusion in the adults with incapacity statute so adults at risk of harm might be assured of appropriate services. Mental health service users are hoping that this principle will stimulate an improvement in services. The principle underlines that any intervention is a major event in a person's life and as a result agencies who work under this Act have a duty of care to that person.

This Act has tested the role and capacity of independent advocacy. They have been effective in giving the person's viewpoint and asking questions of those presenting evidence at hearings (Gammock 2007). However, advocates seem to be involved only in tribunal work rather than having an ongoing role in the person's care. There has been a specific problem about their presence at hearings where someone has been assessed as being incapable of understanding the legal process and a Curator ad Litem[7] has been appointed. Some tribunals have ruled if a person cannot instruct a solicitor, then they cannot instruct an advocate either. This can also be seen as reducing their legal right to advocacy (Mental Health Tribunal Service User Reference Group 2007).

There are two other new measures designed to safeguard the person. First advanced statements were created where people can record how they would like or not like to be treated if they become subject to compulsion under the Act. This could include whether they wished to avoid certain drugs. Professionals have to take the advance statement into account but can overrule it.

Second, the Named Person was created as a direct response to concerns about the abuse of powers vested in nearest relatives under the old Act (Atkinson 2006). An adult with mental health problems can nominate a Named Person who then has a number of rights when that person becomes subject to the Act: to attend hearings, request a review of an order and their views sought about the care plan. The Named Person gives their *own opinion* of what they believe to be in the best interests of the person. Where there is no

---

7   Curator ad Litem is a legal representative who is appointed where there are legal proceedings about a person who does not have the capacity to understand the process or the decisions that might be made. Although Curators ad Litem are often solicitors, their role as a curator is different: they speak for the person as opposed to following their instructions.

Named Person the carer or nearest relative becomes the default named person.

Community-based Compulsory Treatment Orders are the most controversial aspect of the Act due to the potential invasion of privacy and the allied power of coercion by community based personnel responsible for the person's care plan (Ferguson 2003). It was estimated that approximately 200 people at any one time in Scotland would be subject to such an order (Lawton-Smith 2006). They would be used only where there was a history of avoiding treatment and repeated hospital admissions. However after the first year of the operation of the Act, there were already 245 people on these orders (Mental Welfare Commission Monitoring Report 2007). It remains to be seen whether numbers continue to rise. Other trends are evident in the Mental Health Tribunal published statistics. For example, in relation to the conversion rate from short-term detention orders to compulsory treatment orders 'there is large variation in conversion rates from 22% to 88% by Local Authority and Health Board which would suggest different practice in different areas' (Mental Health Tribunal for Scotland 2007, p.25). Such differing practice must be a cause for concern and requires investigation.

Second, the actual number of hearings 'have grown largely due to the increase in Interim Compulsory Treatment Orders which now consistently outnumber full Compulsory Treatment Orders' (Mental Health Tribunal for Scotland 2007, p.25). Interim orders have the effect of keeping a person subject to detention for longer before the application is fully heard. There is concern that solicitors are making the tribunal hearings more adversarial and their actions are not always in the interests of the person. For example requesting an independent medical opinion even where there is no doubt about the extent and severity of the mental disorder. This protraction of proceedings is arguably counter to the principle of minimum intervention.

Whilst the mental health tribunals are considered to be a much improved forum by mental health professionals (Mental Health Officer Newsletter 2006) there does appear much that can be improved in both practice and procedures.

CONCLUSIONS

The three Acts individually are complex and raise ethical dilemmas about personal freedom of action and human rights. Together they provide a range of unprecedented powers to intervene in the lives of people, most of whom have committed no crime and may or may not have had crimes committed against them. They range from the right to see someone and have this imposed by a Court Assessment Order to Guardianship Orders that enforce residence and finally community-based compulsory treatment orders which can impose a range of treatment on a person including regular restriction of liberty in their own home or care facility. Whilst some argue the adult support and protection statute has tight criteria (Patrick 2007), the author believes that many people could fall under its remit and yet the rights to representation and due process are the most limited of the three Acts. This led the Scottish Association for Mental Health to lobby against mental disorder being included, given the powers of investigation under the mental health statute.

Whilst rights to advocacy are included in the adults with incapacity statute and revisions to the statute, there must be questions about the capacity of existing independent advocacy services to meet these new and diverse range of situations into which they might enter. The adults with incapacity statute amendments also contradict the developing practice under the mental health statute that incapacity to engage a solicitor means an advocate's role is defunct. Capacity in this instance is not assessed by a doctor who knows the person but a *man of skill*, appointed by the Tribunal and usually a solicitor. There is much work to be done in rationalising the rights to representations and legal *vis à vis* professional processes. Also, if a Sheriff Court is unsuitable for mental health statute, why not the other Acts?

Any law like ethical codes does not of itself resolve practice dilemmas of if, when and how to intervene in the lives of adults. It remains to be seen whether the use of the adult support and protection statute will develop cautiously or whether like Guardianship Orders and possibly community Compulsory Treatment Orders (CTOs), professionals will use these new powers. Whilst it may be argued that to remove a person for up to seven days is minor in comparison, the effect on that person at the time and in the long term could be considerable. It is early days for the adult support and protection statute. Guidance, training and, one hopes, new resources have yet to come online. The hope is that the best possible practice will emerge and further legislation will address some of the anomalies highlighted in this chapter.

STATUTES

Adult Support and Protection (Scotland) Act 2007. Edinburgh: The Stationery Office.
Adults with Incapacity (Scotland) Act 2000. Edinburgh: The Stationery Office.
Human Rights Act 1998. London: The Stationery Office.
Mental Health (Care and Treatment) (Scotland) Act 2003. Edinburgh: The Stationery Office.
Scots Law Commission (1995) *Incapable Adults Report 151.* Edinburgh: Scots Law Commission.
Scots Law Commission (1997) *Vulnerable Adults Report 158.* Edinburgh: Scots Law Commission.
Social Work (Scotland) Act 1968. Edinburgh: The Stationery Office.

REFERENCES

Age Concern (2006) *Response to Call for Evidence on the Adult Support and Protection (Scotland) Bill.* Edinburgh: Age Concern.

Atkinson, J. (2006) *Private and Public Protection, Civil Mental Health Legislation*. Policy and Practice in Social Care Series Number 1. Edinburgh: Dunedin Academic Press.

Clarke, C. (2006) 'Moral Character in Social Work.' *British Journal of Social Work 36*, 1, 75–89.

Department of Health (1998) *Frank Dobson Outlines Third Way for Mental Health*. Press release, 29 July. Available at www.dh.gov.uk/en/Publicationsandstatistics/Pressreleases/DH_4024509, accessed 25 August 2008.

Ferguson, I. (2003) 'Mental Health and Social Work.' In Baillie, D., Cameron, K., Cull, L.A., Roche, J. and West, J. (eds) (2003) *Social Work and the Law in Scotland*. Open University Publication. Basingstoke: Palgrave.

Ferguson, I. (2005) 'Social Work and Social Care in the 'New' Scotland.' In Mooney, G. and Scott, G. (eds) *Exploring Social Policy in the 'New' Scotland*. Bristol: The Policy Press.

Gammock, G. (2007) 'Independent Advocacy and the Mental Health Tribunal System.' *Newsletter for Mental Health Officers in Scotland 14*, 3. Edinburgh: Scottish Executive.

Killeen, J., Myers, F. and MacDonald, F. (2004) *The Adults with Incapacity (Scotland) Act 2000: Implementation, Monitoring and Research*. Edinburgh: Scottish Executive.

Lawton-Smith, S. (2006) *Community-based Compulsory Treatment Orders in Scotland – The Early Evidence*. London: The Kings Fund.

Mental Health Officer Newsletter Advisory Group (2006) 'MHO Experiences of the New Act and Tribunals.' *Newsletter for Mental Health Officers in Scotland 11*, 6–7. Edinburgh: Scottish Executive.

Mental Health Tribunal Service User Reference Group (2007) *Minutes of the April 2007 Meeting*. Hamilton: Mental Health Tribunal for Scotland.

Mental Health Tribunal for Scotland (2007) *Mental Health Tribunal Service Quarterly Statistics April 2007 – June 2007*. Hamilton: Mental Health Tribunal for Scotland.

Mental Welfare Commission (2007) *Monitoring Report: Community Based Compulsory Treatment Orders under the Mental Health (Care and Treatment)* (Scotland) Act 2003. Edinburgh: Mental Welfare Commission.

Mooney, G. and Scott, G. (eds) (2005) *Exploring Social Policy in the 'New' Scotland*. Bristol: The Policy Press.

Paterson, L., Brown, A., Curtice, J., Hinds, K., McCrone, D., Park, A., Sproston, K. and Surridge, P. (2001) *New Scotland, New Politics?* Edinburgh: Polygon.

Patrick, H. (2004) *Authorising Significant Interventions for Adults who Lack Capacity*. Edinburgh: Mental Welfare Commission.

Patrick, H. (2005) *Adult with Incapacity Act: When to Invoke the Act Summary*. Edinburgh: Mental Welfare Commission.

Patrick, H. (2007) 'The Adult Support and Protection Bill.' *Newsletter for Mental Health Officers in Scotland 14*, 11. Edinburgh: Scottish Executive.

Pilgrim, D. (2007) 'New "Mental Health" Legislation for England and Wales: Some aspects of consensus and conflict.' *Journal of Social Policy 36*, 1, 79–95.

Poole, L. and Mooney, G. (2005) 'Governance and Social Policy in the Devolved Scotland.' In Mooney, G. and Scott, G. (eds) *Exploring Social Policy in the 'New' Scotland*. Bristol: The Policy Press.

Scottish Association for Mental Health (2006) *SAMH Written Evidence on the Adults Support and Protection (Scotland) Bill*. Glasgow: SAMH.

Scottish Executive (1998) *Galbraith Announces Review of Mental Health Act*. Press release, 8 December. Available at www.scotland.gov.uk/News/Releases/1998/12/92678f4b-2db7-4406-8f2e-0e83a9f3f4a7, accessed 25 August 2008.

Scottish Executive (2003) *An Introduction to The Mental Health (Care and Treatment) (Scotland) Act 2003*. Edinburgh: Scottish Executive.

Scottish Executive (2005) *Protecting Vulnerable Adults – Securing their Safety: Third Consultation Paper on the Protection of Vulnerable Adults and Related Matters*. Edinburgh: Scottish Executive.

Scottish Executive (2005) *Analysis of Responses to the 3rd Consultation Paper on Protecting Vulnerable Adults – Securing their Safety*. Edinburgh: Scottish Executive.

Scottish Executive (2007) *Report to Ministers by Working Group Investigating the Role of Curators Ad Litem*. Edinburgh: Scottish Executive.

Tannahill, C. (2005) 'Health and Health Policy.' In Mooney, G. and Scott, G. (eds) *Exploring Social Policy in the 'New' Scotland.* Bristol: The Policy Press.

Ward, A. (2007) 'Adult support: a new generation.' *The Journal, the Member Magazine for the Law Society of Scotland 22,* 6. Available at www.journalonline.co.uk/article/1004240.aspx (page 20), accessed 21 July 2008.

ACKNOWLEDGEMENT

The author would like to thank Ann Ferguson, Age Concern Scotland and Paul Donnelly, previously of the Mental Welfare Commission, for their time and stimulating discussion which helped to inform this chapter.

CHAPTER 3

How Police Investigate Crimes Against Vulnerable Adults

ANONYMOUS

I have worked as a police officer for ten years, starting as a constable. The majority of my service has been as a divisional detective: this includes experience in major investigations such as murder enquiries. Three years ago I started working in a Family Protection Unit (now a Public Protection Unit), which investigated child protection matters, domestic violence and, more recently, vulnerable adult enquiries. The purpose in writing this chapter is to describe how the police respond to crimes against vulnerable adults.

DEALING WITH VULNERABLE ADULTS

It may be helpful to the reader to begin with a historical perspective of how the police force who employs me has dealt with vulnerable adults who have been abused. The force recognised that vulnerable adults were being subjected to incidents of crime. Such incidents were being dealt with as with other reported offences by uniformed officers, but additional measures were needed to deal with these victims, both at the investigation stage and in the court process. On a national level it was agreed that measures should be put in place to offer specialist investigation skills, and capable of providing the level of service required. It was also agreed that a single agency approach, that is, the police in isolation dealing with incidents of crime, was insufficient and that there needed to be a greater working partnership between the relevant agencies. Often the police is just one link in the chain of events when a safeguarding alert is made. Working in partnership with the other agencies and using the local Safeguarding Coordinator as a hub, also increases the number of sources of information and makes us all more aware when a vulnerable adult needs protection.

Historically, the police may respond to an incident involving a vulnerable adult which does not result in a crime being recorded. For example, an older person may have had a fall in their home; the police are called to force entry for the ambulance or a neighbour. Once entry has been gained then it could be argued that the police's involvement is no longer necessary and officers will leave the scene on to the next call. However the police's involvement does not necessarily stop there anymore.

It would be hoped that support measures would be requested via the family general practitioner, hospital or a friend or maybe a relative asking for assistance from the local adult social care department. With the referral from the police, even though no crimes have been committed, the required support will be put in place to prevent further incidents.

WHEN TO ALERT AND WHY

Many health and social care workers ask 'Will I know what is and what isn't a crime?' Common sense should always prevail and it is always better to report straight away and be thanked for being so conscientious, than to stay quiet and realise later that your suspicions were right all along. Of course, the wishes of the individual have to be considered, but at the end of the day it is easier to report and then stop any further investigation rather than to try and start one days or weeks after the event. Where a crime has been committed against a vulnerable adult prompt action by any worker can mean the difference between successfully proving a case or allowing offences to continue unnoticed.

I appreciate that in many places of work there are protocols that must be observed when dealing with incidents; however, it must be stressed that unnecessary delays in reporting a crime can make the world of difference. Obviously every worker has their policies and procedures to follow and the necessary managers or supervisors should be informed. However, it is the responsibility of each and every one of us to make sure the offence is reported promptly to the police. It is no use discovering a criminal offence has been committed, only to hope that the police will get to hear about it over the next few days, when it has eventually reached either an adult social care team, a Safeguarding Adults Coordinator or someone else takes the initiative to tell the police.

Early complaints can allow the police to preserve and capture vital evidence. When an alleged assault has occurred DNA evidence begins to deteriorate the very second after an offence. The sooner the police know what has happened the sooner we can arrange the required examinations to obtain the evidence, which may well be vital in proving an offence. It will also mean that the alleged offender can be apprehended and examined for forensic evidence in support of the complaint. In cases of physical and sexual offences early complaints are also seen as good corroborative evidence, indicating that the complaint is genuine.

In the event when a worker suspects that a crime has or is being committed, the number one priority is the safety of the vulnerable adult. All efforts must be made to protect the adult from further abuse. In my mind the secondary factor is the detection of the offence. A worker's first concern will be the immediate well-being of the victim but efforts to preserve evidence are vital. Police investigations will be planned alongside managing and dealing with the health and social care issues of the vulnerable adult.

HOW POLICE RESPOND

Every operational police officer will have the necessary knowledge and skills to take immediate steps to preserve evidence. This will be done in cooperation with other agencies. Once the initial call is received by the force control room, an officer will be despatched. They will record sufficient information for a crime report to be recorded and take the initial action to arrange for examinations, recording of statements, video interview, arrest and detention of suspect etc. Dependent on the type of offence, it may well be that the officer will retain the investigation and support will be provided by myself or another officer from the Public Protection Unit as required. In possession of the facts of the case the officer will complete a police safeguarding alert form, which is sent to the Public Protection Unit for my attention.

This will then be shared with the Safeguarding Adults Coordinator, who will facilitate the notification and involvement of other agencies. It is of course expected that the Safeguarding Adults Coordinator should be hearing about the same incident from other sources as well as the police, if the system works correctly.

At the early stages of the investigation, the police will meet with the other agencies to discuss the circumstances of the case and what actions need to be taken. Any strategy meeting will not interfere with the police investigation and the criminal investigation will take precedence over other aspects of the case, say, disciplinary matters. However, the agencies will be kept up to date on the investigation's progress.

PRESERVING EVIDENCE

When police involvement is required following suspected physical or sexual activity they are likely to be on the scene quickly. To enable the police to investigate effectively, it is imperative that potentially vital evidence is preserved.

A higher standard of proof is required in criminal proceedings (beyond reasonable doubt) than is required for disciplinary or regulatory proceedings, and police will always seek the 'best evidence'. Their early involvement will ensure that forensic evidence is not lost or contaminated.

For that short time before the police arrive, what a worker does or does not do can make a vital difference. To ensure that forensic evidence is not lost, destroyed or contaminated prior to the arrival of the police it is imperative that potentially vital evidence is preserved in the interest of the vulnerable adult and in the interest of justice.

What follows is a checklist which may help to ensure that evidence is not destroyed. In all cases, the following apply:

GOOD PRACTICE POINTS: PRESERVING EVIDENCE

- Obtain consent before examining the victim.

- Where possible, leave things where they are. If anything has to be handled, keep this to a minimum. Do not clean up. Do not wash anything or in any way remove fibres, blood etc.

- If you have been given items of possible interest, e.g. a weapon, avoid handling them wherever possible. Keep them in a safe, dry place until the police are able to collect.

- Preserve the clothing and footwear of the victim. Handle these as little as possible.

- Preserve anything used to comfort or warm a victim – e.g. a blanket.

- Note in writing the state of clothing of both alleged victim and alleged perpetrator.

- Note injuries in writing. Make full written notes on the condition and attitudes of the people involved in the incident.

- Note and preserve any obvious evidence such as fingerprints or footprints.

- Secure the room and do not allow anyone to enter until the police arrive.

- It is crucial for both victim and alleged perpetrator to be medically examined for forensic evidence at the earliest opportunity. An appropriately trained forensic surgeon will always carry out this examination.

- Try not to have physical contact with both the victim and alleged perpetrator, as cross-contamination can destroy evidence. This may be difficult if you are alone and need to comfort both parties but be aware that cross-contamination can easily occur.

- Preserve bedding where appropriate.

- Note and preserve any bloody item.

- Preserve any used condoms.

- In any instance where a victim is seriously injured and is taken to hospital, ask that a sample of blood be taken before any transfusion is given as a transfusion will invalidate evidence in relation to blood.

- For most things, use clean brown paper, a clean brown paper bag or a clean envelope. If using an envelope, do not lick it to seal.

- For liquids use clean glassware.

These are obviously ideal solutions but may not be possible at a time of trauma. Workers have to do the best they can in the circumstances. If they are unable to comply with these guidelines, they must communicate any issues to the investigating officers.

It must be stressed that forensic matters are a complex issue and early contact for advice/consultation/referral to the police will enable them to establish whether a criminal act has been committed and will give them the opportunity of determining if, and at what stage, they need to become involved. Early contact will also ensure the vulnerable adult is not subjected to repeated interviews/medical examinations, and vital evidence is secured. The evidence can be recorded in different ways, dependant on the abilities of the persons involved.

INTERVIEWING

For some vulnerable adults it may be that it is sufficient that a written statement is taken describing the incident. In other cases it may be necessary to capture the person's evidence in a video interview. Specially trained officers will interview the victim in a purpose-built suite. This video will then be used as their evidence-in-chief. This can then be played to the Court, in place of the victim having to attend Court in person and getting into the box to give their evidence. It also means that the events are described in the person's own words, rather than being the statement taker's perception of what the victim is trying to say happened.

On occasion a complaint can also be recorded from someone acting as an advocate for the vulnerable adult. This is a case where the victim, say of a financial abuse, no longer has capacity to understand what has happened and complain for themselves.

The investigation will follow its course and may require the collation of documentary evidence, some of which may well consist of the paperwork workers have been part of preparing.

RECORD KEEPING

The vulnerable adult's case notes, medical records, in fact any paperwork or notes recorded for the person, which may be relevant to the case could form part of the prosecution case file; or, more importantly, be examined by the defence, looking to introduce evidence to undermine the prosecution's case. As part of the investigation the police may request to see the case notes to establish a person's capacity prior to an offence or see evidence of previous incidents.

The best advice I can give any worker is the notes they make must contain one thing above all – FACT. It is essential that comments recorded in the notes should be based on facts not a worker's interpretation of what it is. Many times comments have been noted giving an opinion on a person's capacity. These comments although harmless in themselves could be damaging to the prosecution's case, where capacity becomes an issue. If the records made are accurate and transparent, then they will be able to stand any form of scrutiny in the future.

It is understandable that on occasions workers may not be able to update records as necessary and there may be some delay in their endorsements. It is also feasible that sometimes mistakes can be made. This again is a natural and understandable occurrence. I must stress that when this happens honesty and openness are essential. Where an omission is made a worker should never try to insert an entry into the existing text, by overwriting or squeezing words in. It is necessary to clearly mark the entry as an addition and to comment on why the entry is late.

I would also stress that where a mistake is made, then a worker should not try to scribble out or erase the writing. A single line should be drawn through the mistake, so it can still be read, with the alteration initialled and the correct entry written below. Again this will make obvious to any future reader what happened and why.

DISCLOSURE RULES

As previously mentioned it may be necessary to examine records relating to the alleged victim as part of the case. Furthermore it may be necessary to allow the suspect's solicitors an opportunity to examine the records. In the interests of a fair trial the judicial system offers disclosure of all relevant information to the defence.

During the disclosure stage I am instructed as the investigator to review all material and disclose to the defence anything which may undermine the prosecution's case or assist the defence. This may include information regarding the victim's history, which casts doubt on the reliability of the complaint. Capacity of the victim is one such example.

There are certain exceptions to this ruling, where information is identified as being sensitive, but withholding this information requires the permission of a judge, who will review the details in confidence and issue an order that these details remain confidential. However, the judge will not withhold information that clearly assists the defence's case in Court.

CAPACITY ISSUES

From my experiences one of the recurring factors when investigating crimes involving vulnerable adults is the question of capacity. This means the adult's ability to consent to certain key facts at the time the offence took place. The question raised could be: 'Did the person have capacity to understand what they were agreeing to at that time?'

A prime example of this is during a financial abuse enquiry, where another person is suspected of abusing the position of trust when having an Enduring Power of Attorney. Unfortunately these are the sort of cases which are not necessarily discovered immediately and it may take several weeks or months before the financial irregularities are found. The big question is whether the victim had capacity to make the important decisions and give permission for the person(s) to act on their behalf.

I interviewed a suspect recently who had obtained a Power of Attorney for an older woman. The woman, who had a form of dementia, was unable to manage her own finances and moved into residential care. In the absence of any next of kin, the suspect was able to spend the woman's money as if it was her own. However, when interviewed the suspect claimed to have been gifted the money by the woman prior to her losing capacity.

This is a very difficult thing to prove or disprove and here is where the relevance of records comes into play. With the benefit of detailed notes documented by the care staff, it could be proven that the older woman clearly had lost the capacity to make these sort of decisions prior to the theft occurring. However, in the absence of such records, the only person who would have been able to refute the suspect's claims would have been the victim herself and since she no longer had capacity, this was impossible.

Another example of the capacity issue can be found in sexual offences. Accurate and detailed records, along with professional assessments, will assist in determining whether a person has or more importantly had sufficient capacity to give consent.

DECISION TO PROSECUTE

At some point or another a worker may well be involved in a case where a person's guilt is, in their mind, without question. However, for inexplicable reasons the case does not proceed to court and the worker may consider a travesty of justice has occurred.

The decision to prosecute is not taken by the police, but by the prosecuting authority. In England and Wales this is the Crown Prosecution Service (CPS) who are guided by the Code for Crown Prosecutors.[1] During various points of an investigation I will discuss the case with the CPS and they will advise on any lines of enquiry which they feel should be pursued. Once the investigation is concluded the CPS will review the file and apply a two-part test. This in its simplest terms means they will evaluate the case and decide whether any charges should be brought against the suspect and therefore whether the case should proceed to court or not. The first part of the test is the *Evidential Test.*[2] Under the Evidential Test the CPS prosecutor must be satisfied themselves that there is sufficient evidence to provide a realistic prospect of conviction. If the case does not pass this test then it will not proceed, no matter how serious or important.

When a case passes the evidential test, the prosecutor must then apply the *Public Interest Test*[3] to decide whether the prosecution is in the public's interest. It will usually be in the public interest to prosecute where there is sufficient evidence, unless there are factors which weigh against rather than in favour of prosecution. One such consideration could be where an offender is already serving a prison sentence for a more serious offence.

The future well-being of the victim or witnesses is also considered when making this decision. On the assumption the case passes both the evidential and public interest tests, it must also remembered that the most important test is still to be faced.

In a civil court the burden of proof is that guilt can be found based on the *balance of probabilities*. The standard is met if the proposition is that the offence

1   This is available in different languages at
      www.cps.gov.uk/victims_witnesses/code.html.
2   For more information see www.cps.gov.uk/about/principles/html.
3   *Ibid.*

is more likely to be true than not true. Effectively, the standard is satisfied if there is greater than 50 per cent chance that the proposition is true.

When a criminal case is heard, the magistrates, judge or jury must be satisfied *'beyond reasonable doubt'*. This means that the proposition or offence must be proven to the extent that there is no 'reasonable doubt' in the mind of a reasonable person (usually this means the mind of the magistrate, judge or jury). There can still be a doubt, but only to the extent that it would be 'unreasonable' to assume the falseness of the proposition.

SPECIAL MEASURES

Most people have had little or no experience with the police or criminal courts. People's perception of the police and courts is based on television dramas and although I am sure most TV producers try to be factually accurate, to make good TV they sensationalise the cases and perhaps give the public the wrong impression. The *Youth Justice and Criminal Evidence Act 1999* provides the legislative framework for the range of Special Measures (Criminal Justice System 2007; Home Office 2002). These are several different ways in which a vulnerable witness may be assisted in giving their evidence.

The first is in what form the witness's evidence is collected, but remember age alone does not make a victim vulnerable. These Special Measures could include the use of:

- *Video recorded evidence in chief.* As I have previously mentioned, the witness' main oral evidence is videotaped and played to the Court. It is therefore possible to record a victim's evidence by means of video recording. This is acceptable where due to circumstances such as illness or disability the victim is unable to provide written evidence. The video suite is set out as a lounge and is specially equipped with video-recording equipment. The victim will be interviewed in comfort by a specially trained officer. The evidence recorded on to a DVD will then be presented to the Court as the evidence-in-chief. This will mean the victim does not have to stand in open court and provide their own evidence. It is however necessary for the victim to be cross examined or questioned by the defence regarding their evidence. When this situation arises, there are certain applications that can be made.

- *Screens around the witness box.* A screen is placed around the witness box to prevent the witness from seeing the defendant.

- *Evidence via live link.* The witness can sit in a room outside the courtroom and give their evidence via a live television link to the courtroom. They will be able to see everything that goes on in the courtroom and those in the courtroom can see the witness via the link.

- *Removal of wigs and gowns.* The judge and lawyers in the Crown Court do not wear gowns and wigs.

- *Evidence given in private.* This is when the public gallery is cleared.

- *Use of communication aids.* For example an alphabet board.

- *Examination through an intermediary.* This is where a person is appointed to help the witness give their evidence.

As investigator I will make the necessary arrangements and make the applications to the court through the CPS for the Special Measures. More Special Measures are gradually being introduced in criminal courts in England and Wales. Most of the measures are available in the Crown Court for both vulnerable and intimidated witnesses (where applicable).

Never forget that the police, along with all other services, are here to support and assist the witnesses through the whole process and most importantly nothing will be done without the permission of the vulnerable person concerned. All actions taken will be with their best interests in mind.

What follows is a case study which I have used when delivering presentations and training courses. I am including it as a fitting conclusion to this chapter; it can be used for groups of workers or in individual supervision sessions.

CASE STUDY 3.1

PART 1

May is 85 years old and lives alone, with no known next of kin. She has limited mobility, due to the need of a hip replacement. She has become forgetful in recent years and relies heavily on a domiciliary care worker from a private domiciliary care agency, who visits her twice daily to provide support and assistance. She is also assisted by older neighbours and friends. Her general health has been getting progressively worse more recently.

Following a fall at home and visit to the local accident and emergency department, her social worker arranges for her to be moved by ambulance to a care home for respite. Two days after arriving at the home a colleague brings to your attention the fact that May has several small brown bruises on her inner and outer upper arms. May has made no disclosures as to how she has received these marks.

Questions for Group Work:

1.1 What if any are your immediate concerns and why?

1.2 What do you think the first course of action should be and why?

1.3 Who do you think should be involved/informed at this early stage and why?

1.4 What other signs and symptoms *could* be present which might lead you to suspect abuse is occurring?[4]

Possible answers (not exhaustive):[5]

QUESTION 1.1

- This is evidence of physical abuse by staff of care home, domiciliary care worker, resident, friend, neighbour

- The bruises are self inflicted

- The bruises are the result of an accident

- There are manual handling issues

- May has a medical condition

- What is the age of the bruising?

- Could these be non-accidental injuries

- Does May need medical treatment

- May's capacity to give an explanation

- May has dementia.

QUESTION 1.2

- Speak to May

- Seek medical attention (photographic evidence to be taken by police forensic surgeon/hospital staff if needed)

- Notify supervisors

- Report to Adult Social Care

- Notify Safeguarding Adults Coordinator

- Record incident

---

4   This question is put in to find out how much workers know about signs and symptoms of abuse in general.
5   Examples of typical responses received in training sessions, some of which could be debated when being mindful of contaminating evidence.

- Take preventative measures
- Conduct a risk assessment.

QUESTION 1.3

- Manager of the care home
- Supervisors
- Other care staff
- Adult Social Care
- Safeguarding Adults Coordinator
- Police
- Commission for Social Care Inspection
- GP
- Hospital.

QUESTION 1.4

- Unexplained or inconsistent injuries or burns
- Finger- or object-shaped bruises
- Clustered bruising
- Bruising on normally well-protected areas e.g. inside thigh or inside upper arms
- Finger marks – from gripping or poking
- Burns in unusual places or of an unusual type
- Injuries in well-protected areas or soft parts
- Injuries/bruising found at different stages of healing that would suggest a non-accidental cause
- Keeping arms and legs covered in hot weather
- An injury shape similar to an object
- Injuries to head, face or scalp
- Pressure sores and being left in wet clothing
- Bald patches
- History of falls or minor ailments
- Hypothermia
- Malnourished/dehydrated without an illness-related cause or when not living alone

- Often being unkempt or unwashed; smelling of urine/faeces

- Incontinence – smearing or recent changes

- Reluctance to seek medical help

- Withdrawal from physical contact

- Aggression to others.

PART 2

The GP has examined May and is of the opinion that the bruises are finger marks, but he cannot give any indication as to how old they are or how they were inflicted. There is no record in any of the case notes making mention of any of these bruises previously. A neighbour visits May who tells her the domiciliary care worker is 'a bit rough sometimes'. The neighbour encourages May to tell staff.

May tells you that her domiciliary care worker is very snappy and rough sometimes, becoming frustrated because 'I am so slow'. She pulls at May to get her to move more quickly.

Questions for group work:

2.1 What other agencies should now be notified as part of the case and why?

2.2 Of the agencies now involved, what role will they play?

2.3 With the disclosures now made, what actions are necessary?

2.4 What sources of information could be explored to account for May's injuries?

Possible answers (not exhaustive):

QUESTION 2.1

- Adult Social Care

- Safeguarding Adults Coordinator

- Police

- Commission for Social Care Inspection

- GP

- Hospital

- Domiciliary care agency.

QUESTION 2.2

- Adult Social Care – convene strategy meeting; coordinate investigation; support for May
- Police – carry out a criminal investigation
- Commission for Social Care Inspection – advice; monitoring of care home and domiciliary care agency
- Domiciliary care agency – suspension of domiciliary care worker.

QUESTION 2.3

- Record disclosure
- Record complaint
- Take statements from witnesses
- Suspend the domiciliary care worker
- Assess risk to other service users
- Record injuries
- Have a specialist examine the bruises (police forensic surgeon; hospital staff)
- Have a specialist photograph injuries (police forensic surgeon; hospital staff).

QUESTION 2.4

- May (ask her carefully)
- Other staff
- Other service users
- GP's notes
- Hospital records
- Ambulance reports
- Domiciliary care worker's notes
- Any other relevant records
- Friends
- Neighbours.

PART 3

May is interviewed by the police and a social worker. She tells them that her domiciliary care worker regularly grabs her by the arms and pulls her about, when she will not do as she says, the last incident being when May could not find her debit card. When questioned May confirms that the domiciliary care worker regularly withdraws cash from her bank account for her and has known her PIN since May got her new debit card. May is clearly very frightened of the carer.

You examine a recent bank statement belonging to May and see large regular cash withdrawals from her account, even whilst she was resident in the care home. Her current balance is now only a few hundred pounds.

Questions for group work:

3.1. What methods of interview are available for police and Adult Social Care interviewers and under what conditions?

3.2. Prior to the interview of a vulnerable adult like May, what considerations should be made by the interviewers and why?

3.3. What additional concerns or offences now exist and what course of action should be taken?

3.4. What sources could now be explored to prove or disprove the whole case?

Possible answers (not exhaustive):

QUESTION 3.1

If May has a mental or physical disability she would be considered a vulnerable adult and a video interview could be applicable. She is not a vulnerable adult by age alone, but Special Measures are available e.g. use of the video suite.

QUESTION 3.2

- Time of the interview
- Duration
- Exhibit
- Visual aids
- Refreshments
- Transportation
- Medical condition/medication needed (if any)
- Support by worker/friend
- Language

- Gender of interviewers
- Accessibility
- Aftercare/victim support.

QUESTION 3.3

- Financial abuse is now a concern
- Change bank card/PIN
- Make assessment of mental capacity
- Arrange Lasting Power of Attorney
- Arrest and interview domicillary care worker
- Start financial investigation
- Gain support from Adult Social Care
- Convene a case conference under Safeguarding procedures.

QUESTION 3.4

- May's video interview
- Medical records
- Bank accounts
- Witness statements
- CCTV at ATM
- Domiciliary care worker's bank accounts
- Search of address
- Court of Protection
- Office of Public Guardian
- Other victims
- Friends
- Neighbours.

PART 4

The domiciliary care worker is arrested and interviewed. She admits to having domestic and financial problems, having access to May's bank accounts, withdrawing £1200 over the last four months. The carer admits that to access the bank, she obtained a Lasting Power of Attorney. She also admits to causing the bruising to May's arms, when shaking her in temper as she could not find her bank card.

The domiciliary care worker is charged with theft and assault and is bailed to appear at Court.

Questions for group work:

4.1.   What aftercare support could be offered to May?

4.2.   What actions could be considered against the domiciliary care worker?

4.3.   What further actions need to be taken and by whom?

4.4.   What Special Measures could be put in place to assist May in the event she is required to give evidence?

Possible answers (not exhaustive):

QUESTION 4.1

- Ongoing care package from adult social care
- New domiciliary care worker
- Victim support
- Friends
- Neighbours
- Counselling/therapy re abuse.

QUESTION 4.2

- Conditional bail pending Court
- Imprisonment
- Disciplinary action by employer
- Assets frozen as part of financial investigation
- Referral to the Protection of Vulnerable Adult (POVA) register
- Court Order to repay money.

QUESTION 4.3

- Application to POVA register by employer
- Commission for Social Care Inspection to continue with examination of Domiciliary Care Agency
- Police – enquiries to trace any other victims
- Adult Social Care – continued support for May

QUESTION 4.4

- Video evidence-in-chief
- Screens around box
- Live link
- Removal of wigs/gowns.

STATUTES

Youth Justice and Criminal Evidence Act 1999. London: The Stationery Office.

REFERENCES

Criminal Justice System (2007) *Achieving Best Evidence in Criminal Proceedings: Guidance on Interviewing Victims and Witnesses, and Using Special Measures.* London: Home Office and Criminal Justice System.

Home Office (2002) *Achieving Best Evidence in Criminal Proceedings: Guidance for Vulnerable or Intimidated Witnesses including Children.* London: Home Office Communication Directorate.

CHAPTER 4

CRIMINAL JUSTICE AND VULNERABLE ADULTS: WHO DOES WHAT?

KATHRYN STONE

INTRODUCTION

As a society, we have historically been very poor at understanding the needs of anyone who is perceived as somehow different from others. The criminal justice system is one place where any difference is heightened and which is often used against people. Sadly, even today, people with learning disabilities and people with mental health problems are still labelled 'incompetent' or 'unreliable' witnesses. This chapter sets out some of the roles in the criminal justice system and the part they play in supporting vulnerable adults to have equal access to justice. Witness supporters, intermediaries and appropriate adults all have a part to play in ensuring that vulnerable adults – either as victims, witnesses or suspects – have equal access to the criminal justice system.

HOW WE GOT WHERE WE ARE TODAY

The history of our society shows how we have developed and civilised ourselves; and a mark of civilisation is the law. The law tells us what is acceptable and what is not. The law should allow us to live equally and fairly. But does it? We have laws that say people must not be raped or abused. That shows we are civilised. But people are raped and are abused, and then we look to bring them to justice. However, if you are a vulnerable victim your chances of justice are slim. Rapists and abusers go unpunished because we cannot give all our citizens justice. Vulnerable adults remain prey to rape and abuse and crime because we – in essence – do not treat them as equal citizens.

In the past 25 years, there have been many great strides taken in seeking justice for vulnerable adults. In August 1992 the government published the *Memorandum of Good Practice on Video Recorded Interviews with Child Witnesses for Criminal Proceedings* (Home Office and Department of Health 1992). This supported provisions in the *Criminal Justice Act 1991* which permitted video recordings for children's evidence in criminal proceedings, particularly in cases involving allegations of sexual abuse, and in civil proceedings involving the care and custody of children. The 1989 report of the Advisory Group on Video Evidence chaired by Judge Thomas Pigot QC (commonly known as the Pigot Report), recommended that once the suggested changes to the child evidence measures had been introduced, those should be extended to adult vulnerable witnesses at the discretion of the court (Pigot 1989).

This eventually led, in June 1998, to the Home Office publishing *Speaking Up for Justice*; the report on the treatment of vulnerable or intimidated witnesses, including children, in the criminal justice system (Home Office 1998). It made 78 recommendations for improvements including the reporting of crime, identification of vulnerable or intimidated witnesses, and measures to assist witnesses before, during and after the trial. Its opening recommendation suggested a definition of 'vulnerability'. You were to be considered vulnerable 'as a result of personal characteristics' (a disorder or disability) or if your 'vulnerabilities depend on circumstances' such as emotional trauma or intimidation (Home Office 1998, Chapter 3).

The report also recommended, in line with Pigot, extending the existing special measures introduced for child witnesses (use of screens, live closed circuit television links (CCTV) and video-recorded evidence-in-chief) to vulnerable or intimidated adults, together with a range of other measures. Some of these, which required legislation, were included in Part II of the *Youth Justice and Criminal Evidence Act 1999*. The implementation programme for the 78 recommendations, *Action for Justice*, began in 1999 and was revised in 2002 (Home Office 1999 and 2002a). This was followed by government guidance – *Achieving Best Evidence in Criminal Proceedings: Guidance for Vulnerable and Intimidated Witnesses, Including Children* (Home Office 2002b). This replaced and extended the *Memorandum of Good Practice*. This was part of the implementation plan *Action for Justice* to see through the reforms recommended in *Speaking Up For Justice*. Other related publications included *Vulnerable Witnesses: A Police Service Guide* (Home Office 2002c). In 2007 *Achieving Best Evidence* was revised and re-issued as *Achieving Best Evidence in Criminal Proceedings: Guidance on Interviewing Victims and Witnesses, and Using Special Measures* (Criminal Justice System 2007).

WHO IS A VULNERABLE WITNESS?

Section 63 of the *Youth Justice and Criminal Evidence Act 1999* defines a witness as 'any person called, or proposed to be called, to give evidence in proceedings'. Thus anybody, except a suspected offender, who is likely to be called to give evidence in a trial, is a witness.

Section 16 of the same legislation also sets out who are to be regarded as potential vulnerable witnesses either through personal characteristics or age. It states that every child or young person who is under 17 years old could be a vulnerable witness. Anyone aged over 17 whose evidence may be affected because they have a mental health problem or learning disability or physical disability is also to be considered a possible vulnerable witness.

The law defines a mental health problem as a 'mental disorder' as defined by the *Mental Health Act 1983*. The *Mental Health Act 1983* describes mental disorder as 'mental illness, arrested or incomplete development of mind, psychopathic disorder and any other disorder or disability of mind' (Section 1: 1 (2)). The same section then defines four subcategories of mental disorder:

- *Severe mental impairment* means a state of arrested or incomplete development of mind which includes severe impairment of intelligence and social functioning and is associated with abnormally aggressive or seriously irresponsible conduct on the part of the person concerned.

- *Mental impairment* means a state of arrested or incomplete development of mind (not amounting to severe mental impairment) which includes significant impairment of intelligence and social functioning and is associated with abnormally aggressive or seriously irresponsible conduct on the part of the person concerned.

- *Psychopathic disorder* means a persistent disorder or disability of mind (whether or not including significant impairment of intelligence) which results in abnormally aggressive or seriously irresponsible conduct on the part of the person concerned.

- *Mental illness*. Despite being the most common form of mental disorder for which people are dealt with under the Act, this is not defined.

The *Youth Justice and Criminal Evidence Act 1999* then goes on to define a person with learning disabilities as someone having 'a significant impairment of intelligence and social functioning'; while a person with physical disabilities is someone having 'a physical disability or physical disorder' (Part 2, Chapter 1, 16:2(a) (ii))

Government research, which sampled 500 random cases, suggested that as many as 54 per cent were possibly vulnerable and intimidated witnesses (Burton, Evans and Sanders 2006). However, *Speaking Up for Justice* estimated that 5–7 per cent would be potentially vulnerable (and a further 2–3% would be vulnerable through intimidation).

In practice, decision-makers apply a three-stage test:

1. Is the prospective witness potentially vulnerable or intimidated or both?

2. If yes, is this vulnerability/intimidation likely to affect whether they will be willing to testify in Court, to affect their capacity to give their 'best evidence' in Court (evidence that is complete, coherent and accurate), and to cause them undue stress in or before Court?

3. If yes, what type of support or assistance will be most likely to alleviate these difficulties?

Applying this three-stage test to the random sample, researchers concluded that 'on a very conservative estimate, 24 per cent of witnesses were probably vulnerable and intimidated witnesses (VIWs). The gap between this and the official estimate (between 7–10%) was considerable' (Burton *et al.* 2006, p.vi).

The report went on: 'Early identification by the police and the CPS is vital but the police continued to have difficulty in identifying VIWs, particularly those with learning disabilities, mental disorders or those who are intimidated. The CPS rarely identified witnesses as VIW if they had not been identified by the police, even those that were categorically VIW' (Burton *et al.* 2006, p.vi).

Four years earlier, the then Home Office minister Keith Bradley acknowledged that 'the identification of vulnerable witnesses at the investigation stage is fundamental to the operation of the whole *Speaking up for Justice* scheme' (Home Office 2002, p.1). And yet as a landmark Australian police report had already conceded: 'Identification of intellectual disability is one of the most difficult issues for personnel in the criminal justice system' (New South Wales Law Reform Commission 1996, section 4). However, despite the acknowledged difficulty, failure to identify potential vulnerable witnesses is a contravention of *The Code of Practice for Victims of Crime* which requires 'police to take all reasonable steps to identify vulnerable or intimidated victims' (Home Office 2005, p.7).

A number of those reasonable steps had been covered in *Vulnerable Witnesses: A Police Service Guide* (Home Office 2002c), which provided a series of prompts to help police officers identify vulnerable witnesses. These include a list of behavioural characteristics which, although in themselves do not necessarily mean a witness should be classed as vulnerable, can indicate a degree of vulnerability. Police are advised to look out, for example, for difficulty in communicating without assistance/interpretation; difficulty understanding questions and instructions; difficult to understand or no or limited speech; the use of signs and gestures to communicate; inappropriate or inconsistent responses to questions; a focus on what could be deemed irrelevant small points, but not the important points; short attention span; inability to read or write; difficulty in telling the time or remembering their date of birth, age, address, telephone number; and appearing very eager to please, or to repeat what you say.

These attempts to improve identification of vulnerable witnesses are to be welcomed. For once identified as a vulnerable victim or witness, a person may be eligible for 'Special Measures'. Special Measures (see below) were intended to improve the way that vulnerable or intimidated witnesses were dealt with by the criminal justice system and help them give best evidence in criminal proceedings. Those measures that required legislation were included in Part II of the *Youth Justice and Criminal Evidence Act 1999.*

Examples of Special Measures available to vulnerable witnesses with the agreement of the Court (from the *Youth Justice and Criminal Evidence Act 1999*)

- Screens (section 23).
- Live link (section 24).
- Evidence given in private (section 25).
- Removal of wigs and gowns (section 26).
- Video-recorded interview (section 27).
- Video-recorded cross examination (section 28).
- Examination of a witness through an intermediary (section 29).
- Aids to communication (section 30).
- Mandatory protection of witness from cross-examination by the accused person (sections 34 and 35).
- Discretionary protection of witness from cross-examination by the accused in person (section 36).
- Restrictions on evidence and questions about complainant's sexual behaviour (section 41).
- Reporting restrictions (sections 44–46).

For more detail see Criminal Justice System 2007, sections 1.9–1.19.

All of the above Special Measures are available for vulnerable witnesses in Crown Courts and Magistrates' Courts in England and Wales. The only exception is saying what happened on videotape and presenting this as the main evidence. This is available in Crown Court but is only available in certain cases in Magistrates' Courts. Special Measures are available to prosecution and defence witnesses but not defendants.

In addition to these new and improved measures, there are now a number of identified roles to support and assist vulnerable adults in giving their very best evidence, including supporters, intermediaries and appropriate adults. However, often their roles are confused and the boundaries between different approaches are blurred. We will now look at these in turn.

SUPPORTERS

Being a witness can be an anxious and worrying time for anyone – and particularly so if you are a vulnerable adult. Having a friend, relative or someone trusted with you can help alleviate some of those pressures. Vulnerable adults may feel very isolated when giving their evidence and can sometimes be reassured by having someone sitting near them, either in the courtroom or in the television link room. This person is known as 'a supporter'.

WHAT DOES A SUPPORTER DO?

A supporter can support a vulnerable victim or witness just by being present when they are giving their evidence. A supporter can also offer support and reassurance before someone has to give evidence and, if the Court allows, they can keep a vulnerable witness company during any breaks.

The supporter can help explain what is happening and make sure that the needs of the witness are known to police, the Crown Prosecution Service (CPS), the Court and so on. They can help reassure the witness. The supporter will be able to sit alongside the vulnerable witness when they are using any of the other Special Measures approved by the court.

They must not discuss the details of the case with the witness or anybody else. Although discouraging the witness from discussing the case, should the witness discuss an important part of the crime, the supporter should record what has happened, and note things such as:

- What time did it happen?
- Who said what to whom?
- Who was present?
- Where did the conversation take place?
- What exactly was said?

These notes should be handed to the police officer in charge of the investigation.

There are three distinct stages that a supporter can be involved: interview, pre-trial and court witness. It is unlikely that the same person will support a witness through all three stages.

The interview supporter

This supporter – a friend, relative, advocate or other person – is independent of police and is not party to the case being investigated. They provide support during the original investigative interview. *Achieving Best Evidence* advises that:

> interview supporters must be clearly told that their role is limited to providing emotional support and that they must not prompt or speak for the witness, especially on any matters relevant to the investigation. (Criminal Justice System 2007, 3.124)

It also warns that:

> in some circumstances it has been found that the use of a person who is *well-known* to the witness as an interview supporter can prove counterproductive by inhibiting the disclosure of information (e.g. as a result of embarrassment arising from sensitive information being disclosed in the presence of a person seen by the witness on a day-to-day basis). For this reason, discussions as to the identity of any potential interview supporter should take account of the nature of their relationship with the witness and its potential impact on the interview process. Wherever possible, the views of the witness should be established prior to the interview as to whether they wish another person to be present and, if so, who this should be. (Criminal Justice System 2007, 3.121)

Pre-trial supporter

This supporter provides support after the original interview and before the start of any trial. Quite often a Victim Support volunteer performs this role.

The court witness supporter

This supporter provides support during the trial. They may be known to the witness but must not be party to any proceedings and know nothing of the case. Quite often a member of the Witness Service performs this role (see also Criminal Justice System 2007, Appendix G).

When a vulnerable witness is nominating a potential supporter, consideration should be given to how they might react if they hear the evidence. For example, a vulnerable witness may want to protect certain family or friends from hearing the details of the evidence. If a family member might get upset or angry in court, this may also upset the witness. In those cases it may be best to decide to have someone from outside the family.

WHO CAN AND CANNOT BE A SUPPORTER?

A supporter can be someone trusted by the witness. This could be a friend, relative or advocate with no connection to the case. Equally it could be someone from a specialist support organisation or social services department who may already be working with the vulnerable adult in some way unconnected to the case (this person may also give advice on who would be best placed to support the witness).

A supporter cannot be someone aware of the details of the case or involved in the case in some way – for example, as a witness themselves. Nor can a supporter be someone who wants to advise and influence the witness.

GOOD PRACTICE POINTS FOR A SUPPORTER

DOS

- Make sure the witness is as comfortable as possible.
- Make sure enough breaks are taken.
- Check that the witness understands the questions and the police understand the answers.
- Escort the witness to the interview room.
- Challenge inappropriate questions or behaviour of the police.
- Take pens and paper if you think the witness will use them.
- Make sure the police are aware of the needs of the witness.

DON'TS

- Help the witness with any part of the evidence.
- Interfere or try to influence evidence in any way.
- Prompt the witness or interrupt while they are giving evidence.
- Threaten or pressurise the witness.
- 'Legally advise' – if legal advice is required get a lawyer.
- Use negative body language (yawning, stretching and so on).

INTERMEDIARIES – WHAT DO THEY DO?

Following assessment of the witness, the intermediary's role at investigative interview and trial is to make sure that the witness is able to give their best evidence, that which is 'complete, coherent and accurate'. They are approved for use by the Court and are allowed to explain questions and answers to the witness, but not to change the substance or meaning of evidence. The role may assist questioners to test the witness's evidence but cannot provide an opinion on whether the witness is truthful (Plotnikoff and Woolfson 2007).

Even though Section 29 of the *Youth Justice and Criminal Evidence Act 1999* makes it clear that an intermediary can assist a witness to communicate by explaining questions put to and answers given by a vulnerable witness, this rarely happens in practice. *Achieving Best Evidence* states:

> It is more common for intermediaries to assist during the planning phase of an interview by providing advice on how questions should be asked and then to intervene during the interview where miscommunication is likely by assisting the interviewer to rephrase the question or by repeating the witness's answers where they might otherwise be inaudible or unclear on the recording. The extent to which the intermediary is actively involved in the communication of questions and answers will vary from witness to witness depending on the witness's particular needs and communication style. It will also depend on the degree of compliance with the intermediary's recommendations by the interviewer. It is very important to remember that the intermediary is there only to assist communication and understanding – they are not allowed to take on the function of investigator. (Criminal Justice System 2007, 2.97)

WHAT IS AN INTERMEDIARY?

Intermediaries are a go-between for a vulnerable witness and the Court. They are independent – which means they do not take sides. They are not investigators (someone trying to find out the facts of what happened), advocates (someone who represents and speaks up for the vulnerable witness), supporters (someone known to the vulnerable witness who can reassure them) or appropriate adults (someone who can support and advise a vulnerable witness who is being kept at a police station). Intermediaries work for the Court, want to make sure justice is done but must do what the judge or magistrate says. They do not ask their own questions or make up answers for vulnerable witnesses.

The role of an intermediary is thus separate from that of the court or witness supporter and they should be available during pre-trial preparation to improve the witness's understanding. 'An intermediary will usually have undertaken an assessment of the witness at an early stage in the proceedings, and will have produced a written report for the judge, the prosecution and the defence. That report should highlight matters such as limited concentration spans and particular types of questioning that should be avoided' (Criminal Justice System 2007, 5.72).

All sorts of people from different walks of life have become intermediaries. They include people who are speech and language therapists, psychologists, teachers, social care workers and health professionals (Home Office press release 11 January 2006).

As with all Special Measures, not everyone who could have an intermediary will need one. Some vulnerable adults will be able to understand and answer questions on their own. Some people might just need a little help in understanding what is going on or what is being asked.

An early evaluation of the scheme concluded that 'feedback from witnesses and carers in trial cases was uniformly enthusiastic. Carers felt that intermediaries not only facilitated communication but also helped witnesses cope with the stress of giving evidence. Appreciation of the role was also almost unanimous across the judiciary and other criminal justice personnel in pathfinder cases' (Plotnikoff and Woolfson 2007, p.4).

In 2007, intermediaries were available in eight police areas; Merseyside, West Midlands, Thames Valley, South Wales, Norfolk, and Devon and Cornwall were the original six 'pathfinder areas' in 2004/5. They were joined in 2007 by Derbyshire and Leicestershire. Experience from these areas will inform the plan to introduce the scheme in all the other areas in England and Wales. By the end of February 2006, there were 76 registered intermediaries and 206 requests for an intermediary had been received (Plotnikoff and Woolfson 2007). By the summer of 2007, over 600 witnesses have been supported by 120 registered intermediaries – with an average of over 30 referrals a month being made (Hopkins 2007, p.37). Recruitment is ongoing. By January 2008, a recruitment advertisement issued by the government put the number of witnesses supported past the 1000 mark. In essence, this shows that over 1000 people have accessed a justice that perhaps would have previously been denied them.

WHEN TO USE AN INTERMEDIARY

If a police officer or lawyer thinks that a vulnerable witness needs help in understanding or answering questions then an intermediary should be brought in as soon as possible. The intermediary can meet the vulnerable witness and can decide with police officers and the CPS whether a case should go to court or not. An intermediary does not have to be used from the start. The court can be asked to use an intermediary at the trial even if one had not been used during the interviews. Neither does an intermediary need to stay on until the case is finished. They can be called upon at any time to help for as long as needed.

As a Special Measure the court will usually approve the use of an intermediary if it believes the witness is vulnerable, and if it believes that an intermediary will help the witness provide better evidence. In deciding on whether an intermediary is needed the court will think about all aspects of the case, including what the vulnerable witness thinks – do they wish to have an intermediary? The best evidence a court can hear is that which is complete (nothing is missed out), clear (easy to understand) and true (just the facts).

TASKS

An intermediary can do a lot of things that help vulnerable witnesses and those who work in criminal justice – such as police, solicitors, lawyers, magistrates and judges.

What an intermediary can do

- Meet the witness.
- Provide advice.
- Help the witness understand questions.
- Help prepare the witness for court.

Meet the witness

An intermediary will meet with the vulnerable witness first to find out what help they might need. However, they will not talk about the case at this time. This meeting is to:

- find out what help might be needed
- make sure that the intermediary is the right person help the witness
- get to know each other.

Provide advice

An intermediary can provide advice that can help interviews go well and get the best evidence for court. This advice could be on:

- how a vulnerable witness communicates
- the level of understanding of a vulnerable witness
- the best way to question a vulnerable witness in order to get the best answers
- what sort of questions to avoid
- how long a vulnerable witness might take to answer a question
- how often a vulnerable witness will need a break from being asked questions.

Help the witness understand questions

An intermediary can help a vulnerable witness understand questions that may be asked during interviews with police or lawyers. Sometimes the way police and lawyers ask questions can be confusing or complicated. Sometimes the words they use are not clear. Intermediaries can help with this. They can also help make clear what a vulnerable witness has said in answer to any questions.

Help prepare the witness for court

If police get good evidence and the CPS decide to prosecute, the case will go to court. This can make a vulnerable witness worry about what might happen. An intermediary can help make this more comfortable by explaining what will happen and why. Before the trial, an intermediary can take a vulnerable witness to visit the court where the trial will take place to have a look around and get used to what it feels like.

CASE STUDY 4.1

BACKGROUND

Sarah[1] a young woman with learning disabilities, said that she had been raped. The police decided that because Sarah had problems making herself understood she could not be a witness. However, when the police heard about the new scheme they asked for an intermediary to help.

WHAT HAPPENED

In police interviews the intermediary picked out questions that were too complicated for Sarah, and repeated some of Sarah's answers that the police could not work out.

In court, the intermediary told the judge and lawyers about how to deal with Sarah's communication difficulties. The intermediary also helped Sarah use pictures to pick out the rooms where she said she had been raped.

RESULT

The man who raped Sarah was sent to prison for ten years.

---

1   All names have been changed.

CASE STUDY 4.2

BACKGROUND

Brian was a 64-year-old man with severe learning disabilities. At first he gave his evidence to police using a video recording. However, when he was asked to give evidence in Court in person an intermediary was asked to help Brian give his side of the story with as little upset as possible.

WHAT HAPPENED

The intermediary wrote a report for the judge and those asking questions in court about Brian. The intermediary explained about Brian's difficulties and how he should be treated.

RESULT

The judge was able to stop the way Brian was being questioned in court because the questions were the type that the intermediary had said Brian would be unable to answer. Without this the questions would have gone on and made Brian seem like someone who was unsure of what he was saying. This would have meant that people might not trust what he had to say.

APPROPRIATE ADULTS

So far this chapter has concentrated on the needs of vulnerable adults if they are the victims or witnesses of crime. Things are different if they are suspected of causing the crime. If a vulnerable adult is to be questioned they should be supported by an 'appropriate adult'.

The Police and Criminal Evidence Act 1984 (PACE) *Code C: The Detention, Treatment and Questioning of Persons by Police Officers* sets out the circumstances that a person 'who is mentally disordered or mentally vulnerable' should be accompanied by an appropriate adult when being questioned (Home Office 2008, PACE Code C, 1.7(b)).

Appropriate adults are there to make sure that the detained person understands what is happening to them and why. Their role is a positive one – they are not there simply to observe. However, a person cannot act as an appropriate adult if they have received admissions or denials from the detained person before they came to the police station. Nor must they seek to provide the detained person with legal advice (conversations with the detained person are not covered by legal privilege).

WHAT DOES AN APPROPRIATE ADULT DO?

An appropriate adult is there to support, advise and assist the detained person, particularly while they are being questioned. It is also their role to observe whether police are acting properly, fairly and with respect for the rights of the detained person. And to tell them if they think they are not. An appropriate adult can also assist with communication between the detained person and police, and has a responsibility to make sure that the detained person understands their rights, and takes a role in protecting their rights.

LEGAL ADVICE

An appropriate adult should consider whether legal advice from a solicitor is required. They should normally speak to the detained person in private before deciding whether legal advice should be requested. The detained person can speak to a solicitor at the police station at any time. It will cost them nothing and they can speak to the solicitor privately either on the telephone or at the police station. Even if the appropriate adult decides that a solicitor is not necessary upon arrival at the police station, they can change their mind about that at any time. However, if the detained person is adamant that they do not want to see a solicitor, that wish must be respected. If the detained person does wish to see a solicitor the appropriate adult must inform the custody officer immediately.

THE RIGHTS OF A VULNERABLE ADULT AS A DETAINED PERSON

If detained, a vulnerable adult has the right to have someone informed of their arrest. They also have the right to consult privately with a solicitor and be made aware of the fact that independent legal advice is available free of charge. Finally, they have the right to consult the Codes of Practice setting out the powers, responsibilities and procedures of the police. The custody officer must also give the detained person a written notice of these basic rights, together with an additional notice of their other entitlements such as reasonable standards of physical comfort, adequate food and drink, access to toilet and washing facilities, clothing, medical attention, and exercise where practicable.

THE RIGHTS OF AN APPROPRIATE ADULT

An appropriate adult has the right to be told why the detained person is being held. They must be allowed to speak to the detained person in private at any time. They have the right to inspect the written record of the person's period in detention (the custody record) at any time. They can also see copies of the notices of rights and entitlements mentioned above, including a copy of the Codes of Practice setting out the powers, responsibilities and procedures of police.

An appropriate adult can intervene in an interview if they feel it is necessary and in the interests of the detained person to help them communicate effectively with police. They can also ask for a break in any interview, either to seek legal advice or consult with the detained person (particularly if the interview is a lengthy one or if the detained person is distressed or ill).

The appropriate adult also has the right to be present during any procedure requiring information to be given by or sought from the detained person. They may also be present when any form of consent is sought from the detained vulnerable adult or if the vulnerable adult is asked to agree or sign any documentation or both.

The appropriate adult is allowed to be present when the custody officer informs the detained person of their rights and entitlements; when the detained person is cautioned; during any police interview with the detained person at a police station; when the detained person is charged; during any search of the detained person involving the removal of more than outer clothing (subject to strictly limited exceptions); when the need to keep the person in detention is reviewed; during any form of identification procedure such as an identification parade; during any process involving the fingerprinting or photographing of the detained person or when a sample is taken from them. However, the appropriate adult is not entitled to be present during private legal consultations between the detainee and their legal representative.

QUESTIONING

One of the main reasons for detaining a person at a police station is to ask them questions. The police should only ask them questions in the presence of an appropriate adult. Before any questioning begins the detained person should be cautioned in the following terms: 'You do not have to say anything. But it may harm your defence if you do not mention when questioned something which you later rely on in court. Anything you do say may be given in evidence.'

The appropriate adult's main role is to ensure that in any interview which follows the person detained understands the questions which are being asked and that the police do not ask questions in a way which is confusing, repetitive or oppressive. They should always make sure that when questions are asked the person detained understands them and that the police understand the reply.

Almost all interviews are audio or videotape recorded. There is a procedure for recording. In an interview the appropriate adult should not feel that they have to remain silent. They are entitled to intervene at any stage. If the appropriate adult is unhappy about the way in which the interview is being conducted then they are entitled to ask to stop the interview so that legal advice can be taken from a solicitor. Any queries or complaints about the conduct of the interview should be made to the custody officer.

CONCLUSION

This chapter has discussed some of the ways in which vulnerable adults can be supported in the criminal justice system. We have come a long way in the last ten years, but that there is still some distance to travel. As I write there are more discussions and seminar papers being published on the role of the CPS and police in identifying and charging cases of disability hate crime; evidence of hostility because of a disability can be seen as an aggravating factor and the tariff increased accordingly.

We have undoubtedly come some distance in beginning to understand how vulnerable adults can get a fair access to justice. But, equally, there is still some way to go. For, if we cannot have justice for the most vulnerable people in our society, we have no justice.

STATUTES
Criminal Justice Act 1991. London: HMSO.
Mental Health Act 1983. London: HMSO.
Police and Criminal Evidence Act 1984. London: HMSO.
Youth Justice and Criminal Evidence Act 1999. London: HMSO.

REFERENCES
Burton, M., Evans, R. and Sanders, A. (2006) *Are Special Measures for Vulnerable and Intimidated Witnesses Working? Evidence from the Criminal Justice Agencies.* Home Office online report, 1 June. Available at: www.homeoffice.gov.uk/rds/pdfs06/rdsolr0106, accessed 29 July 2008.

Criminal Justice System (2007) *Achieving Best Evidence in Criminal Proceedings: Guidance on Interviewing Victims and Witnesses, and Using Special Measures.* London: Criminal Justice System.

Home Office (1984) *Guidance for Appropriate Adults: The Police and Criminal Evidence Act 1984 (PACE) Codes of Practice.* London: Home Office.

Home Office (1998) *Speaking Up For Justice: Report of the Interdepartmental Working Group on the Treatment of Vulnerable or Intimidated Witnesses in the Criminal Justice System.* London: Home Office.

Home Office (1999 and 2002a) *Action for Justice.* London: Home Office Communication Directorate.

Home Office (2002b) *Achieving Best Evidence in Criminal Proceedings: Guidance for Vulnerable or Intimidated Witnesses including Children.* London: Home Office Communication Directorate.

Home Office (2002c) *Vulnerable Witnesses: A Police Service Guide.* London: Home Office.

Home Office (2005) *The Code of Practice for Victims of Crime.* London: Home Office.

Home Office (2006) Press release 11 January 2006. Available at www.cjsonline.gov.uk/the_cjs/whats_new/news-3265.html, accessed 29 July 2008.

Home Office (2008) *Police and Criminal Evidence Act 1984 (PACE) Code C: Code of Practice for the Detention, Treatment and Questioning of Persons by Police Officers.* London: Home Office.

Home Office and Department of Health (1992) *Memorandum of Good Practice on Video Recorded Interviews with Child Witnesses for Criminal Proceedings.* London: HMSO.

Hopkins, G. (2007) 'In the cause of justice...', *Community Care*, 21 June, p.37.

New South Wales Law Reform Commission (1996) *Report 80: People with an Intellectual Disability and the Criminal Justice System*. New South Wales: Law Reform Commission. Available at: www.lawlink.nsw.gov.au/lrc.nsf/pages/R80TOC, accessed 29 July 2008.

Office for Criminal Justice Reform (2006) *What's My Story? A Guide to Using Intermediaries to Help Vulnerable Witnesses*. London: OCJR.

Pigot, Judge Thomas (1989) *Report of the Advisory Group on Video-recorded Evidence*. London: HMSO.

Plotnikoff, J. and Woolfson, D. (2007) *The 'Go-Between': Evaluation of Intermediary Pathfinder Projects*. London: Ministry of Justice.

USEFUL ORGANISATIONS

National Autistic Society
The National Autistic Society champions the rights and interests of all people with autism and aims to provide individuals with autism and their families with help, support and services that they can access, trust and rely upon and which can make a positive difference to their lives.
www.nas.org.uk
National helpline: 0845 070 4004

Respond
Respond provides a range of services to both victims and perpetrators of sexual abuse who have learning disabilities and those who have been affected by other trauma.
www.respond.org.uk
National helpline: 0808 808 0700

Victim Support
Victim Support is the national charity which helps people affected by crime. It provides free and confidential support to help you deal with your experience, whether or not you report the crime.
www.victimsupport.org.uk
National helpline (England and Wales): 0845 30 30 900
National helpline (Scotland): 0845 603 9213

Voice UK
Voice UK is a national charity supporting people with learning disabilities and other vulnerable people who have experienced crime or abuse. It also supports their families, carers and professional workers
www.voiceuk.org.uk
National helpline: 0845 122 8695

CHAPTER 5

CONFIDENTIALITY AND INFORMATION-SHARING

SIMON LESLIE

INTRODUCTION

As a solicitor working with local authorities I am often asked to advise and provide training on information-sharing and confidentiality. The responses of practitioners vary enormously, particularly in adult protection situations. There are some who feel that no information about service users should be shared without consent. At the opposite end of the spectrum there are people who feel that information should be fairly freely exchanged wherever there is or may be a risk to vulnerable adults.

It is clear that information-sharing dilemmas run throughout adult protection work. These are legal dilemmas, as well as ethical and professional ones. There are limits to confidentiality and we need to be clear where these lie. For example we may need to encroach on one person's rights to privacy and reputation in order to uphold the right of another person to be kept safe and free from fear.

1. The work is predominantly inter-agency and multi-professional. It is probably rare for best practice in safeguarding adults from serious risk to involve only one agency. Much more commonly, the assessment and response draw in skills and resources from a number of agencies. This inevitably involves sharing information across the boundaries between disciplines and organisations.

2. Appropriate sharing of information involves striking a balance between the right to confidentiality on the one hand and the right to be protected from harm on the other. This is not straightforward, even conceptually, because the right to confidentiality and the right to be protected are not directly comparable with one another. But clearly we need sound professional judgements about risk and an awareness of the legal principles involved – as well as access to advice in individual cases.

3. The consequences of making the wrong decision could be serious. If we are too cautious about sharing sensitive information because of concerns about confidentiality, someone could be avoidably harmed. If we share information without proper justification, we encroach on people's rights and risk criticism and worse. Unjustified breach of confidence can itself be abusive.

SUMMARY OF THE LAW GOVERNING INFORMATION-SHARING

The law governing confidentiality and sharing information has three strands to it: data protection, human rights and case law.

The Data Protection Act 1998

The *Data Protection Act* covers all 'processing' of information from which individuals can be identified. We 'process' information whenever we obtain it, or record, store or share it. Anyone who processes personal information in this way must abide by the data protection principles set out in schedule 1 to the Act. These mean that information must be:

- fairly and lawfully processed – people must be told at the time that information is being collected and the purposes it will be used for

- processed for limited purposes – information obtained for one or more purposes must not be put to other uses without further consent

- adequate, relevant and not excessive – is there enough information to achieve the stated purposes, without going beyond what is needed?

- accurate and up-to-date – all obsolete and incorrect information should be removed and inconsistencies should be pursued

- not kept for longer than is necessary – records should not be kept once they are clearly no longer needed, unless required by statute to be retained

- processed in line with people's rights

- kept securely

- not transferred to other countries without adequate protection.

It is particularly important to ensure that adult protection information is reliable and up-to-date, as detailed as it needs to be (but no more than this) and that it is only shared (even within agencies) on a 'need to know' basis.

Personal information can only be shared (or processed in other ways) if one of the *conditions* in the *Data Protection Act* is met. The three conditions most relevant to adult protection are:[1]

1. That the *data subject* (the person the information is about) *has given their consent*. With some less sensitive information this consent could be tacit, for example by the person not objecting. However, it is clearly preferable for both practitioner and service user if consent is explicit, and recorded, though this is not feasible in every situation. If the person is incapable of giving informed consent to the disclosure, a judgement needs to be made on their behalf about whether it is in their best interests for the information to be disclosed. Consent to disclosure should always be carefully considered, particularly where we are thinking of sharing information without seeking consent, or despite an objection.

2. That the processing is *necessary because of a public duty or function*. This includes any statutory duty, and 'functions of a public nature exercised in the public interest by any person'. This is likely to include most (if not all) disclosures by statutory and voluntary bodies which are aimed at public protection, or safeguarding against identified risk.

3. That the disclosure is *necessary to protect the vital interests of the data subject*. The Information Commissioner treats this as only applying to life or death situations.

If the information is 'sensitive', the conditions under which it can be shared are more restrictive.[2] This applies to information including a person's racial or ethnic origin, physical or mental condition, or sexual life; also allegations of any criminal behaviour and information about criminal proceedings.

If information is 'sensitive':

1. Any consent to disclose it has to be explicit rather than tacit.

2. It may be disclosed where this is necessary to perform a statutory duty, but not a non-statutory function; individuals, and practitioners working outside the statutory sector, may need to obtain advice before disclosing sensitive personal information.

The *Data Protection Act* also sets out four factors to consider in deciding whether to disclose third party information. Although these relate to subject access requests (people asking to see records about themselves) they are also

---

1   See schedule 2 *Data Protection Act 1998*.
2   See schedule 3 *Data Protection Act 1998*.

relevant to decisions about sharing information in order to safeguard adults. The four factors are[3]

(a) any duty of confidentiality owed to the other individual (which will almost invariably apply in safeguarding work)

(b) any steps taken by the data controller with a view to seeking the consent of the other individual (seeking consent should be the starting point unless risk, incapacity or other reason indicates otherwise)

(c) whether the other individual is capable of giving consent (do they have capacity to give an informed consent?), and

(d) any express refusal of consent by the other individual (an objection cannot prevent disclosure, but we need good reason to override it).

Human rights

Under section 6 of the *Human Rights Act 1998*, public authorities must not act incompatibly with people's human rights. Although this legal duty is essentially a negative one (to avoid breaching human rights), it is clearly good practice for staff in all agencies to work to positively promote human rights, particularly for those who are vulnerable.

Four Articles in the European Convention on Human Rights are particularly important in deciding whether to disclose information for the purpose of safeguarding adults. The four Articles are:

ARTICLE 8 – THE RIGHT TO RESPECT FOR PRIVATE AND FAMILY LIFE

This right can be 'engaged' – or brought into play – not only when we share information which would usually be private, but also by most aspects of assessing and responding to risk to adults.

However, the right to privacy under Article 8 is not absolute. Sharing information is lawful provided it is both *justified* and *proportionate*. Public authorities can only interfere with the right to privacy in ways which are '*in accordance with the law* and…necessary in a democratic society in the interests of

- national security

- public safety or the economic well-being of the country

- the prevention of disorder or crime

---

3   See section 7 (6) *Data Protection Act 1998.*

- the protection of health or morals, or

- the protection of the rights and freedoms of others'.[4]

Is the disclosure justified? If we are clear that by sharing the information we are likely to contribute to public safety, the prevention of crime or disorder, the protection of health or morals or the protection of other people's rights and freedoms – then the disclosure is likely to be *justified*. Particularly important are those disclosures which we make in order to protect other people's right under Article 3 not to be subjected to inhuman or degrading treatment (see below).

Is the disclosure proportionate? This involves thinking about the scale of the intrusion on someone's rights and balancing it against the risk we are trying to avert in sharing the information. The *Mental Capacity Act*[5] speaks of risk as comprising both the *likelihood* of someone suffering harm and the *seriousness* of that harm if it does occur. It would be disproportionate to address a relatively low-level risk with a significant intrusion on someone's privacy. For example, if we are proposing to share information with someone's employer, we need to consider the likely impact on their livelihood and to be clear that the risk is sufficiently serious to warrant making the disclosure.

ARTICLE 3 – THE RIGHT NOT TO BE SUBJECTED TO TORTURE, OR INHUMAN OR DEGRADING TREATMENT

The European Court of Human Rights has given 'degrading treatment' a broad interpretation:[6]

> Where treatment humiliates or debases an individual, showing a lack of respect for, or diminishing, his or her human dignity, or arouses feelings of fear, anguish or inferiority capable of breaking an individual's moral and physical resistance, it may be characterised as degrading and also fall within the prohibition of Article 3…

Many serious forms of physical and emotional abuse will fall into this definition of degrading treatment. If someone is suffering degrading treatment – or is at risk of suffering it – this may well justify sharing information we would otherwise keep confidential. And although, as we saw above, section 6 of the *Human Rights Act* only imposes a negative duty to avoid breaching human rights, the House of Lords has held that it does not matter whether the public authority has itself inflicted degrading treatment by its own act (on the one hand) or has only allowed degradation to continue by failing to intervene

---

4   Article 8 (2) *European Convention on Human Rights* (emphasis added).
5   See sections 6 (3) and 11(4) *Mental Capacity Act 2005*.
6   *Diane Pretty* v *UK*, European Court of Human Rights case no. 2346/02, judgment para. 52 (emphasis added).

when it should have.[7] A failure to act (including by sharing information in order to safeguard someone) could also amount to a breach of Article 3.

ARTICLE 6 – THE RIGHT TO A 'FAIR HEARING' WHEN ONE'S 'CIVIL RIGHTS AND OBLIGATIONS' ARE BEING DECIDED

This right should be treated as applying not only to court and other formal adjudications, but to any decision made by a public authority which may produce a benefit or detriment to the person concerned. Certainly, all decisions whether or not to share information should be reached by a fair process.

What are the key elements of a fair hearing for someone whose information may be shared to protect a vulnerable adult?

- *The right to have access to the evidence.*[8] People – whether possible perpetrators or victims – should be told (at least in outline) what information might be shared, and why.

- *The right to present one's case.*[9] People should be allowed to comment on the accuracy of the facts presented and on the risk assessment. They should be allowed to suggest ways of averting the risk which do not involve sharing the proposed information. Their views should be carefully recorded and considered.

- *The right to a reasoned decision.* A failure to give adequate reasons for a decision is automatically a breach of the right to a fair hearing.[10] The reasons should explain the logic of the decision and the alternatives rejected. Lack of stated reasons is also unfair because it makes it harder for the person to challenge the decision.

ARTICLE 14 – THE RIGHT NOT TO BE DISCRIMINATED AGAINST

Although Article 14 only outlaws discrimination in the way that people access the Convention rights (as opposed to their other legal rights),[11] it is nonetheless important to ensure that the approach to information-sharing decisions is demonstrably non-discriminatory. This would include not presuming guilt without sufficient proof, and ensuring that the threshold of risk which is used to justify disclosure is applied consistently across all parts of the community.

---

7   *R (Limbuela, Tesema and Adam)* v *Home Secretary* [2005] UKHL 66, paras. 55 and 77.
8   *Edwards* v *UK* 15 EHRR 417.
9   *Dombo Beheer BV* v *The Netherlands* 18 EHRR 13.
10 See the case of *H* v *Belgium* 10 EHRR 339.
11 Protocol 12 to the European Convention would create a general ban on discrimination in the exercise of any legal right, i.e. even where Convention rights were not engaged. The UK has not to date ratified this Protocol and it is not therefore incorporated into UK law.

Other statutes covering information-sharing

Section 115 of the *Crime and Disorder Act 1998* contains a general power for anyone to disclose information to social services, probation, the police or health. Such disclosure has to be 'necessary or expedient' for one of the purposes set out in the Crime and Disorder Act, which include 'preventing or reducing crime'. This power goes in tandem with the duty under the Data Protection Act to seek consent to disclosure if possible. This power is particularly relevant for those working in non-statutory settings.

The *Freedom of Information Act 2000* gives people rights to ask public authorities for a wide range of information, which has to be provided unless one of the exemptions applies. In particular, a request for information about an identifiable individual can only be met if disclosure is consistent with the *Data Protection Act*.[12] This means that the *Freedom of Information Act* cannot be used to gain access to information about individuals which is not accessible under the *Data Protection Act*.

Whistle-blowing – the *Public Interest Disclosure Act 1998* amended the *Employment Rights Act 1996* so as to make it unlawful to dismiss or discriminate against someone for making a 'protected' whistle-blowing disclosure.

A disclosure is 'protected' if it is about an actual or possible crime or breach of a legal obligation; or about miscarriage of justice, or danger to health and safety or the environment, or about attempts to cover up such malpractice. The disclosure must be made in good faith and the person making it must reasonably believe it to be true. The disclosure is still protected even if the whistle-blower, though reasonable turns out to be wrong.[13]

Section 5 of the *Domestic Violence, Crime and Victims Act 2004* can give rise to a positive duty to share information which may prevent serious harm. Section 5 creates the offence of failing to take reasonable steps to protect a child or vulnerable adult from significant risk of harm which in fact results in the victim's death. The offence only applies to those living in the same household and people who visit sufficiently frequently to be reasonably regarded as part of the household (this might include people who, although sleeping elsewhere, spend the majority of the daytime in the household). However, one of the steps which could be expected in these cases, which are sometimes referred to as 'familial homicide', is to notify the police of incidents or threats of violence.

---

12   See section 40 Freedom of Information Act (personal information) and section 41 (information provided in confidence).

13   *Babula* v *Waltham Forest College* [2007] EWCA Civ 174.

Case law

Apart from the *Data Protection Act* and the *European Convention on Human Rights,* the common law (case law) defines and regulates confidentiality. Information is confidential if it is only available to one person (or a group) who do not intend it to become generally available.[14] Information received in confidence should usually be kept confidential. This applies whether the confidentiality was explicit, or clear from the situation (as for example in the case of most consultations with social workers and similar practitioners).[15]

The 1998 case of *R* v *North Wales Police ex parte AB and CD*[16] concerned a married couple who had each served 11 years in prison for serious sexual offences, mostly against their own children. Following release they had had to move a number of times because of publicity which risked leading to reprisals. After they moved to a caravan site in North Wales, the local police received a probation assessment that the couple posed a considerable risk to children and vulnerable adults in the community, and were likely to target such people for sexual abuse.

Following a multi-agency case discussion, police and probation officers told the couple about the concerns. They agreed to move from the site before the impending Easter holidays, when numbers of children would be staying at the site. When they did not move, the police shared with the site owner press articles about the couple's history. This led to the couple being asked to leave the caravan site. They applied for a judicial review of the decision by the police to share their backgrounds with the site owner.

The Court of Appeal held that confidential information should only be disclosed where there is a 'pressing need'. The couple should have been given the opportunity to comment on the gist of the information against them. In this case, however, nothing they might have said could have affected the decision to disclose the information, which was appropriate given the risk assessment. The Court of Appeal held that the public interest in disclosure overrode the couple's right to confidentiality.

However, the Court also stressed that a general policy to disclose this type of information (irrespective of the circumstances of the individual case) was not justified, including because this would 'obstruct the rehabilitation of ex-offenders who have not offended again and who are seriously bent on reform'.

---

14   See the case of *Douglas* v *Hello! Ltd (No 3)* [2005] EWCA Civ 595, Court of Appeal at para. 55.
15   'The key is whether the information comes into the possession of its holder in circumstances that import an obligation of confidence...' Mr Justice Beatson in *R (application of A)* v *National Probation Service* at para. 46.
16   (1998) 3 All ER 310 Court of Appeal.

On the other hand, the case of *ex parte LM*[17] concerned someone who had not been convicted of harming children or vulnerable adults. However, LM had been alleged in the past to have sexually abused his daughter, aged four, and an 11-year-old boy in his care at what was described as a local authority hostel. LM's contract to provide school transport was terminated when these allegations came to light. Soon after, he received threats and verbal abuse, apparently as a result of rumours suggesting his contract had been terminated because he was a paedophile. LM asked the police and local authority to agree not to disclose the allegations to another local authority where he was providing school transport and had been asked to give archery lessons.

The police and local authority declined to give such assurances and LM applied for a judicial review of their decisions.

In this case the High Court overruled the information-sharing decisions of both the police and local authority because they were based on blanket considerations rather than the facts of the specific case. For example the local authority did not put forward a risk assessment, but argued in general terms that the information should be disclosed because the welfare of children was paramount.

The High Court also set out more general points about information-sharing to protect children, which are also relevant to work to safeguard adults:

1. The police and local authorities have the power to disclose information about allegations of sexual abuse of children if they genuinely and reasonably believe that such disclosure is necessary to protect children from the risk of sexual abuse.

2. The 'pressing need' test set out in the North Wales case when considering sharing information with members of the public also applies when sharing between agencies – rather than some lower, less demanding standard.

3. The approach to possible information-sharing should be to examine the facts of the case carefully, and carry out the exercise of balancing the public interest in the need to protect children against the need to safeguard the right of an individual to a private life.

4. Particular factors in the balancing exercise will be:

    (i)   The agency's own belief as to the truth of the allegation. The stronger the belief that the allegation is true, the more pressing the need for disclosure.

17   See the case of *R v A Local Authority in the Midlands and a Police Authority in the Midlands ex parte LM* (2000) 1 FLR 612 Dyson J.

(ii) The validity of the third party's reason for obtaining the information. At one extreme are local authorities with a statutory responsibility for the protection of children. At the other are members of the public whose sole interest is to expose those whom they consider to be child sex abusers.

(iii) The degree of risk posed by the person if disclosure is not made.

In the case of *Re C*,[18] the issue was whether serious findings made by a civil court (in care proceedings concerning children) should be disclosed to the parents' landlords, a housing association. The purpose was to prevent families with children from being moved to live nearby.

The father, Mr C, had no convictions against children, though he had been cautioned in 1970 (at age 15) for indecent assaults against two six-year-old girls and he had been convicted of violence towards adults. In care proceedings concerning the couple's baby son, the judge found that over a period of almost 30 years Mr C had seriously sexually abused a number of boys and girls ranging in age between three and eight. He found that Mr C had a personality disorder and posed 'a considerable risk to any child, any child who is young or vulnerable, [and] he poses a great risk to a vulnerable adult whom he can seek to dominate'.

The judge found that the risk had been appropriately assessed as high. Although the housing association did not have statutory child protection duties, nonetheless there was a clear purpose to be achieved by disclosing to the current landlord. The judge, however, refused permission to share information about the risks posed by Mr C with any other landlord who might house the couple in future, as such an open-ended arrangement would make it harder to control the confidentiality of the information and respond flexibly to changes in circumstances.

In *R (application of A) v National Probation Service*,[19] Mr A was aged 70 and was about to be released from prison on life licence. Six years before, he had been convicted of murdering his wife. Mr A was proposing to buy a flat in a sheltered accommodation complex. The probation service considered that he posed some continuing risk to women with whom he might form a relationship, particularly as he had not sufficiently addressed his offending behaviour while in custody. He was acknowledged to be at low risk of re-offending, but if he did re-offend 'there will be extremely serious consequences for victims'. The risk of future harm was thus assessed as medium. This would be more likely to occur living close to older, vulnerable people, particularly if Mr A's mental state were to deteriorate or he experienced difficulties in a relationship.

18   *Re C (Sexual Abuse: Disclosure)* [2002] EWHC 234 (Fam) Bodey J.
19   [2003] EWHC 2910 (Admin) Beatson J.

There was policy guidance from the Prison Service Management Board that 'there was a presumption in favour of disclosure' of parolees' offences to partners, employers and accommodation providers. In other words the policy was to tell such people about convictions unless there were good reason not to.

Mr A brought the matter to court to prevent the manager of the sheltered accommodation being informed about his conviction.

The judge agreed with much of the approach taken by the probation service. There was no difficulty with sharing information with the unit manager confidentially. There was no reason 'to believe that a reputable organisation dealing with the elderly will not recognise and heed the importance of confidentiality'. There had been a careful risk assessment. The alternative of sharing information later if necessary – for example once a relationship formed or Mr A's health declined – had been considered and rejected. The impact of the disclosure on Mr A had also been thought through.

The problem – as the Court found – with probation's approach was that its starting point was the presumption in favour of disclosure, whereas the proper test is that disclosure must be justified in the particular circumstances and must meet a pressing need. The judge therefore ruled that the unit manager was not to be told about the conviction, though he did not exclude the prospect of probation making a fresh information-sharing decision on the correct basis.

The case of *A Local Authority* v *SK & HK*[20] concerned proposed information-sharing with a care home, one of whose staff had been found to have seriously and repeatedly assaulted her eight-year-old daughter.

In care proceedings Mr Justice Sumner had found that the mother had assaulted her daughter, causing marks and bruises to her eye, three linear marks and a bruise to her shoulder. Altogether she had 30 marks on her body, and the judge found that she had suffered considerable pain and distress. Her mother had struck her in the face, beaten her with sufficient force to cause marks, and bitten her. When questioned, the daughter had clearly felt under pressure from her mother not to admit the truth. She had influenced the daughter subsequently to write letters asking to go home. The mother denied responsibility and even forged a confession from a friend, whom the judge found did not exist. Her daughter remained in care.

The local authority sought the Court's permission to disclose the judge's findings to the residential care home for older people where the mother worked, and to the local authority for that area.

The judge noted the POVA (Protection of Vulnerable Adults) list (DH 2006)[21] maintained under Part V of the Care Standards Act 2000, which requires people to be referred for inclusion if they have been dismissed as a care worker for misconduct which significantly harmed a vulnerable adult or placed them at risk of suffering such harm. (People on the POVA list are barred from work caring for vulnerable adults.)

The judge acknowledged the possibility that a more positive risk assessment might be reached by safeguarding adults professionals. However, in giving permission for the disclosure, he also stressed the links between abuse of adults and of children:

> the standards to be expected of those looking after children may be no less than those looking after vulnerable adults.

> If a mother can seriously harm her child without explanation, I consider that other children and vulnerable adults are or may be at risk from her and are entitled to be protected.[22]

Considerations of public safety were sufficient to override the mother's right to respect for her privacy, which included the risk to her livelihood if her employer was informed about the assaults on her daughter.

SUMMARY OF THE LAW ABOUT INFORMATION-SHARING

Where information-sharing is concerned, data protection, human rights and case law complement and reinforce one another. To summarise the key legal rules about information-sharing to protect vulnerable adults:

1. The disclosure of personal information should be 'the exception not the rule'.[23] Personal information should only be disclosed where there is a 'pressing need' to do so.

2. Deciding whether there is a pressing need to disclose will depend on carefully assessing the risk of harm to vulnerable adults and deciding if this outweighs individual rights to privacy and confidentiality.

3. Agencies and professionals should not adopt a policy of routinely disclosing information without gauging whether risk (or some other good reason) justifies disclosure in the particular circumstances.

4. Consent should always be addressed. If the person has capacity to make an informed decision whether their information should be

21   www.dh.gov.uk/en/Publicationsandstatistics/Publications/PublicationsPolicyAnd Guidance/DH_4085855.
22   [2007] EWHC 1250 (Fam) Sumner J at paras. 49, 56.
23   *Ex parte LM* [2000] 1 FLR 612 at 622C.

shared, their views should be elicited and only overridden for good reason. If they lack capacity to make this decision, it needs to be decided on their behalf if disclosure is in their best interests.

INFORMATION-SHARING IN SAFEGUARDING ADULTS PRACTICE

So how do we apply these legal rules to safeguarding situations as they arise? Consider the following scenarios.

Scenario 1

A is a man who previously sexually abused a vulnerable adult. A social worker in the local authority learning disability team who knows A's history becomes concerned when A forms a relationship with the mother of one of her service users. The daughter has a learning disability. Should the social worker share any information about A with a view to safeguarding the daughter?

The starting point will be to assess what risk (if any) A poses to the daughter:

- When did the previous abuse occur and over what period?
- What form did the abuse take?
- What is A's attitude towards the earlier assault(s)? Has he undergone therapy and what insight does he exhibit?
- What contact does A appear to have with the learning-disabled daughter, particularly on his own?
- From what is known of A's history, does this contact offer opportunity for similar abuse?
- What is known of A's new relationship?
- Do we know if the mother is likely to be able to protect her daughter?
- How far would the daughter be able to protect herself?

If disclosure is indicated (to either the mother or the daughter), A should be forewarned of the concerns and invited to comment. It may be appropriate for him to be involved in sharing the information – though probably not to take sole responsibility for doing so. A clear rider of confidentiality should be attached to any information shared.

Scenario 2

B is a man facing a serious criminal charge who believes his alleged victim has made similar, untrue allegations against others. What action might he take?

Alleged victims may have had contact with professionals in the past, for example in children's or adult social services, or for psychological or psychiatric assessment, or counselling or therapy. The notes of such involvement will usually be highly confidential. But can they ever be relevant to the issues in a criminal trial?

The answer is that if records held by a third party (i.e. neither the prosecution nor the defence) affect the credibility of a witness, they could be relevant. The third party material may support what the witness has said or may undermine it. This will particularly apply if the alleged victim has made similar allegations in the past. If these were found plausible – even though there may not have been a prosecution – this will tend to make the current allegations more likely to be true. If the previous allegations were not substantiated, the defence may ask for disclosure because this may reduce the person's credibility before the Court.

The Court will then need to balance the public interest in upholding the confidentiality of what may be very sensitive records against the public interest in ensuring that the alleged perpetrator receives a fair trial.

One question is: who is responsible for protecting the rights of the alleged victim, particularly if they are vulnerable? Until recently the holder of the records was expected to liaise with the alleged victim and present their views on disclosure to the court. However, the 2006 case of *Re TB*[24] establishes that the holder of the records cannot be expected to do this; and that the Court must itself make sure that the alleged victim (or other witness) is aware of the application for disclosure of their records and has had the opportunity to present their views direct to the Court:

> I would firmly reject the suggestion that it would have been sufficient for the interest of TB [the alleged victim] to be represented only by the NHS Trust [as holder of the records]. The confidence is hers, not theirs. Their interests are different. They have a wider public interest in patient confidentiality generally and may have particular interests relating to her care which could conflict with hers…the Trust should not be saddled with the heavy burden of

24   *R (on the application of TB)* v *Stafford Combined Court and Others* [2006] EWHC 1645 (Admin).

making enquiries of the patient, finding reasons why he or she might object and putting those reasons before the court...the burden of protecting TB's privacy should not be placed on the Trust. The burden resides with the court and she herself was entitled to notice and proper opportunity for representation.[25]

Scenario 3

C is a woman who has given her therapist highly sensitive information in the belief this has been received in strictest confidence.

It is always important to stress on first contact with a service user that their confidentiality will be respected so far as possible and high importance attached to doing so; but that there may be exceptional circumstances in which information has to be divulged. Such information-sharing may be required where

1. There is a risk to other vulnerable adults, or children.
2. The information needs to be shared to aid the prevention, detection or investigation of serious crime.
3. There is serious risk to the life or health of the person themselves.
4. There is a legal duty to disclose, including under a Court Order (see the case of B above).

Scenario 4

D is a person who has been repeatedly assaulted by a close family member and does not want the police to know or take action.

The fundamental issue here is *capacity*. Does D have the capacity to make an informed decision about what action (if any) to take to keep himself safe? Does he have an understanding of the risks he is exposed to, of the actions which could be taken and what each of these would involve? If D is capacitated to make these decisions, then his wishes should only be overridden for very clear

---

25   *Re TB*, Lord Justice Forbes at paras 25–28.

reasons. These will be broadly those reasons that might justify overriding C's wishes in the case example above.

Practitioners can quite properly go through with D the ways in which D might be protected: for example by involving the police, or helping D to see a solicitor about an injunction. D could also be offered further support if he should change his mind. But a capacitated refusal should be respected unless there are exceptional grounds to override it. The *Mental Capacity Act* and Code of Practice stress that the test is whether the person has capacity, not whether they make a decision that others believe is best for them:

> A person is not to be treated as unable to make a decision merely because he makes an unwise decision.[26]

If the person lacks the capacity to decide whether to agree to information-sharing (or other action) to protect them, then this decision will need to be made on their behalf by gauging whether disclosure is in their best interests.

In adult protection situations, it should be explained to service users that information is preferably shared with other agencies who may have relevant expertise, statutory powers or resources. The user should be invited to consent in writing to such sharing. Any capacitated refusal of consent should only be overridden for pressing reasons, which should be clearly recorded.

CONCLUSION

Effective work to protect adults from risk is almost invariably interdisciplinary and inter-agency. This means that practitioners need to think carefully about what information to share with each other, and the purposes that are being served by sharing it. The checklist below may be helpful in addressing these questions.

GOOD PRACTICE POINTS: INFORMATION-SHARING TO SAFEGUARD ADULTS – A CHECKLIST

When considering sharing information in order to protect a vulnerable adult, it may be helpful to think through the following:

- What is the information we might share – and have we checked its source, accuracy and consistency?

26   See section 1 (4) *Mental Capacity Act 2005.*

- What risk does the information point to – nature, degree, to whom and in what situations?

- Who would need to know – who can do something meaningful to protect themselves or others?

- How much would they need to know – enough to decide for themselves about the risk (rather than taking the risk on trust) but no more than necessary?

- Who has rights of confidentiality in this information and do they have capacity to decide if they agree to it being shared?

- What would disclosure mean for the people the information is about – especially risk or heightened risk, possible loss of accommodation and/or livelihood?

- Balancing risk against confidentiality – does the balance come down in favour of disclosing or not?

- Planning the disclosure – oral/written, confidentiality rider.

- Other protective action – the information-sharing should be part of a wider protection plan.

CHAPTER 6

THE VULNERABLE ADULT AND THE *MENTAL CAPACITY ACT 2005*

DAVID HEWITT

INTRODUCTION

This chapter discusses how the *Mental Capacity Act 2005* (MCA) might be used to protect vulnerable adults who have been abused, and it asks whether the Act might itself increase the incidence of abuse. Although it will consider many of the provisions of the Act, it will not do so systematically. (For that, see Bartlett 2005; Greaney, Morris and Taylor 2005; Jones 2005.)

MCA came fully into force on 1 October 2007. It is the first Act to cover the care given to adults that lack capacity and it aims to provide a comprehensive framework within which interventions can be made. It applies to every decision made on behalf of such people, whether that decision concerns life-changing events or every day matters (Department for Constitutional Affairs 2007, para 1.1).

WHO IS COVERED?

MCA will apply where someone is incapable; in other words, if they are unable to make a decision in relation to a matter and that inability is the result of an impairment of, or a disturbance in the functioning of, their mind or brain (MCA, s 2(1)). A person will be unable to make a decision in relation to a matter if they are unable: to understand, retain, use or weigh information relevant to that decision (MCA, s 3(1)).

The test for whether someone is incapable, and therefore falls within MCA, is very different from the one used in the Department of Health's guidance *No Secrets* (Department of Health) to determine whether someone is a vulnerable adult. The latter test looks for a person who is or may be, amongst other things:

- in need of community care services by reason of mental or other disability, age or illness and

- unable to take care of himself or herself, or unable to protect himself or herself against significant harm or serious exploitation (Department of Health 2000, para 2.3).

This means that while an incapable person may be vulnerable, the reverse is not necessarily so; and that MCA will only protect a vulnerable adult if he or she is also incapable. In fact, the MCA conception of incapacity should be broad enough to encompass a large number of vulnerable adults. (Furthermore, the High Court has hinted that it will use its powers to safeguard incapable people as well as vulnerable adults, and that it sees the two as different things: *The City of Sunderland* v *PS & CA* 2007.)

The circumstances in which abuse might occur will be as varied as its perpetrators, and there will be no *typical* victims. Nevertheless, there will be scenarios in which abuse is seen to recur. In the context of MCA, they might include the examples given below. (All examples given in this chapter are derived from the six categories of abuse set out in paragraph 2.7 of *No Secrets*.) It will be noted that although MCA powers will often be a safeguard against abuse, they might in some cases also provide an opportunity for it.

Abuse of incapable people

- Peter has a learning disability and can be noisy. One of his carers gives him a powerful sedative. MCA doesn't apply, because the sedative is given, not in Peter's best interests, but so that his carers can get some sleep.

- Mary has dementia. Whenever her carers wash her, they are covered by MCA. One day, however, a carer sexually assaults Mary and thereby forfeits the protection of the Act.

- Kamlesh lives in a care home, where he is kept on a strict diet for good medical reasons. He often complains of feeling hungry, but a social worker tells him that if he does not stop doing so, he will not be allowed to see his relatives. While the diet might be permitted by MCA, the threat will not.

- Bud appointed Lou as his attorney under a Lasting Power of Attorney. Lou makes sure that Bud's nursing home fees are paid on time, but she is also using some of his money to buy shares for herself.

- Hermione, who has no religious beliefs, needs a blood transfusion. Her attorney, Harry, will not consent to it because he is a Jehovah's Witness. Although he has the power to give or

> withhold consent, Harry might lose it if he does not act in Hermione's best interests.
>
> • Winston sustained serious head injuries in a car crash and now lives in a rehabilitation unit. Every Thursday, his sister, Julia, takes him out in his wheelchair. One day, however, Julia begins to abuse him, calling him a 'damned cripple' who is 'a drain on the state'. Although the trips might once have been beneficial to Winston, and so have fallen within MCA, that might no longer be the case.

It will be noted that although MCA powers will often be a safeguard against abuse, they might in some cases also provide opportunity for it.

WHAT COVER IS AVAILABLE?

MCA offers two main forms of protection: some guiding principles and the obligation of best interests.

Principles

MCA contains five guiding principles, which will apply to any act done or decision made under the Act. They are intended to assist and support incapable people, not to control or restrict their lives. The principles are as follows:

- 'A person must be assumed to have capacity unless it is established that he lacks capacity' (MCA, s 1(2)).

- 'A person is not to be treated as unable to make a decision unless all practicable steps to help him to do so have been taken without success' (MCA, s 1(3)). This resembles the injunction in *No Secrets* to 'ensure that when the right to an independent lifestyle and choice is at risk the individual concerned receives appropriate help, including advice, protection and support from relevant agencies' (para 4.3(vii)).

- 'A person is not to be treated as unable to make a decision merely because he makes an unwise decision' (MCA, s 1(4)). This recalls two aspects of *No Secrets*: first, that services should 'act in a way which supports the rights of the individual to lead an independent life based on self-determination and personal choice' (para 4.3(iii)); and second, that they should 'recognise that the right to self determination can involve risk and ensure that such risk is recognised and understood by all concerned, and minimised whenever possible' (para 4.3(v)).

- 'An act done, or decision made, under this Act for or on behalf of a person who lacks capacity must be done, or made, in his best interests' (MCA, s 1(5)).

- 'Before the act is done, or the decision is made, regard must be had to whether the purpose for which it is needed can be as effectively achieved in a way that is less restrictive of the person's rights and freedom of action' (MCA, s 1(6)).

Although the two sets of principles might resemble each other, they are not interchangeable and an act purportedly performed under MCA will not be lawful merely because it appears to fall within *No Secrets*.

Where, in the case of a vulnerable adult who is also incapable within MCA, someone does or proposes to do something that would infringe the principles, it might be possible to take the protective steps described below.

Best interests

Any intervention for an incapable person must be in his or her best interests (MCA, s 1(5)). This is probably the most significant protection MCA offers. It binds everyone, from doctors, nurses and social workers to an attorney under a Lasting Power of Attorney (LPA), a deputy appointed by the Court of Protection and even a judge of that Court. The best interests requirement, too, has its parallels in the vulnerable adult guidance, for under *No Secrets*, services must: 'recognise people who are unable to take their own decisions and/or to protect themselves, their assets and bodily integrity' (para 4.3(iv)); and 'actively promote the empowerment and well-being of vulnerable adults through the services they provide' (para 4.3(ii)).

Anyone assessing an incapable person's best interests must take into account all relevant circumstances (MCA, s 4(2)–(9)). The assessor must also consult: anyone named by the person for the purpose; anyone engaged in caring for the person or interested in their welfare; any attorney under any LPA; and any deputy appointed by the Court of Protection. (If there is no one to be consulted, it might be necessary to appoint a specialist advocate: see Chapters 8 and 9.) These people need only be consulted if it is practicable and appropriate to do so, and their views need only be taken into account and will not be binding. It might be permissible, therefore, to ignore a carer or relative who has abused an incapable person, or at least to disregard the information they supply, or afford their views comparatively little weight.

If an assessor fails to consider the requisite information, or to consult the requisite people, their intervention will not be in the incapable person's best interests and it might be possible to use the protective steps described below.

There are, however, some situations in which the best interests obligation will not apply. For example: if the person concerned is capable, any intervention must have their consent; and a valid advance decision will be binding, even if its result is not in the person's best interests. In addition, best interests will not apply to professionals where decisions are made by the incapable person's attorney, or by a deputy appointed for them by the Court of Protection. (In either case, however, the obligation *will* bind the attorney or deputy.)

THE POWER TO ACT

MCA is designed, not only to safeguard incapable people, but also to protect those that care for them (Department for Constitutional Affairs 2007, para 5.8). The way it does that is by providing a general power to act (MCA, s 5). If someone uses the general power improperly, it might be possible to take the protective steps described below.

What the general power covers

In giving examples of the sort of interventions that might be covered by MCA, the Code of Practice divides them into the two groups (DCA 2007, paras 6.5 and 6.15–6.19):

- *Health care and treatment.* This includes tests; actual medical or dental treatment; nursing; giving medication; taking someone to hospital; and other, related procedures (such as physiotherapy).

- *Personal care.* This includes help with such things as daily living; educational, social or leisure activities; shopping or arranging essential services; and moving home.

The examples below consider how the general power might be used to protect an incapable person who is subject to abuse.

Preventing abuse

- Terry lives in a care home but is visited every day by his friend, June. Staff suspect that when the two are alone together, June slaps Terry and calls him unpleasant names. They think it would be in Terry's best interests for a member of staff to be present whenever he sees June, and the general power would allow appropriate steps to be taken. (If June's behaviour were to deteriorate further, those steps might even include banning her from the premises. That, however, would be a last resort: MCA says that less restrictive steps must be taken before more restrictive steps; and the *Human Rights Act 1998* requires that any interference with a person's private and family life be proportionate to the desired result.)

- Mr Keppel lives at home and although he gets confused about money, he can still care for himself. A social worker, Wilson, discovers that Mr Keppel has been giving a neighbour, Betty, £250 every time she visits him. Betty is coming up the path now. Wilson can use the general power to hide Mr Keppel's wallet until Betty has gone away.

- A few years ago, there were concerns that Faith was being abused by her niece, Hope. Suddenly, however, Hope disappeared from the scene and has not been heard of since. It seems that when Faith's sister, Charity, heard what was going on, she made sure that Hope left the country. Charity is Hope's mother. Faith now says that Hope is back in the country and came to see her yesterday. Even though she asks that this information be kept confidential, the general power might allow it to be communicated to Charity. (The issue of information sharing is dealt with more fully in Chapter 5.)

- Marie is an older person who lives at home with her son, Louis. She is frail and has a form of dementia. Lately, she has begun to exhibit symptoms of what her GP thinks might be a tumour. Further investigations are required, but Louis will not permit them. He says the Lord will keep his mother safe from harm. It will be possible to use MCA to perform the relevant investigations, and also to move Marie into hospital.

In these examples, of course, the general power is not the only solution, and it would almost certainly be possible – and prudent – to refer the matter to the Court of Protection as well. The Court might, for example, be able to appoint a deputy for Mr Keppel; to restrict Hope's contact with Faith (and approve any restrictions placed on June); and to make a declaration about the treatment given to Marie. In the first three examples, it might also be necessary to alert the police.

What the general power does not cover

Because the general power will apply in such a broad range of situations, it might be used to try and cover up abuse. So, for example, inappropriate sexual contact might be excused as an instance of intimate personal care; or a person suspected of stealing cash might say he was simply recovering money an incapable person owed to him. For this reason, the general power is not without its critics. There are, however, some interventions that even the MCA says are beyond the general power. They are set out below.

Not covered by MCA

- When Peter and Paul care for Mary, they are covered by MCA. Peter has sex with Mary and says it is all right because Paul consented on her behalf (MCA, s 27).

- Elsie looks after her sister, Doris, who has a mild learning disability. On polling day, Elsie is caught voting a second time. She says she is casting this vote on behalf of her sister, because it is in Doris's best interests for there to be a British National Party government (MCA, s 29).

- George helps Gracie to kill herself. He says it was in her best interests to die (MCA, s 62).

These cases should be reported to the police.

Using the general power

In order to be covered by the general power, anyone using it must:

- take reasonable steps to check that the person concerned is indeed incapable with regard to the act or decision

- reasonably believe first, that the person is incapable, and second, that the act is in his or her best interests (MCA, s 5(1)), and

- act without negligence; in other words, in a manner consistent with a practice accepted as proper by a responsible body of relevant professional opinion (*Bolam* v *Friern Hospital Management Committee* 1957).

In the next box, there is a list of circumstances in which an act that might have been covered by MCA is not, in fact, so covered.

The use of force

Where an intervention is thought to be in the best interests of an incapable person, those concerned may use force to ensure that it is made. So, for example, there are circumstances in which an incapable person may be held down so that they can be given an injection, or to prevent them coming to harm.

No MCA protection

- Roy gives Siegfried some medicine, even though he does not want it and without considering whether it is in his best interests.
- Bert, a social worker, moves Ernie into a care home, not because it is in Ernie's best interests, but because Bert thinks it will save money for the local authority.
- It is in Martha's best interests to go into a care home, but in the course of moving her there, Mary manages to destroy all of Martha's most cherished possessions.

There is clearly a danger that force will be used inappropriately and, once again, that MCA will be invoked in an attempt to hide instances of real abuse. It should be borne in mind, however, that force will only be lawful where:

- the person using it reasonably believes it is necessary to prevent harm to the incapable person
- it is a proportionate, both to the likelihood of the incapable person suffering harm and to the seriousness of that harm, and
- it does not amount to a deprivation of that person's liberty (MCA, s 6).

Even if force appears to be justified, it will not be so if it conflicts with a decision properly made by an attorney under a LPA or a deputy appointed by the Court of Protection (MCA, s 6(6)).

In the case of an incapable person, although a mere *restriction* on their liberty might be covered by MCA, a *deprivation* of liberty will not. The Code of Practice provides some guidance on distinguishing between the two states (Department for Constitutional Affairs 2007, paras 6.49–6.53). Since MCA came into force, powers have been added to it that will eventually allow incapable people, not just to have their liberty restricted, but to be deprived of their liberty (*Mental Health Act 2007*, s 50 and scheds 7–9).

The next box sets out some circumstances in which the force used on an incapable person will not be covered by the MCA general power.

CAST OF CHARACTERS

As well as the professionals and carers with whom many vulnerable adults will be familiar, MCA might send through their lives other people, with

---

Unlawful force

- Margot gets hold of Jerry in order to give him his fifth bed-bath of the day.

- Bruce cuts Anthea's nails so close that her fingers begin to bleed.

- Because Tony's appearance disturbs the neighbours, Cherie puts him in a low chair so that he cannot go near the window.

- When Anne walks towards the lounge door, Henry holds her back, even though her attorney has asked him not to do so.

- At dinnertime, David bangs his knife and fork on the table, so Victoria locks him in his room for the rest of the day.

- Catherine keeps walking down the hall, so the manager of the home, Michael, locks the front door and puts the key in his pocket.

---

wholly new functions and perspectives. They include attorneys, deputies and advocates, and although many of them will be a force for good, some might not.

Attorneys

If someone has an attorney, it will be because they appointed one under a LPA and have subsequently become incapable within the meaning of MCA.

The maker of a LPA is called the 'donor', and the attorney (or 'donee') is the person in whose favour it is made. If a LPA is to be valid, it must conform to certain requirements (MCA, s 9(2)). An attorney can only use the LPA to make decisions if the donor has become incapable and the LPA has been registered with the Public Guardian (PG) (see below). A LPA can be registered by the donor while they are still capable, or by the attorney at any time. Any concerns about the validity of a LPA may be referred to the PG.

An attorney will be able to make decisions about such things as the donor's day-to-day care, medical treatment and leisure activities (MCA, s 9(1)). Although the donor might have restricted the attorney's powers (MCA, s 11(7)(a)), a decision made by an attorney is as binding as one made by the donor while they were still capable, so there will be plenty of scope for abuse. There are, however, several situations in which, despite the LPA, an attorney will not be able to make decisions on behalf of the donor. They include where the donor is capable of making the decision him- or herself; and the decision is about life-sustaining treatment, but the LPA does not give the attorney the power to make it (MCA, ss 11(7) and (8)(a)).

An attorney will have very significant powers, and a donor should think carefully about whom they appoint to the role. The attorney does not, however, have *carte blanche*. They will have to have regard to the MCA principles and the Code of Practice, and act in the donor's best interests; and to respect any restrictions imposed by the LPA itself (or, indeed, by the Court of Protection). In addition, an attorney cannot use force unless the appropriate conditions are met, and must not deprive the incapable person of liberty. An attorney will also be the legal agent of the donor and so have responsibilities other than those set out in MCA. So, for example, they must perform the role with a reasonable standard of care and skill (which will vary according to whether or not they are being paid); not use the position to benefit him- or herself; act in good faith; and respect the donor's confidentiality (Department for Constitutional Affairs 2007, paras 7.59–7.68).

In the next box are some circumstances in which an attorney might be guilty of abusing a donor.

Abuse by attorney

- William decides to move Mary into a care home, even though he knows she could be looked after perfectly well in her own home.

- Eric needs an operation, but although he has the power to do so, his attorney, Ernie, will not consent to it.

- Vicky deals with Bob's money, even though the LPA appointing her relates only to his personal care.

- Stephen puts Matilda's money into a unit trust because he likes its name.

- Katharine decides not to move Spencer into a care home. It would clearly be in his best interests, but she hopes to inherit under his will and does not want his estate to be depleted in any way.

- Philip writes a blog about his life as Elizabeth's attorney. No names are changed.

- When Elizabeth reads Philip's blog, she becomes very upset and starts to shout at Philip, so he locks her in her bedroom.

Where an attorney fails to meet his or her MCA or more general obligations, it might be possible to take the protective steps set out below.

Where someone purports to be an attorney under a LPA and thereby entitled to make decisions about an incapable person's care, they may be asked to produce the LPA, and to prove both that they are the attorney named in it and that it has been registered with the Office of the PG. An attorney might also be asked to point to the provision that gives them the power to give (or withhold) consent to life-sustaining treatment.

Deputies

If a person has a deputy, it will be because they are incapable within the meaning of MCA and one was appointed for them by the Court of Protection. A deputy may make decisions about an incapable person's personal welfare and/or property and affairs (MCA, s 16(2)(b)).

A deputy should inform everyone concerned of the capacity in which they act. There will be documents to substantiate their appointment, and they should expect to be asked to produce them (Department for Constitutional Affairs 2007, para 8.48).

A deputy must not fail to make a decision that falls within their remit (Department for Constitutional Affairs 2007, para 8.49). Like an attorney, they must respect the MCA principles and Code and act in the incapable person's best interests. A deputy will also have to work within the confines set by the Court of Protection and respect decisions of any attorney. They will not be able to prevent contact between the incapable person and someone else or refuse consent to life-sustaining treatment. These steps would require an order of the Court. Finally, of course, a deputy must neither use force on an incapable person unless the appropriate conditions are met, nor deprive them of liberty. A deputy will also be the legal agent of the incapable person in respect of whom they were appointed (MCA, s 19(6)). This means that, like an attorney, they will have all the obligations of an agent (Department for Constitutional Affairs 2007, paras 8.55–8.67).

If they involved not an attorney but a deputy, the circumstances set out in the previous box might also constitute abuse. The next box sets out some other circumstances in which a deputy might be guilty of abusing an incapable person.

Where a deputy fails to meet their MCA or more general obligations, it might be possible to take the protective steps set out below.

Advocates

The new statutory advocacy service is discussed elsewhere (see Chapters 8 and 9).

Abuse by deputy

- Ferdinand says Isabella can have a hip operation, even though the Court of Protection has only given him power over her financial affairs.

- Marge books a holiday for Homer, even though his attorney, Lisa, has decided that it will not be in his best interests.

- Neil, who is Christine's deputy, objects to her meeting Louis and tells him that he must not come to the house.

CRIMINAL OFFENCE OF ILL-TREATMENT OR NEGLECT

MCA contains a new criminal offence, which consists of (i) ill-treating or (ii) wilfully neglecting an incapable person (MCA, s 44). These terms are not defined in the Act, but they also form part of the similar offences under MHA 1983 (s 127). It seems that:

- they are separate offences

- ill-treatment must be deliberate, or at least reckless, but it might consist of a single act; and a perpetrator will be guilty even if they did not intend the incapable person to be harmed (and even if there was no harm)

- a violent act will not necessarily constitute ill-treatment, as it might be necessary to control the incapable person (*R* v *Holmes* 1979; *R* v *Newington* 1990)

- a perpetrator will be guilty of neglect if they deliberately (or recklessly) failed to perform an act they knew there was a duty to perform (*R* v *Sheppard* 1981).

The MCA offence will be committed where the victim is incapable within the meaning of the Act, but also where, although the victim is actually capable, the perpetrator *believes* them to be incapable. (This distinction marks one of the few situations in which MCA might be used to assist someone who is capable. It might be especially relevant in the case of an adult who, though certainly vulnerable, would not otherwise fall within MCA.) In addition, the perpetrator will have to 'have care' of the incapable person, be their attorney under a LPA or have been appointed their deputy by the Court of Protection (MCA, s 44(1)). It will be for the Court to decide whether such a relationship existed between the alleged perpetrator and victim.

Upon conviction, a perpetrator might be fined and/or imprisoned for a maximum of 12 months (in the Magistrates' Court) or five years (in the Crown Court) (MCA, s 44(3)).

Is it criminal?

Victoria is an incapable person within the meaning of MCA and lives in a care home. One day, Albert punches her in the face. The punch almost certainly constitutes a criminal offence (because it would be difficult to say it was necessary for the purposes of controlling Victoria). It will only be punishable under MCA, however, if Albert has care of Victoria (because he is an employee of the home, for example, or a community psychiatric nurse), or if he is her attorney or deputy. If he is merely a visitor to the home, the punch will not be punishable under MCA, although it will certainly be punishable by other means (and should therefore be reported without delay). Of course, if Albert cared for Victoria (or was her attorney or deputy), the punch would be punishable under MCA if he merely thought she was incapable, and even if she was actually capable.

There are other offences that might be committed in the case of a vulnerable person (see Chapter 1). For example: where the person has created a LPA, the attorney will commit an offence where they dishonestly abuse their position, intending to make a gain or to cause a loss to someone else (such as the donor) (*Fraud Act 2006*, s 4).

PROTECTIVE STEPS

Where MCA powers are concerned, it is the Court of Protection that offers the greatest bulwark against abuse (and because those powers are so wide, it should prove possible to obtain the Court's protection in a large number of situations).

The Court of Protection

The Court of Protection is a specialist court that deals with decision-making for adults who lack capacity to make decisions for themselves (MCA, s 45). It can hear cases about their property and affairs, and also about their health care and personal welfare (which were previously dealt with by the High Court, under its inherent jurisdiction).

The Court, like everyone that acts under MCA, must do so both in accordance with the statutory principles and also in the incapable person's best interests (MCA, ss 1(1) and (5), 4(8)(b) and 16(3)). It may make a declaration or a decision about the person, or appoint a deputy (MCA, ss 15(1) and 16(2)). The Court will also have certain powers in respect of a LPA.

(I) DECLARATIONS

The Court may decide (and then declare) whether a person is incapable within the meaning of MCA; and if so, whether a particular intervention (or, indeed, a failure to intervene) would be lawful (MCA, s 15(1)). This is the power that used to be enjoyed by the High Court as part of its inherent jurisdiction.

(II) DECISIONS

The Court of Protection may make decisions about an incapable person's personal welfare and/or property and affairs, and even if no one has asked it to do so (MCA, s 16(3) and (6)). It might wish to do so where, for example, it is not clear whether an advance decision to refuse medical treatment is valid and applicable; there is disagreement about where an incapable person should live; or there are concerns that an incapable person is at risk of harm from someone else. The Court may make an order to ensure that all parties comply with its decision, or appoint a deputy to make decisions on its behalf. The former is preferable to the latter (MCA, s 16(2) and (4)).

(III) DEPUTIES

Where decisions about an incapable person are mundane and will have to be made repeatedly, the Court might appoint a deputy to make them on its behalf (see above). It will also have the power to revoke a deputy's appointment, and may do so where they have exceeded the powers given by the Court or acted against the incapable person's best interests (MCA, s 16(8)).

(IV) THE COURT AND THE LPA

The Court has the power to decide whether a LPA has been validly created or revoked, or has otherwise come to an end, and to clarify how it should be used. It may also order an attorney to explain their dealings, or even revoke a LPA or prevent it being registered at all (MCA, ss 22 and 23). Revocation might be appropriate where fraud or pressure was used to induce a donor to create the LPA, or where an attorney has exceeded their powers or acted against the donor's best interests (MCA, s 22(2)–(4)).

Responding to concerns

Where there are concerns about someone who is both a vulnerable adult and incapable within the meaning of MCA, the means by which they are addressed will vary according to the nature of the concerns themselves. In almost all the cases mentioned in this chapter, of course, it will be appropriate to invoke *No Secrets* and the relevant adult protection procedures.

(I) THE PUBLIC GUARDIAN

In many cases, it will be appropriate to report concerns to the Office of the Public Guardian (OPG) (MCA, s 57). That might be so whether the concerns relate to professionals, family members, or formal or informal carers. The PG has special responsibilities with regard to attorneys and deputies (MCA, s 58).

(II) BEST INTERESTS

As has been noted, anyone that intervenes on behalf of an incapable person will lose the protection of MCA if they do not at least believe the intervention to be in the person's best interests; and they might be vulnerable to civil suit and/or criminal prosecution, and, if a professional, to disciplinary or regulatory proceedings.

An act that is believed to breach MCA may be reported to the OPG, or to any attorney under a LPA or deputy appointed by the Court of Protection. (Protection from abuse *by* attorneys or deputies is discussed below.)

(III) ATTORNEYS

A LPA is a private arrangement between the donor and their attorney. As such, it will not be subject to regular monitoring, whether by the Court of Protection or any other body. If it gives cause for concern, however, the conduct of an attorney may be reported to the OPG, which might in turn (and in a serious case) refer it to the Court of Protection. As has been noted, the Court has the power to remove an attorney from office.

(IV) DEPUTIES

In contrast to the position with attorneys, the OPG *is* responsible for supervising and supporting deputies, and for making sure that they do not abuse their position. A deputy remains accountable to the Court of Protection for the way he or she performs his or her duties. If the conduct of a deputy is giving cause for concern, it might be reported to the OPG.

(V) PROFESSIONALS AND SERVICES

Where it breaches MCA, or is thought to constitute a more general mischief, the conduct of a health care or social care professional might be reported to the OPG, or to any attorney, deputy or advocate. Alternatively, it might be reported to the professional's employer and/or to the relevant regulatory body (such as the General Medical Council, the Nursing and Midwifery Council or the General Social Care Council).

Where the circumstances or frequency of abuse are such as to implicate not just individual practitioners but a whole service, it might be appropriate to refer the matter to the relevant NHS trust, local authority or registered provider, or to the Healthcare Commission or the Commission for Social Care Inspection. This might also be so where abuse is thought to have arisen, not through individual shortcomings, but as a result of defective systems or policies. (See, for example, *No Secrets*, para 2.9.)

(VI) ADVOCATES

The conduct of an IMCA might be referred to any steering group set up by the relevant NHS bodies and local authority to monitor MCA advocacy arrangements (see also Chapters 8 and 9).

(VII) ACTS FALLING OUTSIDE MCA

An intervention for an incapable person might be questionable because, quite simply, it constitutes a criminal offence. If so, consideration should be given to reporting it to the police.

CONCLUSION

The *Mental Capacity Act 2005* was not introduced for the benefit of vulnerable adults. It might, it is true, protect large numbers of them, at least where they are also incapable, but that is a result of the very broad ambit of the Act. And the breadth of MCA is itself problematic. Its elements include the new general power and the various individuals it will send into the lives of incapable people. Though it might well make new forms of protection available to incapable people, it will also increase the possibilities of abuse. And if the new Act makes a significant difference to the lives of those vulnerable adults that also happen to fall within its reach, what does that say about the mechanisms that already existed to protect them? Does the need for the MCA suggest that *No Secrets* is not fit for its purpose?

CASES

Bolam v *Friern Hospital Management Committee* (1957) 1 WLR 583.

City of Sunderland v *PS & CA* [2007] EWHC 623 (Fam).

Re A (Medical treatment: Male sterilisation) (1999) 53 BMLR 66.

R v *Holmes* [1979] Crim LR 52.

R v *Newington* (1990) 91 Cr App R 247, CA.

R v *Sheppard* [1981] AC 394, HL.

STATUTES

Fraud Act 2006, c 35.

Mental Health Act 1983, c 20.

Mental Capacity Act 2005, c 9.

Mental Health Act 2007, c 12.

REFERENCES

Bartlett, P. (2005) *Blackstone's Guide to the Mental Capacity Act 2005.* Oxford: Oxford University Press.

Department for Constitutional Affairs (2007) *Mental Capacity Act 2005 Code of Practice.* London: The Stationery Office.

Department for Constitutional Affairs, Department for Health, Public Guardianship Office and Welsh Assembly Government (2005) *Mental Capacity Act 2005 – Summary.* London: DCA.

Department of Health (2000) *No Secrets: Guidance on Developing and Implementing Multi-Agency Policies and Procedures to Protect Vulnerable Adults from Abuse.* London: DH.

Greaney, N., Morris, F. and Taylor, B. (2005) *Mental Capacity Act 2005: A Guide to the New Law.* London: The Law Society.

Jones, R. (2005) *Mental Capacity Act Manual.* London: Sweet and Maxwell.

CHAPTER 7

CAPACITY AND FINANCIAL ABUSE

PENNY LETTS

WHAT IS 'FINANCIAL ABUSE'?

Of course, we all know what we mean when we talk about financial abuse. But, do we? If that is the case, how come it is often ignored or goes undetected, or just not recognised as abuse; particularly when it affects those who lack the capacity to complain or take action to protect themselves? Even when financial abuse is suspected, how come it is rarely reported? Or is it just a minor problem affecting few people, as the statistics (or lack of them) would have us believe?

So what is financial abuse? Perhaps the most widely accepted definition of the term 'abuse' is that set out by the Department of Health/Home Office (2000) guidance *No Secrets* (DH 2000) and also adopted by the National Assembly of Wales (2000) guidance *In Safe Hands*:

> Abuse is a violation of an individual's human and civil rights by any other person or persons... Abuse may consist of single or repeated acts. It may be physical, verbal or psychological, it may be an act of neglect or an omission to act, or it may occur where a vulnerable person is persuaded to enter into a financial or sexual transaction to which he or she has not consented, or cannot consent. Abuse can occur in any relationship and may result in significant harm to, or exploitation of, the person subjected to it. (Department of Health and the Home Office 2000, p.9)

Financial or material abuse is further described in *No Secrets/In Safe Hands* as '...including theft, fraud, exploitation, pressure in connection with wills, property or inheritance or financial transactions, or the misuse or appropriation of property, possessions or benefits'(Department of Health and the Home Office 2000, p.9).

Along similar lines, but with a different emphasis, is the often quoted definition of 'elder abuse' developed by Action on Elder Abuse (also adopted by the World Health Organisation (2002)), that abuse is:

a single or repeated act or lack of appropriate action occurring within any relationship where there is an expectation of trust, which causes harm or distress to an older person. (Action on Elder Abuse n.d.)

It is the 'expectation of trust' – trust of family members, other carers, social care providers, lawyers or other professionals – that makes abusive actions hard to prevent and where they do occur, difficult to find sufficient evidence to take action against the abuser.

Financial abuse is further defined by Action on Elder Abuse (AEA) as 'stealing from, defrauding someone of, or coercing someone to part with, goods and/or property' (Action on Elder Abuse 2007, p.1). According to an AEA survey of calls to their helpline, this can involve:

- the direct theft of money or other possessions from an older person

- the withholding of benefits from an older person

- the misuse of a Power of Attorney, Enduring Power of Attorney or other systems giving power to a third party to act in financial matters on behalf of an older person

- older people being forced to sell their homes, having their homes sold against their wishes, or significant assets from the value of the property removed without their consent or knowledge

- older people being tricked into scam/rogue investments.

(Action on Elder Abuse 2007, p.2)

The Public Guardianship Office (PGO), which until October 2007 provided services to protect the financial well-being of people who lacked capacity to manage their own financial affairs, commissioned research to work towards a comprehensive definition of financial abuse (Brown 2003) and to explore the PGO's role in preventing such abuse (Brown, Burns and Wilson 2003). As a result of this work, the PGO suggested that the term 'financial abuse':

describes the situation where an abuser **misappropriates** a vulnerable person's money and/or other assets through various means (e.g. theft or fraud); **misuses** or wrongfully spends a vulnerable person's assests while having legitimate access to these; or **fails to use** a vulnerable person's assets to meet that person's needs. (Public Guardianship Office 2004, p.2)

Subsequently the Office of the Public Guardian (OPG), which replaced the PGO in October 2007 with the implementation of the *Mental Capacity Act 2005*, has reverted to using a definition of abuse similar to that used in *No Secrets*, but with no additional description of financial abuse (Office of the Public Guardian 2007).

CASE STUDY 7.1

Frank has learning disabilities and lives in a group home with other learning disabled adults, assisted by support workers. The residents all receive social security benefits and contribute to the household budget. Frank enjoys going to the pub where he has made some friends. For the last few weeks he has stopped contributing to the household budget and has had to borrow money from the other residents to buy food and other essentials. When questioned by his support worker, Frank tells him that his new 'friends' at the pub insist that he buys their drinks and cigarettes, or they won't be friends with him any more.

THE PREVALENCE OF FINANCIAL ABUSE OF VULNERABLE ADULTS

The variety of meanings, definitions and descriptions used for financial abuse, together with the complex and diverse nature of the range of acts that might constitute abuse, make it difficult to determine just how often it occurs. The most recent study of abuse of older people confirmed that financial abuse is one of the most prevalent forms of abuse – the survey found that approximately 57,000 people (0.66%) aged 66 and over living at home in the UK reported experiencing financial abuse by a close friend, relative or care worker in the year of the study (O'Keeffe *et al.* 2007). The same study estimated that over 100,000 UK older people (1.2%) had experienced financial abuse by a close friend or relative since the age of 65. The risk of financial abuse increased for those living alone, those in receipt of services, those in bad or very bad health, older men, and women who were divorced or separated, or lonely. Family, other than partners, were the most common perpetrators of financial abuse.

But this study only covered people aged 66 and over living at home, not those in care homes, whose financial management processes have often been found lacking (Commission for Social Care Inspection 2007). It also excluded older people with severe dementia, mental health problems or other disabilities affecting their capacity to manage their own financial affairs – the people who are likely to be most at risk of abuse through their inability to protect themselves from it. As the study was only concerned with elder abuse, it did not look at the prevalence of abuse of other 'vulnerable adults', such as younger adults with physical or learning disabilities, mental health problems or acquired brain injury.[1] It is also recognised that any prevalence estimates of financial abuse are likely to be underestimates through under-reporting (Centre for Policy on Ageing 2007).

Defining those groups of people who are 'vulnerable' and at risk of abuse is also problematic. *No Secrets* and *In Safe Hands* both define vulnerable adults as people aged 18 and over who:

- need community care services due to a mental disability, other disability, age or illness, and

- may be unable to take care of themselves or protect themselves against serious harm or exploitation.

However, the term 'vulnerable adult' has itself been criticised, since it directs attention to the individual and locates 'the cause of the abuse with the victim, rather than placing the responsibility with the actions or commissions of others' (Association of Directors of Social Services 2005, p.4). But there can be little doubt that the most 'vulnerable' are those adults who lack capacity to manage their own finances or make decisions to protect themselves. Their reliance on others, who may not always measure up to the expectation of trust placed in them, puts those lacking capacity at increased risk of abuse or exploitation.

CASE STUDY 7.2

Enid Johnson is 87 and is finding it difficult to deal with her finances. She had previously made an Enduring Power of Attorney[2] appointing her son Robert as her attorney, so he suggests that he should now take over managing her financial affairs. Over the next 18 months, Robert spends over £300,000 of his mother's assets on himself and his family and friends, without her knowledge. This only came to light when Enid was admitted to residential care and a means assessment was carried out by the local authority. Both police and social services felt unable to take any action against Robert since he was Enid's appointed attorney. However, he had clearly abused his powers as attorney and had used his mother's money unlawfully and without proper authority.

1   For more information on this subject see Naven, L. and Parker, J. (2008) 'Brain Injury, Case Management and Financial Abuse: A Complex Affair.' In J. Pritchard (ed.) *Good Practice in Safeguarding Adults: Working Effectively in Adult Protection.* London: Jessica Kingsley Publishers.
2   See p.129.

WHAT IS CAPACITY?

It has always been an important legal principle that every adult is assumed to have the mental capacity to make a decision for themselves unless there is proof that they are unable to make it. This principle is now set out in the *Mental Capacity Act* (MCA) *2005* (section 1(2)). People must not be assumed to lack capacity to make a decision simply because they have a medical condition or disability or because of their age or appearance (MCA section 2(5)). The Act also states that everyone should be given all appropriate help and support to enable them to make decisions for themselves (section 1(3)) – this may be through using different ways of communicating such as words, pictures or signs or providing information in different formats. The MCA Code of Practice (Department for Constitutional Affairs 2007, Chapter 3) provides guidance on the sort of help that may be appropriate.

The Act goes on to define what it means to lack capacity to make a decision (MCA section 2). Capacity is 'decision-specific' – this means a person's capacity must be assessed in terms of their ability to make a particular decision at the time that decision needs to be made, not their ability to make decisions generally. The Act sets out a two-stage test of capacity:

- Does the person have an impairment of, or disturbance in the functioning of, their mind or brain? (It doesn't matter if this is permanent or temporary.)

- If so, does that impairment or disturbance cause the person to be unable to make the particular decision at the time it needs to be made?

The person will be unable to make a decision (MCA section 3) if, after all appropriate help and support has been given, they cannot:

- understand the information relevant to that decision

- retain that information

- use or weigh that information as part of the process of making the decision

- communicate the decision (whether by talking, using sign language or any other means).

An assessment of capacity must be made on the balance of probabilities – that it is more likely than not that the person lacks capacity to make the decision in question. The definition also covers people with partial capacity (who can make some decisions but not other, perhaps more complex, decisions) or and those whose capacity fluctuates (they are able to make decisions at some times, but not at others, for example during an acute phase of illness). These groups may be particularly vulnerable to abuse.

THE LAW AND FINANCIAL ABUSE

The law regulating the protection of vulnerable adults from abuse derives from a complex mixture of legislation, guidance and case law resulting from court decisions. This must all be seen in the context of human rights legislation, since the *Human Rights Act 1998* (section 6) places a duty on public authorities to comply with the *European Convention on Human Rights* (ECHR) (Council of Europe 1950). The particular ECHR rights which are relevant to protection from abuse include:

- *Article 3: Freedom from torture or inhuman or degrading treatment:* Everyone has the absolute right not to be tortured or subjected to treatment or punishment that is inhuman or degrading – this may extend to treatment in care homes or hospital.

- *Article 8: Private life and family:* Everyone has the right to respect for their private and family life, their home and their correspondence. This right can only be restricted in specified circumstances.

- *Article 14: Freedom from discrimination:* Discrimination means treating people in similar situations differently, or those in different situations in the same way, without proper justification. Article 14 gives individuals the right to protection from discrimination in relation to all the other rights guaranteed under the ECHR. Everyone must have equal access to these rights, whatever their status.

- *Protocol 1, Article 1: Property:* Everyone has the right to the peaceful enjoyment of their possessions. This means that public bodies cannot usually interfere with things individuals own or the way that they use them except in specified circumstances.

Until implementation of the *Mental Capacity Act 2005* in October 2007, the civil courts had to develop a procedure, known as 'declaratory relief', in an effort to fill gaps in the legislation when making decisions to protect the health and welfare of people who lacked capacity to make those decisions for themselves (see for example, *Re F (Adult: Court's Jurisdiction)* [2000] 2 FLR 512). In relation to financial abuse amounting to theft, fraud or dishonest gain of property or possessions, the criminal law should be sufficient to bring alleged abusers to justice, but the difficulty in finding evidence to prove such abuse if the victim lacks capacity to provide it often makes a criminal prosecution hard to achieve.

Legislation to protect adults from abuse has been described as falling into four broad groups (Clements and Thompson 2007):

1. Measures to prevent abuse, for example by advance planning or setting up protocols and procedures to safeguard against abuse.

2. Barring certain individuals from working with vulnerable people.

3. Imposing legal duties to act in the best interests of someone who lacks capacity to make specific decisions, and restricting actions that can be taken on their behalf.

4. Making certain actions in relation to vulnerable adults a criminal offence and therefore a deterrent to potential abusers.

1. Measures to prevent financial abuse

There are enormous difficulties in investigating and proving financial abuse, and recovering lost money or possessions, once the abuse has occurred. Therefore the most effective way of protecting vulnerable people from financial abuse is taking steps to prevent the abuse happening in the first place. This may be achieved both by simple, informal arrangements for managing money and by more formal legal arrangements – including advance planning in financial matters which everyone should do, as well as the protocols and procedures that agencies working with vulnerable adults should put in place to prevent opportunities for abuse.

INFORMAL ARRANGEMENTS

Anyone caring for or working with vulnerable adults should encourage them to take precautions in arranging their financial affairs that would prevent their money being stolen or used without their agreement. Such arrangements might include:

- keeping money in bank or building society accounts rather than storing large amounts of money at home
- avoiding carrying large amounts of cash
- arranging for pensions or benefits to be paid directly into a bank account
- paying bills by direct debit
- not disclosing bank details or PIN
- putting a limit on the amount of money that can be withdrawn from a bank account
- checking bank statements carefully.

Helping to educate vulnerable adults about financial management and improving their financial skills and awareness can go a long way to preventing opportunities for abuse.

ADVANCE PLANNING IN FINANCIAL MATTERS: ENDURING POWERS OF
ATTORNEY AND LASTING POWERS OF ATTORNEY

It is important to encourage everyone, while they are still capable, to plan in
advance for a future time when they may lack capacity, so that preventive
measures are then already in place. The most common methods of advance
planning are Enduring Powers of Attorney (which could only be made before
1 October 2007) or Lasting Powers of Attorney (made since 1 October 2007).

A power of attorney is a legal document that allows someone (the
'donor'), while they have the capacity to understand what they are doing, to
appoint another person or group of people (the 'attorneys' or 'donees') to
manage their financial affairs. Any decision made by an attorney can be
treated as if made by the donor themselves. Only the donor can decide to
create a power of attorney – it cannot be done on someone else's behalf, either
by the proposed attorney or anyone else. This enables the donor to choose
who they want to take over their affairs if they can no longer manage for themselves – the choice of attorney is entirely the donor's, but it is important to
choose attorneys who are both trustworthy and competent in dealing with
financial matters.

Prior to the *Enduring Powers of Attorney Act 1985*, every power of attorney
automatically became invalid once the donor lacked capacity to make their
own decisions – just at the time when it was most needed. That Act, however,
introduced the Enduring Power of Attorney (EPA) – a particular type of
power of attorney that allowed the attorney(s) to continue to make financial
decisions on behalf of the donor even after the donor ceased to have capacity
to manage their own affairs. An EPA must be registered with the Public
Guardian (see below) when the donor has become, or is becoming, incapable
of managing their affairs. EPAs made before 1 October 2007, whether registered or unregistered, will continue to be valid and can be used at any time
after that date.

The *Mental Capacity Act 2005* (which repealed the *Enduring Powers of
Attorney Act 1985*) introduced a new form of power of attorney, a Lasting
Power of Attorney (LPA), to replace EPAs as the primary way of choosing a
decision-maker to act when the donor no longer has capacity to make specific
decisions. The MCA also extends the areas in which donors can authorise
others to make decisions on their behalf – there are now two types of LPA:

- *a property and affairs LPA* – similar to an EPA, which can be used
  both before and after the donor lacks capacity to make financial
  decisions

- *a personal welfare LPA* – this allows donors to appoint attorney(s)
  to make decisions concerning their personal welfare, including
  health care and consent to medical treatment, which can only be

used when they lack capacity to make such decisions for themselves.

Either the same or different attorneys can be appointed to take different types of decisions, depending on the donor's choice.

Attorneys are in a position of trust, so there is always a risk of them abusing their position. They are not supervised and there are no automatic checks that they are fulfilling their duties properly. It was estimated that financial abuse occurred in around 10–15 per cent of cases involving registered EPAs and more often with unregistered powers (Lush 2001, para 12.1). The LPA scheme was designed to provide greater safeguards against abuse and improper use, in the following ways:

- The LPA form includes a certificate, which must be completed by an independent person (called a certificate provider), confirming that the donor understands the purpose and scope of the LPA and that no fraud or undue pressure is being used to persuade the donor to make the LPA. The certificate provider can be someone who has known the donor for at least two years, or a professional, such a solicitor, doctor or social worker.

- LPAs must be registered with the Public Guardian (a new public office created under the MCA) before they can be used – this can be done before or after the donor lacks capacity to make decisions that the LPA covers. This puts the LPA on the public record. It is important to confirm registration, either by checking the register or looking for the Public Guardian's stamp on the LPA form. If the LPA is not registered, it cannot be used.

- When making the LPA, the donor may name up to five people who must be notified when an application to register the LPA is made. Those people may raise objections if they have concerns about the validity of the LPA. But if the donor chooses not to name anyone to be notified, they will need two certificate providers to confirm their understanding of the LPA.

- Attorneys making decisions under a registered EPA or LPA must follow the principles set out in the *Mental Capacity Act* and must always act in the best interests of the donor.

- The *Mental Capacity Act Code of Practice* (Department for Constitutional Affairs 2007, Chapter 7) sets out the duties of attorneys and gives guidance on the standard of conduct expected of them. The Act requires attorneys to have regard to the Code of Practice and comply with it wherever possible.

- The OPG is responsible for dealing with any concerns raised about attorneys – such concerns can be raised by family members, carers, care workers or anyone who has doubts that an attorney may not be acting in the donor's best interests. The OPG may ask a Court of Protection Visitor to visit an attorney to investigate the matter, or it may make a referral to the local safeguarding adults authorities. In cases where the Public Guardian considers there may be grounds to justify the removal of an attorney or where there is a need for directions or an adjustment to the attorney's powers, he can apply to the Court of Protection (the specialist court dealing with capacity issues) for the required decision to be made.

- The Court of Protection has considerable powers – for example, to decide whether an LPA is valid, to give directions to attorneys or require them to produce accounts, or to revoke (cancel) an LPA if it considers that an attorney is not acting in the donor's best interests, thereby removing the attorney's powers. If this happens, the Court can appoint a deputy to make decisions about property and financial affairs on behalf of someone who lacks capacity – deputies are accountable to the court and their actions are supervised and monitored by the OPG. In some cases, the Court can authorise the deputy to apply to the Chancery Division of the High Court to try to recover any assets lost through the attorney's dishonesty. But the Court of Protection has no criminal jurisdiction and no power to set aside a fraudulent transaction.

However, no scheme that relies on trust can be completely watertight. Anyone caring for or working with vulnerable adults has a role to play in looking out for possible signs of abuse or exploitation. The *MCA Code of Practice* describes some signs that are sufficient to raise concerns that an attorney may be exploiting the donor or failing to act in the donor's best interests. They include the attorney:

- not allowing relatives or friends to have access to the donor – either where the attorney actively prevents contact or where the donor suddenly refuses visits or telephone calls from family or friends for no apparent reason

- making sudden unexplained changes in living arrangements, such as where someone moves into care for the donor when they had little previous contact with them

- not allowing a doctor or care worker to see the donor

- discharging the donor from hospital against medical advice, while the donor is undergoing necessary medical treatment

- leaving bills unpaid, such as arrears of residential care or nursing home fees

- opening a credit card account for the donor

- spending money on things that are not obviously related to the donor's needs

- spending money in unusual or extravagant ways

- transfering assets to another country.

(Department for Constitutional Affairs 2007, para 7.70)

Anyone who suspects abuse by an attorney should contact the OPG immediately. In cases of suspected theft or serious fraud, the matter should also be reported to the police.

1. Protocols and procedures to prevent abuse

Where vulnerable people are receiving health or social care services, the providers of those services must have protocols and procedures in place, with effective monitoring, to prevent opportunities for abuse.

In relation to care services, all providers of care covered by the *Care Standards Act 2000* must register with the Commission for Social Care inspection (CSCI) in England[3] or the Care and Social Services Inspectorate for Wales (CSSIW). These agencies are responsible for ensuring that care providers act in accordance with the *Care Standards Act* and the associated Regulations (*Care Homes Regulations 2001* and *Domiciliary Care Agencies Regulations 2002*). The Regulations make clear that care providers have a legal duty to establish robust financial management procedures.

In addition, the Department of Health publishes National Minimum Standards (NMS) (Department of Health 2007) for care providers[4] which include standards that relate to the prevention of abuse and specifically on safeguards for the handling of people's money and financial affairs. Independent health care providers (such as private hospitals or nursing homes) are required to meet similar standards, but their compliance is monitored by the Healthcare Commission (the independent watchdog for health care in England)[5] or by the Healthcare Inspectorate for Wales.

CSCI has agreed a protocol with the Association of Directors of Adult Social Services and the Association of Chief Police Officers (Commission for Social Care Inspection, Association of Directors of Social Services and the

---

3   The Health and Social Care Bill introduced in Parliament in November 2007 establishes a new body, the Care Quality Commission, responsible for the registration, review and inspection of health and social care services in England, replacing the CSCI and the Healthcare Commission.

4   Each type of care service (care homes for adults, care homes for older people, domiciliary care, adult placement schemes, nurses agencies, independent health care providers etc.) has its own set of National Minimum Standards.

5   See Footnote 2 above.

Association of Chief Police Officers 2007), setting out the action to be taken by the appropriate bodies (the police, social services, service providers, Healthcare Commission or CSCI) in response to allegations of abuse or neglect.

2. Barring certain people from working with vulnerable adults

The *Care Standards Act 2000* Part 7 sets up controls to prevent unsuitable people from working with vulnerable adults in England and Wales. The Protection of Vulnerable Adults (POVA) list names those people who have been barred from working with vulnerable adults (Department of Health 2006). Employers providing care in a residential setting or domiciliary care in a person's own home must check whether potential employees are on the list, and if so, must refuse to employ them or only employ them in a position that does not give them access to vulnerable adults. It is a criminal offence for anyone on the POVA list to apply for a care position.

The *Safeguarding Vulnerable Groups Act* (SVGA) *2006*, due to be implemented in autumn 2008, will replace the POVA scheme and introduce a new vetting and barring scheme for those who work with children or vulnerable adults in health or social care services, either in a paid or volunteer capacity. Individuals will be barred either automatically – if they are convicted or cautioned for certain offences – or following a decision by the Independent Safeguarding Authority, a new public body set up to decide who should be barred, taking account of other offences or cautions or other relevant information.

Under the SVGA, criminal record checks are now compulsory for all staff who have contact with service users in registered care homes, who provide personal care to people in their own homes or who are involved in providing adult placement schemes for vulnerable adults. Pre-employment Criminal Record Bureau (CRB) checks must be carried out for all potential new health care and social care staff, including nursing agency and home care agency staff.

3. Safeguards for people who lack capacity

In addition to allowing people to plan ahead for future lack of capacity, the *Mental Capacity Act 2005* sets out a statutory framework governing how decisions should be made on behalf of people aged 16 and over who may lack capacity to make specific decisions for themselves. The Act sets out five key principles (section 1) that must be followed by anyone caring for or working with someone who may lack capacity which can be summarised as follows:

- The presumption of capacity – every adult has the right to make their own decisions and must be assumed to have capacity to do so unless it is proved otherwise.

- Individuals must be supported to make their own decisions – people must be given all appropriate help before anyone concludes that they cannot make their own decisions.

- People are allowed to make decisions that may seem to others to be unwise or eccentric – they should not be treated as lacking capacity merely because they make an unwise decision.

- Anything done for or on behalf of people without capacity must be in their best interests.

- Anything done for or on behalf of people without capacity should be done in a way that is less restrictive of their basic rights and freedoms (so long as it is in their best interests).

BEST INTERESTS

Of particular importance is the requirement that any act done, or any decision made, for or on behalf of a person who lacks capacity must be done, or made, in that person's 'best interests' (section 1(4)). The Act sets out a 'checklist' of factors which must always be considered when trying to decide what is in someone's best interests (section 4). These can be summarised as follows:

- *Equal consideration and non-discrimination* – Do not make assumptions about someone's best interests merely on the basis of the person's age or appearance, condition or aspect of their behaviour.

- *All relevant circumstances* – Try to identify all the issues and circumstances that are most relevant to the person who lacks capacity to make that particular decision.

- *Regaining capacity* – Consider whether the person is likely to regain capacity (e.g. after receiving medical treatment). If so, can the decision wait until then?

- *Permitting and encouraging participation* – Do whatever is reasonably practicable to permit and encourage the person to participate as fully as possible in any act done or any decision affecting them.

- *The person's wishes, feelings, beliefs and values* – Try to find out the views of the person lacking capacity, including:

  ○ the person's past and present wishes and feelings – both their current views and whether the person has expressed any relevant views in the past, either verbally, in writing or through behaviour or habits

- ○ any beliefs and values (e.g. religious, cultural, moral or political) that would be likely to influence the decision in question

- ○ any other factors the person would be likely to consider if able to do so.

- *The views of other people* – Consult other people, if it is practical and appropriate to do so, for their views about the person's best interests and to see if they have any information about the person's wishes, feelings, beliefs or values. But be aware of the person's right to confidentiality – not everyone needs to know everything. In particular, try to consult:

- ○ anyone previously named by the person as someone to be consulted on the decision in question or matters of a similar kind

- ○ anyone engaged in caring for the person, or close relatives, friends or others who take an interest in the person's welfare

- ○ any attorney of a Lasting Power of Attorney made by the person

- ○ any deputy appointed by the Court of Protection to make decisions for the person.

- *Determining best interests* – Weigh up all of the above factors in order to determine what decision or course of action is in the person's best interests.

ACTS IN CONNECTION WITH CARE OR TREATMENT

The MCA also allows carers (both informal carers, such as family members, and paid carers) and health and social care professionals to carry out certain acts in connection with the personal care, health care or treatment of a person lacking capacity (section 5) and in some limited circumstances to spend their money to pay for necessary goods and services (sections 7–8). These provisions are intended to give legal backing, in the form of protection from liability, for actions which are essential for the personal welfare or health of people lacking capacity to consent to having things done to or for them. Such actions can be performed as if the person concerned had capacity and had given consent. There is no need to obtain any formal powers or authority to act.

However, the Act also makes clear that anyone acting unreasonably, negligently or not in the person's best interests could forfeit that protection and their actions can be challenged, through the courts if necessary. This could potentially be an effective way to challenge alleged financial abuse.

FINANCIAL AFFAIRS

It is recognised that people who care for someone who lacks capacity to make particular decisions often have to spend money on that person's behalf in order to provide the care they need. For example, carers (whether family carers, other carers or paid care workers) may buy food, arrange for milk to be delivered or for a chiropodist to call to provide a service to the person at home. More costly arrangements might be for house repairs or organising a holiday. Where it is appropriate for carers or care workers to arrange such matters, and so long as the arrangements made are in the best interests of the person lacking capacity to consent, the MCA (sections 7–8) allows the carer to use cash in the person's possession to pay for these necessary goods or services. If there is not enough cash available, someone with authority to make financial decisions on the person's behalf must be asked to make appropriate arrangements for payment.

A distinction is drawn between the use of available cash already in the possession of the person lacking capacity on the one hand and the removal of money from a bank account or selling valuable items of property on the other. The MCA does not allow anyone to have access to another person's income, savings or bank accounts or to sell property belonging to a person who lacks capacity to make such decisions, without some formal authority. That formal authority can be given in one of the following ways:

- *EPAs and LPAs* – Attorneys appointed under an EPA or LPA will have the formal authority to make decisions about property and financial affairs on behalf of the donor, even after the donor loses capacity. In this way, the donor's choice of who they wish to deal with their affairs is respected.

- *Appointeeship* – If the person lacking capacity has no assets other than social security benefits or pensions, the Department for Work and Pensions (DWP) can appoint someone (called an appointee) to claim and spend benefits on the person's behalf (*Social Security (Claims and Payment) Regulations 1987*, SI 1987/1968, Reg 33). But an appointee has no right to deal with other assets or savings from sources other than benefits. The appointee is usually a family member or carer, but could be a professional, such as a solicitor. The DWP should check that the appointee is trustworthy. It also investigates complaints that an appointee is not acting appropriately or in the person's best interests.

- *Application to the Court of Protection* – If a person who now lacks capacity has not made an EPA or LPA and has assets other than social security benefits, then an application must be made to the Court of Protection for authority to deal with the person's property and affairs. In most cases, the Court will appoint a deputy to make decisions about property and financial affairs (deputies were previously known as 'receivers' before the *Mental Capacity Act* came into effect). The Court decides who to appoint as deputy – this could be a family member or a professional, depending on what the Court considers to be most appropriate in the person's best interests. The order of appointment will set out the deputy's powers. Deputies have a duty to act in accordance with the MCA principles, and in particular, must make decisions in the person's best interests. They must also have regard to the MCA Code of Practice, in particular the guidance on the duties of a deputy and the standard of conduct expected of them (Chapter 8). Deputies are accountable to the Court of Protection and the OPG is responsible for supervising and supporting deputies, including investigating any complaints or concerns about the way deputies are exercising their powers.

CASE STUDY 7.3

Several years ago, Rekha asked her son Ashok to manage her financial affairs but did not make any formal arrangements. Rekha now has advanced dementia and depression and has moved in with Ashok and his family. The rest of the family is concerned that Ashok is proposing to sell Rekha's house and use the proceeds to carry out various alterations to his own home, arguing that these will help him take better care of his mother. He meets with the family to try to work out what decisions would be in Rekha's best interests, taking account of her past and present wishes and feelings, the views of all members of the family as well as other matters in the best interests 'checklist'. As a result, the family supports Ashok's application to the Court of Protection for authority to sell her property and use some of the proceeds for essential alterations to his house which will assist her future care. The Court agrees that this would be in Rekha's best interests and appoints Ashok as her financial deputy with authority to sell her home and to manage her finances. The order of appointment confirms that every decision that Ashok makes in the future must always be in Rekha's best interests.

4. Criminal offences

Over the last few years there has been an increase in the number of criminal offences which are specific to adults who are in vulnerable situations or may be vulnerable to abuse. The possibility of being charged with a criminal offence is intended to deter people from abusing adults, although it is debatable how effective this is. The majority of these new criminal offences relate to ill-treatment or neglect (*Mental Capacity Act 2005*, section 44), or to physical or sexual abuse (*Sexual Offences Act 2003*, sections 30–44; *Domestic Violence, Crimes and Victims Act 2004*, section 5), although a few are specific to financial abuse. The main criminal offences relating to financial abuse are as follows:

THEFT ACT 1968

Section 1 sets out the legal definition of theft – 'A person shall be guilty of theft if he dishonestly appropriates property belonging to another with the intention of permanently depriving the other of it.' Theft is a criminal offence, regardless of whether the alleged thief is a family member, carer, appointee, attorney or Court-appointed deputy, if they are acting dishonestly or outside the scope of their authority. Any suspicion of theft should be reported to the police.

FRAUD ACT 2006

Section 4 creates a new offence of 'fraud by abuse of position'. Any person who occupies a position which requires them to safeguard (or not act against) the financial interests of another person (such as an attorney or deputy) may be guilty of fraud if they dishonestly abuse that position, intending to benefit themselves or others, or cause loss or expose the vulnerable person to the risk of loss. Again, any suspicion of fraud should be reported to the police.

As well as laws which criminalise specific actions, there are other laws intended to stop abusive or criminal acts or to assist in the prosecution of alleged offenders, as follows:

ENTERPRISE ACT 2002

Part 8 of this Act allows the Office of Fair Trading, Trading Standards Authorities and other designated enforcement bodies, to apply to the courts for an order to stop traders infringing a wide range of consumer protection legislation where those infringements harm the collective interests of consumers. These Stop Now Orders (also known as Enforcement Orders) are intended to stop poor trading practices, such as dishonest doorstep selling or rogue traders.

PUBLIC INTEREST AND DISCLOSURE ACT 1998

This Act encourages people to report malpractice in the workplace (including financial malpractice and abuse) and protects people who report malpractice (sometimes called 'whistleblowers') from being sacked or victimised. The organisation Public Concern at Work provides legal advice and support for whistleblowers.

CASE STUDY 7.4

Jenny works as a care worker in a care home for older people with dementia. She had suspicions that one of the managers was stealing cash from the residents. This manager was responsible for the residents' personal allowances and kept a ledger of sums paid out. Jenny found entries in the ledger that money had been given to particular residents when she knew they had received none. Jenny raised her concerns with the home owner, who carried out an investigation and found she was right. The manager was dismissed and the police were called in. Jenny was criticised by some of her colleagues, and those who had been friends with the manager refused to speak to her and made unfounded accusations of poor practice in her own work. But she was later vindicated when the manager was convicted of stealing over £5000 from the residents.

WHAT TO DO IF FINANCIAL ABUSE IS SUSPECTED

The *Mental Capacity Act Code of Practice* (Department for Constitutional Affairs 2007, Chapter 14) describes the different agencies involved in the prevention of abuse and what they can do if abuse is suspected. This contains guidance on what actions should be taken by those involved in the care of people lacking capacity if they suspect that someone is being abused. The guidance relates to all forms of abuse, but may still be relevant since research has shown that financial abuse is often associated with other forms of abuse (Centre for Policy on Ageing 2007). A summary of the guidance is as follows:

- Always report suspicions of abuse of a person who lacks capacity to the relevant agency.

Concerns about an appointee

- When someone is concerned about the collection or use of social security benefits by an appointee on behalf a person who lacks capacity, they should contact the local Jobcentre Plus. If the appointee is for someone who is over the age of 60, contact Pension Services.

Concerns about an attorney or deputy

- If someone is concerned about the actions of an attorney or deputy, they should contact the Office of the Public Guardian.

Concerns about a possible criminal offence

- If there is a good reason to suspect that someone has committed a crime against a vulnerable person, such as theft or physical or sexual assault, contact the police.

- In addition, social services should also be contacted, so that they can support the vulnerable person during the investigation.

Concerns about possible ill-treatment or wilful neglect

- The Act introduces new criminal offences of ill-treatment or wilful neglect of a person who lacks capacity to make decisions (section 44) – in some cases, financial abuse could amount to ill-treatment or neglect.

- If someone is not being looked after properly, contact social services.

- In serious cases, contact the police.

Concerns about care standards

- In cases of concern about the standard of care in a care home or an adult placement scheme, or about the care provided by a home care worker, or in cases where financial abuse by a care worker is suspected, contact social services.

- It may also be appropriate to contact the Commission for Social Care Inspection (in England) or the Care and Social Services Inspectorate for Wales.

So, if you suspect that a vulnerable person, especially someone who lacks capacity to make decisions for themselves, is being abused financially, or in any other way, do not ignore it – report it!

If the matter cannot be resolved in any other way, the Court of Protection has ultimate powers to resolve disputes or deal with concerns about the best interests of a person lacking capacity. In some cases, the Court's permission will be required for an application to be made, but anyone acting as a 'litigation friend' (someone who is appointed to act on behalf of a person lacking capacity to represent themselves) would not normally need permission. Usually the Official Solicitor can be asked to act as litigation friend, but in some cases it could be argued that a local authority should act as the litigation friend of a person lacking capacity under the broad welfare powers to 'promote well-being' available under the *Local Government Act 2000* (section 2). While the Court of Protection has no criminal jurisdiction and no power to set aside fraudulent transactions, it may be able to resolve the matter in other ways. For example, the Court has the power to:

- request a report from the Public Guardian about the actions of a deputy or attorney

- direct a Court of Protection Visitor to visit a person lacking capacity and report on the actions of an attorney or deputy

- ask the Official Solicitor to act on behalf of the person lacking capacity and to carry out investigations on the person's behalf

- revoke an LPA or EPA if the attorney has abused their authority or not acted in the donor's best interests

- remove a deputy who has abused their authority or not acted in the donor's best interests

- appoint a deputy with authority to investigate and report on the prior dealings of an attorney (or a previous deputy)

- authorise a deputy to apply to Chancery Division for relief or for an order to recover lost assets

- prohibit an alleged abuser from having contact with a person lacking capacity

- refer the case to be dealt with through local safeguarding adults procedures.

CONCLUSION

No specific public body has a statutory function to prevent or investigate financial abuse. The guidance in *No Secrets* (Department of Health 2000) and *In Safe hands* (National Assembly for Wales 2000) places local authorities as the lead agency in coordinating a local multi-agency approach to dealing with abuse. The Public Guardian has a statutory function to 'deal with representations' made about attorneys and deputies, but with wide discretion to refer any concerns to other agencies. It is arguable that both local authorities and the Public Guardian could seize the initiative and use the legal provisions described in this chapter to greater effect to prevent and deal with financial abuse affecting very vulnerable people – those who lack capacity to protect themselves.

STATUTES
Care Standards Act 2000. London: The Stationery Office.
Domestic Violence, Crimes and Victims Act 2004. London: The Stationery Office.
Enduring Powers of Attorney Act 1985. London: HMSO.
Enterprise Act 2002. London: The Stationery Office.
Fraud Act 2006. London: The Stationery Office.
Human Rights Act 1998. London: The Stationery Office.
Local Government Act 2000. London: The Stationery Office.
Mental Capacity Act 2005. London: The Stationery Office.
Public Interest Disclosure Act 1998. London: The Stationery Office.
Safeguarding Vulnerable Groups Act 2006. London: The Stationery Office.
Sexual Offences Act 2003. London: The Stationery Office.
Theft Act 1968. London: HMSO.

STATUTORY INSTRUMENTS
Care Homes Regulations 2001. SI 2001/3965. London: The Stationery Office.
Domiciliary Care Agencies Regulations 2002. SI 2002/3214. London: The Stationery Office.
Social Security (Claims and Payment) Regulations 1987. SI 1987/1968. London: HMSO.

REFERENCES
Action on Elder Abuse (n.d.) *What is Elder Abuse?* London: AEA. Available at www.elderabuse.org.uk, accessed 29 July 2008.
Action on Elder Abuse (2007) *The Cost of Living.* London: AEA. Available at www.elderabuse.org.uk, accessed 29 July 2008.
Association of Directors of Social Services (2005) *Safeguarding Adults.* London: ADSS.
Brown, H. (2003) 'What is financial abuse?' *The Journal of Adult Protection* 5, 2, 3–10.
Brown, H., Burns, S. and Wilson, B. (2003) 'Suspected financial abuse among cases administered by the PGO.' *The Journal of Adult Protection* 5, 2, 26–37.
Centre for Policy on Ageing (2007) *Briefing: The Financial Abuse of Older People.* London: CPA. Available at www.cpa.org.uk/policy/briefings/financial_abuse.pdf, accessed 29 July 2008.
Clements, L. and Thompson, P. (2007) *Community Care and the Law.* 4th edition. London: Legal Action Group.
Commission for Social Care Inspection (2007) 'In safe keeping: Supporting people who use regulated care services with their finance'. *Focus Social Care Policy and Practice* 6, May, 1–32.
Commission for Social Care Inspection, Association of Directors of Social Services and the Association of Chief Police Officers (2007) *Safeguarding Adults Protocol and Guidance.* London: CSCI.
Council of Europe (1950) *Convention for the Protection of Human Rights and Fundamental Freedoms.* Also known as the *European Convention on Human Rights (ECHR).* Rome: Council of Europe. The Convention has subsequently been amended by a number of Protocols, most recently in 2003.
Department for Constitutional Affairs (2007) *Mental Capacity Act 2005 Code of Practice.* London: TSO. Available at www.publicguardian.gov.uk/docs/code-of-practice-041007.pdf, accessed 22 May 2008.
Department of Health and the Home Office (2000) *No Secrets: Guidance on Developing and Implementing Multi-agency Policies and Procedures to Protect Vulnerable Adults from Abuse.* London: Department of Health.
Department of Health (2006) *Protection of Vulnerable Adults Scheme in England and Wales for Adult Placement Schemes, Domiciliary Care Agencies and Care Homes: A Practical Guide.* London: Department of Health.

Department of Health (2007) *National Minimum Standards.* Available at www.dh.gov.uk/en/Policyandguidance/SocialCare/Standardsandregulation/DH_079561, accessed 22 May 2008.

Lush, D. (2001) *Cretney & Lush on Enduring Powers of Attorney.* 5th edition. Bristol: Jordans.

National Assembly for Wales (2000) *In Safe Hands.* Cardiff: National Assembly for Wales.

Office of the Public Guardian (2007) *What Is Abuse?* Available at www.publicguardian.gov.uk/concerns/problems-making-decisions.htm, accessed 22 May 2008.

O'Keeffe, M., Hills, A., Doyle, M., McCreadie, C. *et al.* (2007) *UK Study of Abuse and Neglect of Older People: Prevalence Survey Report.* Prepared for Comic Relief and Department of Health. London: National Centre for Social Research and King's College London.

Public Guardianship Office (2004) *Are You Aware of Financial Abuse?* London: Public Guardianship Office.

World Health Organisation (2002) *Toronto Declaration of Global Prevention of Elder Abuse.* Geneva: WHO.

USEFUL ORGANISATIONS

Public Concern at Work

Website: www.pcaw.co.uk/

THE ROLE OF ADVOCACY AND THE INDEPENDENT MENTAL CAPACITY ADVOCATE (IMCA) IN ADULT PROTECTION WORK

ROB HARRIS

This chapter aims to illustrate the role of advocacy and the Independent Mental Capacity Advocate (IMCA) in cases of adult protection. This book focuses on adult protection issues, however an understanding and awareness of the advocacy 'economy' is beneficial when setting a context for the role of the IMCA. It is also useful to give consideration to some of the developing themes in the advocacy sector to be able to fully appreciate the independent and specialist role that advocacy plays in health and social care in the UK today.

Independent advocacy has always had a role to play in adult protection work, the very nature of the client groups that advocacy serves makes this an inevitable aspect of advocacy work. The concept of advocacy is one of protection and promotion of people's rights and entitlements; it is therefore logical that vulnerable people involved in adult protection proceedings should have an independent person to support and represent their views and ensure that they understand the process that is being applied by statutory agencies. The *Mental Capacity Act 2005* makes provision for a statutory advocacy role in the form of IMCA. The role of the IMCA is described in more detail later in this chapter and in particular the role of the IMCA in adult protection cases.

WHAT IS ADVOCACY?

First, it is useful to provide a summary of independent advocacy in England and Wales starting with an established definition:

Definition of advocacy

Advocacy is taking action to help people say what they want, secure their rights, represent their interests and obtain services they need. Advocates and advocacy schemes work in partnership with the people they support and take their side. Advocacy promotes social inclusion, equality and social justice.

(Action for Advocacy 2002, p.2)

Independent advocacy is a civil form of representation, support and empowerment. There are several models and approaches to advocacy that have developed since the early 1980s in the UK. These models range from citizen advocacy, a volunteer-based advocacy prevalent mainly in community settings through to a professional paid model of advocacy widely utilised in mental health services, hospitals and IMCA services. Action for Advocacy, a national body that supports and campaigns for the continuing development of advocacy services in England and Wales, has summarised the most common models of advocacy as follows:

Different types of advocacy

Citizen advocacy: Citizen advocacy was developed in America and became formalised in the UK in the early 1980s. It is based on one-to-one partnerships. An unpaid advocate works with someone on a long-term basis, sometimes throughout their whole life.

Short-term, issue-based or crisis advocacy: When an advocate speaks up for someone about a particular issue, or speaks up for them to help them through a crisis.

Self-advocacy: When someone speaks and acts for themselves to present their case. Many self-advocates have come together to form a collective voice on issues that impact on their lives. This is also sometimes called 'group advocacy'.

Peer advocacy: When the advocate has something in common with the person they are advocating for. For example, the advocate might be a user or a former user of the advocacy service.

Bilingual advocacy: Bilingual advocates speak the language of the people they work with as well as English. Bilingual advocates often support people through health issues. They are sometimes employed by the statutory sector.

Health advocacy: Like bilingual advocates, health advocates normally support people whose first language is not English. There are health advocates available who speak a range of languages. Health advocates can help people to access GPs, practice nurses, dentists, opticians, pharmacists, health visitors, district nurses, family planning services, health screening services, school nurses, community mental health services, speech and language therapy and other health services.

Non-instructed advocacy: Taking affirmative action with or on behalf of someone unable to give a clear indication of their views or wishes in a specific situation. For example, this could be someone with dementia, profound learning disabilities or brain injury. The non-instructed advocate seeks to uphold the person's rights, ensure fair and equal treatment and access to services, make certain that decisions are taken with due consideration for their unique preferences and perspectives.

Independent Mental Capacity Advocacy (IMCA): Advocacy for people who do not have the capacity to make their own decisions. IMCAs support these people with issues regarding serious medical treatment and/or accommodation moves.

Legal advocacy: This is provided by lawyers and aims to assist people to exercise or defend their legal rights.

(www.actionforadvocacy.org.uk/articleServlet?action=display&article=716&articletype=20, accessed 25 August 2008)

The work of Action for Advocacy and the wider advocacy sector has resulted in significant steps forward in respect of clarity, universal understanding and consensus regarding independent advocacy. England and Wales has experienced significant growth in independent advocacy since 2000 and it looks likely that this will continue. The commissioning of advocacy service contracts throughout the health and social care economy has also increased the number of service users that have genuine access to an independent advocate. An example of this type of focused commissioning can be seen in the North West of England where the strategic intention of the North West Specialised Commissioning Team has been achieved ensuring that all patients admitted to an NHS secure hospital have access to a commissioned independent advocacy service.

It is almost an expectation that the most vulnerable people in society will have easy access to an effective, locally provided independent advocacy service that is able to provide support and representation. There are an increasing number of local authorities that are instigating local advocacy strategies to plan for development of services to meet local needs, one such example being Liverpool City Council (developing a joint advocacy policy and commissioning strategy; Liverpool City Council 2007). These services inevitably support and advocate for people that are subject to adult protection procedures, ensuring that their rights are upheld and their views are heard and fully considered.

Advocacy is and will always be about the rights of the individual to have a voice, to be supported where necessary to be fully involved in decision-making, to understand the processes they are engaged in as fully as possible, and be able to freely exercise their rights in the same way as other members of society. The common themes of all advocacy models are illustrated below:

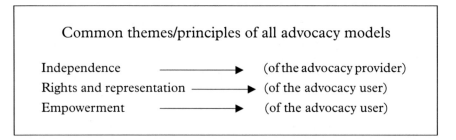

Common themes/principles of all advocacy models

Independence   ⟶   (of the advocacy provider)

Rights and representation ⟶ (of the advocacy user)

Empowerment   ⟶   (of the advocacy user)

A summary of significant developments in advocacy in 2007 is illustrated as follows:

Advocacy Developments 2007

IMCA: Statutory advocacy role detailed in provisions in the *Mental Capacity Act 2005*, implemented in England on 1 April and in Wales 1 October 2007.

IMHA: Amendments to the *Mental Health Act 1983* include a statutory Independent Mental Health Advocate role for people subject to compulsion under the amended *Mental Health Act 2007* (anticipated implementation for the IMHA is April 2009).

> *Award:* Development of a national accredited advocacy qualification due to be launched in 2008. This will include mandatory training for IMCA and IMHA.

These developments affect the whole of the advocacy sector and therefore have relevance to advocacy work in the arena of adult protection. As the IMCA role in adult protection work evolves it is likely that good practice will develop in the advocacy sector that will influence non-statutory advocacy work in this area.

The emergence of advocacy in a statutory role has influenced change and development in the sector. There are individuals and organisations within the advocacy sector that have resisted the 'professionalisation' of advocacy, pre-ferring it to remain at the 'grass roots' level, minimising the possibility of inter-ference or conflicts of interest with the purchasers of advocacy services that may potentially damage the relationship with the advocacy user. There is an argument to suggest that this position must be maintained by the advocacy sector and this has significant ethical value. Conversely, advocacy providers that have championed the development of a professional advocacy role have done so with the gravitas and backing of a larger organisation with infrastruc-ture and influence, ensuring that the principles of advocacy are maintained. I believe that the advocacy sector is now large enough to embrace both ends of the advocacy spectrum and provide a range of models to suit different client groups. It can be legitimately argued that the broad range of advocacy organi-sations and models is one of the UK advocacy sector's biggest strengths and most attractive features.

IMCA SERVICES IN ENGLAND AND WALES

The *Mental Capacity Act 2005* was implemented in full on 1 October 2007 and provides a statutory framework to empower and protect vulnerable people who are unable to make their own decisions. The Act clarifies who can take decisions, in which situations, and how they should go about this. The Act also makes new provisions for people to plan ahead for a time when they may lose capacity. Guidance on the Act is provided in the *Mental Capacity Act Code of Practice* (Department for Constitutional Affairs 2007). The *Mental Capacity Act 2005* places a duty on health and social care professionals to adhere to the Code when taking decisions for people they deem to be incapable. This includes the full range of health and social care professionals such as doctors, social workers, community psychiatric nurses and health care workers. The *Mental Capacity Act 2005*:

applies more generally to *everyone* who looks after, or cares for, someone who lacks capacity to make particular decisions for themselves. This includes family carers or other carers. Although these carers are not legally required to have regard to the Code of Practice, the guidance given in the Code will help them to understand the Act and apply it. They should follow the guidance in the Code as far as they are aware of it. (Department for Constitutional Affairs 2007, p.2)

The *Mental Capacity Act 2005* also created a new statutory advocacy service: the IMCA service. This is the first, and at the time of writing only, statutory form of advocacy available in England and Wales. IMCA services are commissioned jointly by local authorities and primary care trusts, the lead commissioning responsibility resting with local authorities in England, and local health boards in Wales. The Department of Health funded Turning Point to produce guidance for commissioners of IMCA services, *Guidance for Commissioners on the Independent Mental Capacity Advocate Service* (Bradley 2006).

The role of the IMCA is to support vulnerable people who lack capacity who are facing important decisions made by the NHS and local authorities about serious medical treatment – for example, a leg amputation – and changes of residence – for example, moving to a hospital or care home. NHS bodies and local authorities have a duty to consult the IMCA in decisions involving people who have no family or friends that are willing or appropriate to be consulted. This criteria includes people that it is not possible or practical to consult with, for example a relative that lives in a different country; one that has little contact with the person, or simply refuses to be consulted. The IMCA effectively provides a safeguard for those people that lack capacity to ensure that they are as fully involved as possible in the decision-making process applied by statutory agencies.

The IMCA does not, and cannot, replace the friends, family, and relatives ordinarily involved in the consultation process through decision-making processes. An IMCA does not have prior knowledge or experience of the person and is not as well equipped as a friend or relative to describe the person's wishes and beliefs based on personal experience. However, the IMCA is able to uphold the client's rights (in accordance with the principles of the *Mental Capacity Act 2005*), ensure that the decision-making process is applied with vigilance, and gather information about the person to assist decision-makers in coming to a decision that is in the best interests of the person. The IMCA submits a report of their findings including the views and wishes of the person who lacks capacity. The IMCA's report must be considered during the decision-making process. The IMCA's involvement clearly provides an extra safeguard for vulnerable people that otherwise would not be there. The eligibility criteria are illustrated in the box below.

The duty to instruct an IMCA is limited to decisions regarding serious medical treatment and NHS and local authority changes of accommodation.

Eligibility criteria for IMCA[1]

Available to people aged 16 years and over.

The decision-maker *must* refer to the IMCA service in the following circumstances:

- the person lacks capacity to make the particular decision
- the decision is about either serious medical treatment (see Department for Constitutional Affairs 2007 for detail of what this means)

  OR

- a change of accommodation (over 28 days in respect of an NHS move and eight weeks in respect of a local authority move)

  AND

- the person has nobody 'appropriate' to be consulted in respect of the particular decision.

The decision-maker *may* refer to the IMCA service in the following circumstances:

- the person lacks capacity to make the particular decision
- the decision is related to adult protection proceedings or a Care Review[2] (where accommodation is being reviewed)

  AND

- in cases of Care Reviews the person has nobody 'appropriate' to be consulted in respect of the particular decision. This does not apply in cases of adult protection proceedings.

However, regulations passed in autumn 2006 extended the powers of local authorities and NHS bodies to instruct IMCAs in certain cases involving care reviews and adult protection cases. It is not a duty to instruct an IMCA in these situations; however, it is a duty to consider the use of these powers wherever relevant. The decision-maker, otherwise known as the local authority/NHS body, must decide whether referral to an IMCA will or may benefit the client.

---

1   For further information a useful booklet to refer to is *Making Decisions: The Independent Mental Capacity Advocate (IMCA) Service*, written by Speaking Up.

2   The 'Care Review' is defined in Section 7 of the *Local Authority Social Services Act 1970* (it states that there should be a review 'within three months of help being provided or major changes made to services'. There should then be a review every year – or more often if needed (Department for Constitutional Affairs 2007, p.197).

Clearly this is a subjective area that is led by local planning and commissioning arrangements to ensure that consistency is applied and monitored. It is essential that local procedures are developed and instigated to provide a clear framework for decision-makers to refer and adhere to when faced with a decision of this kind. Developing practice suggests that IMCA providers are negotiating protocols with their commissioners to ensure that this extension to the role is used appropriately and fairly discharged by decision-makers. IMCA providers will presumably want to see local accountability embedded in policy to ensure that the discretionary element of extensions of the role does not result in circumnavigation of the IMCA provisions for complex or contentious cases, and arguably the people who should be referred an IMCA more than others.

The IMCA's role cannot be underestimated. It has the scope to have enormous influence for individuals who are unable to state clearly what they want, and are assessed as unable to make certain decisions. This client group represents some of the most vulnerable and potentially disempowered people in society. Furthermore there is a legitimate view that this group has traditionally been overlooked, or at the very least marginalised, in decision-making processes. The role of the IMCA is therefore focused very clearly on individuals who have nobody available or appropriate to be consulted on their behalf. The main principles of the *Mental Capacity Act 2005*, and the duty to deliver services in accordance with them, underpin the necessity of the IMCA role and functions; the best interests process and the consultation that must occur in this process cannot occur effectively if there is nobody available to take that role, or the available people are deemed to be inappropriate. A summary of the role and functions of an IMCA is illustrated below:

The role and functions of the IMCA

- The IMCA must be independent of the person making the decision.

- The IMCA provides support for the person who lacks capacity.

- The IMCA represents the person without capacity in discussions to work out whether the proposed decision is in the person's best interests.

- The IMCA provides information to help work out what is in the person's best interests.

- The IMCA submits a report illustrating the IMCA's findings and any views and wishes illicited from the person.

- The IMCA can view relevant health and social care records.
- The IMCA will raise questions or challenge decisions which appear not to be in the best interests of the person.

WHO ARE THE IMCAS?

The 'What is Advocacy' section of this chapter illustrates the advocacy sector as a broad-ranging sector that includes providers that can be defined as large national organisations through to very small projects consisting in some cases of a small number of community based advocates serving the immediate area. The emergence of advocacy in legislation such as the *Health and Social Care Act 2001*, the *Mental Capacity Act 2005* and the *Mental Health Act 2007* has provided an opportunity for the advocacy sector to formalise approaches and effectively deliver service contracts. As previously described this is a shift that the sector has responded to inconsistently, in that some providers have fully invested in the concept of 'professional advocacy' and have embraced the changes that are necessary to effectively deliver this contracted model; equally, some organisations believe that professionalising advocacy impacts on the independence and freedom of the sector to fully represent and 'fight the corner' of the client, and have therefore chosen to protect their independence and remain embedded in the community, history and 'grass roots' of advocacy.

The training of advocates is one of the core elements in the shift towards professionalising the role. A national advocacy qualification (AWARD) has been proposed and is due to be launched in 2008); this includes the statutory requirement for IMCA training. The current IMCA training delivered by Action for Advocacy will be absorbed into the new qualification. The IMCA training course is a four-day course incorporating the following:

1. Understanding the *Mental Capacity Act 2005*.
2. The role of the IMCA.
3. Working with people who may lack capacity.
4. Non-instructed advocacy.
5. Working with other professionals.
6. Case management.
7. Review and action planning.

The course aims to provide IMCAs with a good knowledge of the *Mental Capacity Act 2005* and the role and responsibilities of the IMCA. It includes a range of training methods including role play, multimedia and group work and has been positively reviewed by the 500 participants that attended the course in 2007. The course includes a section on abuse and the IMCA role in adult protection cases. The IMCA training course is similar to most professional training in that there is an expectation that personal and professional development as well as organisational development will be implemented to further the IMCA's knowledge in the given area of work as the role develops. IMCA providers have a clear responsibility in ensuring that investment in IMCA development work occurs at the outset and that this area is absorbed into personal and professional development plans for IMCAs.

Finally, a person can be an IMCA as long as they attend the training course, are employed by a contracted IMCA provider and are authorised by the commissioning local authority to be an IMCA (see Statutory Instruments 1832/2883 contained within the MCA regulations 2006). IMCA providers have seemingly taken different approaches to the recruitment and resourcing of IMCAs. Some have trained existing advocates and absorbed the IMCA role into their generic advocacy work. Other providers have opted to recruit advocates into an 'IMCA only' role, allowing for development of specialist expertise in the statutory IMCA role. These approaches have resulted in development of current expertise in established advocates and also an influx of new advocates into the sector. It is estimated that the current resourcing of IMCAs has seen an increase of approximately 300–400 full-time advocates in the sector. Interestingly the IMCA role has attracted a significant number of former social workers and nurses into the advocacy sector. Clearly this has provided some relevant expertise in the field of health and social care, however the early signs are that there is a need to complement this knowledge with general advocacy training to 'new' IMCAs so that the IMCA role does not simply become another statutory function, losing some of its independence and unique 'advocacy' characteristics.

IMCA AND ADULT PROTECTION WORK

The regulations regarding the role of the IMCA specify that:

LAs and the NHS have the power to instruct an IMCA if the following two requirements are met:

- where protective measures are being put in place in relation to the protection of vulnerable adults from abuse; and
- where the person lacks capacity.

In these circumstances the LA or NHS body may instruct an IMCA to represent the person concerned if it is satisfied that it would be of benefit to the person to do so...

... the regulations apply equally to

(a)   a person who has been abused

(b)   who has been neglected and

(c)   a person who is alleged to be the abuser.

(Department of Health 2007, p.2)

The Mental Capacity Act 2005 places a duty on decision-makers to consider the extension of the IMCA role to situations for people who lack capacity that are involved in adult protection procedures. Decision-makers, for example the local authority or primary care trust, have powers to instruct an IMCA to support and represent a person who lacks capacity where it is alleged that the person is or has been abused or neglected by another person, or, the person is abusing or has abused another person. The criteria of appropriate friends or family to consult does not apply in cases of IMCA and adult protection. It is important to note that the responsible bodies can only instruct an IMCA if they propose to take, or have already taken, protective measures (these would ordinarily be discussed at a 'strategy meeting'). This clearly represents an appropriate filter for the IMCA service to ensure that the referral criteria are not broadened to the extent that they can fit several situations, and place limited resources under pressure.

The role of the IMCA in adult protection issues is no different in principle to the role taken in other IMCA work. The IMCA's role is one of safeguarding the person's rights and ensuring that they are as fully involved as possible through the process that is being applied. The role of the IMCA does not include investigating the allegations, giving evidence or supporting a case for or against the person. However, there is one significant difference that is clear in referrals to IMCA for adult protection issues and care reviews apart from the fact that the Act only makes it a duty under the MCA to *consider* whether it is in the client's best interests to refer to an IMCA service. In these two areas there is not necessarily a decision to be taken or considered, it is a process that is being applied. For example an older person in hospital who is being considered for a hip replacement who lacks capacity and has nobody available who can be consulted about the decision is clearly eligible for an IMCA. The IMCA's work in this case will focus on this decision and the IMCA work will be completed when the serious medical treatment decision is taken and acted upon, if there is any action to be taken. In cases of adult abuse there is a process to be gone through, following very clear policy set out in local safeguarding/adult protection procedures. In some cases this process will result in something approaching the clarity of a serious medical treatment decision; however, in most cases it will not be as clear cut and may result in a range of interventions or care planning (protective measures) that are not as simple to describe as a hip replacement, for example. Where an IMCA is appointed in relation to an adult protection case the local authority or NHS must take into account any information provided, or submission made, by the IMCA when making any decision about the protective measures in respect of the person concerned.

Early case studies in this area have resulted in practice issues that IMCA providers will discuss locally and nationally and develop at regional IMCA network meetings. The IMCA providers have been appointed partly because of their experience in developing new and best practice in the advocacy arena. The adult protection IMCA work is one of the areas that will develop based on early experiences and close collaboration with adult protection coordinators. The case studies below provide some illustrative examples of the process applied by the IMCA in cases of adult protection. This is followed by some practice dilemmas and issues for development of this work further.

CASE STUDY 8.1

The client is an older man with a diagnosis of vascular dementia. He is being cared for by a number of close relatives who all live locally. The family support is complemented by a care package provided by a care agency. The agreement is that a partial care package is provided by the care agency at specific times and at other times the family provide the care to the gentleman.

The local authority have instigated Protection of Vulnerable Adult Procedures on the basis of allegations that the family are neglecting their relative. A referral was made to the IMCA service prior to the strategy meeting.

The referral was screened and accepted and the IMCA process began. The process began with the IMCA meeting the client and attempting to illicit his views regarding his care package and his future needs and wishes. The IMCA process also involved talking to neighbours, relatives and the care agency providing the care.

The IMCA submitted a report outlining the client's views and wishes and giving a summary of the interviews that had taken place as part of the information-gathering process. The IMCA attended the subsequent case conference and represented the views of the client.

At the time of writing the case is still ongoing. The IMCA will remain involved in the case until the adult protection process has ended.

CASE STUDY 8.2

The client is an older man in residential care. The client suffered a brain injury early in his life that affects his behaviour significantly. The client was referred to the IMCA service from a social services department who were instigating adult protection proceedings against the man due to an allegation of serious sexual assault on another resident. The alleged victim decided not to press charges; however, the Protection of Vulnerable Adults process was progressed. The police were involved in the strategy meeting and the IMCA was also in attendance.

The IMCA had three meetings with the client who lacked any insight into the alleged incident but was able to make known his views and wishes regarding his care. The client also described his sexualised behaviour to the IMCA.

The IMCA's report made a recommendation regarding neuropsychology for the client to have support regarding his sexualised behaviour. The IMCA was also responsible for contacting a social worker based locally who had particular experience in finding placements for this type of client.

The client was moved to an alternative placement, as a protective measure. The IMCA's suggestions were actioned and the views of the client remained at the centre of the process. The IMCA attended both the strategy meeting and the case conference on behalf of the client.

CONCLUSION

The emergence of the IMCA role in statute is a significant development in the advocacy sector. The early signs are that the IMCA role is benefiting some of the most vulnerable people in our society. The apparent weakness in the legislation in making referral to IMCA in cases of adult protection an extension to the role, and optional not obligatory, can be strengthened by ensuring local policy is carefully adapted to fully consider appropriate referral. The advocacy sector must ensure that the independence of advocacy is not affected by the statutory function that IMCA holds and fully represent vulnerable clients that are submerged in what must be a very confusing and sometimes daunting process. I am confident that the advocacy sector will respond professionally and effectively to this new development, and pave the way for more statutory advocacy in the future. If, as planned, the IMCA role protects and empowers people engaged in adult protection procedures then this statutory model of advocacy will have proved its worth and its critical independent position in health and social care provision.

GOOD PRACTICE POINTS

- The IMCA service must work closely with the local authority adult protection coordinator/lead in developing adult protection IMCA processes and being fully consulted on the development of a local authority policy and amendment to Vulnerable Adult and Safeguarding Adults procedures.

- All IMCAs should attend Level 1 and 2 Safeguarding Adults training provided by the local authority.

- IMCA providers must develop or adapt a vulnerable adults policy to reflect the IMCA's role in adult protection work. This policy must be made available to all health and social care staff.

- Referrals to the IMCA service must occur at the earliest opportunity, providing more scope for the alleged victim/abuser to be involved in the process more fully and independently.

- The IMCA service must be involved in all strategy meetings where the alleged victim/abuser lacks capacity.

- The strategy meeting must fully consider and record whether instructing an IMCA will benefit the client or not.

- IMCA providers should prepare for a situation where both the alleged victim and alleged abuser are referred to the IMCA service.

- The IMCA provider must have a legally accurate confidentiality procedure that protects both the IMCA and client throughout the adult protection process. It is wise to check that the IMCA provider's confidentiality policy is consistent with that of the local authority.

- IMCA providers should be equipped to refer cases to generic advocacy services after the IMCA role is performed. The generic advocacy provider must have a non-instructed advocacy policy in place.

- IMCA providers must be resourced sufficiently to provide adequate management support to IMCAs; especially in cases of adult protection where debriefing and sometimes counselling support may be required.

STATUTES

Health and Social Care Act 2000. London: The Stationery Office

Mental Capacity Act 2005. London: The Stationery Office

The Mental Capacity Act 2005 (Independent Mental Capacity Advocate) (Wales) Regulations 2007. In draft.

Mental Health Act 1983. London: HMSO

Mental Health Act 2007. London: The Stationery Office

REGULATIONS

The Mental Capacity Act 2005 (Independent Mental Capacity Advocate) (General) Regulations 2006. London: Crown Copyright.

The Mental Capacity Act 2005 (Independent Mental Capacity Advocate) (Expansion of Role) Regulations 2006. London: Crown Copyright.

REFERENCES

Action for Advocacy (n.d.) 'Are There Different Types of Advocacy?' Available at: www.actionforadvocacy.org.uk/articleServlet?action=display&article=716&articletype=20/, accessed 29 July 2008.

Action for Advocacy (2002) *The Advocacy Charter.* London: Action for Advocacy.

Bradley, A. (2006) *Guidance for Commissioners on the Independent Mental Capacity Advocate Service.* London: Turning Point.

Department for Constitutional Affairs (2007) *Mental Capacity Act 2005 Code of Practice.* London: The Stationery Office.

Department of Health (2007) *Adult Protection, Care Reviews and Independent Mental Capacity Advocates (IMCA): Guidance on Interpreting the Regulations Extending the IMCA Role.* London: DH.

Liverpool City Council (2007) *Developing a Joint Advocacy Policy and Commissioning Strategy – The Vision for Liverpool.* Available at www.liverpool.gov.uk/Health_and_Social_care/Advocacy/index.asp, accessed 29 July 2008.

Speaking Up (2006) *Making Decisions: The Independent Mental Capacity Advocate (IMCA) Service.* London: DCA, PGO, DH, Welsh Assembly.

USEFUL ORGANISATIONS

Advocacy Experience Head Office

4 Harvard Court

Quay Business Centre

Calver Road
Warrington WA2 8LT
Tel: 01925 414443
Fax: 01925 651400
IMCA line: 0844 800 2776
E-mail: headoffice@advocacyexperience.com
Website: www.advocacyexperience.com

Action for Advocacy
PO Box 31856
Lorrimore Square
London SE17 3XR
Tel: 020 7820 7868
Fax: 020 7820 9947
E-mail: info@actionforadvocacy.org.uk
Website: www.actionforadvocacy.org.uk

CHAPTER 9

BEING AN IMCA: EXPERIENCES IN ADULT PROTECTION PROCEEDINGS

TERESA GORCZYNSKA

INTRODUCTION

Advocacy Partners was the first advocacy organisation in the UK. Rights, voices and choices are at the centre of all our work. Since 1981 we have been working to ensure that people who have the greatest needs, are supported to speak out, have greater involvement in decision-making, and have control over their lives. We strive to ensure that no one gets left out or treated as second best. We do this by ensuring that people's rights are respected, their voices heard and their choices responded to.

Advocacy Partners was commissioned by the Department of Health to provide one of the Independent Mental Capacity Advocate (IMCA) pilots and wrote part of the first national IMCA training course (Department of Health 2007). In 2007 Advocacy Partners was awarded contracts in ten local authorities across London and Sussex to provide the Independent Mental Capacity Advocate service. I am the Head of IMCA and Mental Health Advocacy at Advocacy Partners and manage the IMCA services. I provide *Mental Capacity Act* training and at the time of writing am updating the national IMCA qualification and writing guidance on the role of the IMCA in adult protection proceedings. This chapter draws on my experiences and those of the IMCAs I manage; it will discuss when to instruct an IMCA in adult protection proceedings, the role of the IMCA within those proceedings, lessons learnt so far and recommendations to ensure the best use of this valuable safeguard.

The *Mental Capacity Act 2005* (MCA) introduced the first legal right to independent advocacy, the IMCA service. The Act places a duty on local authorities and NHS bodies to refer to an IMCA when adults may lack capacity to make decisions about serious medical treatment, or about a change in accommodation, who do not have family or friends with whom it is appropriate to consult about the decision. Local authorities and NHS bodies also have discretionary powers to refer to an IMCA when someone lacks the capacity to agree to the arrangements made in accommodation reviews and adult protection proceedings. In the first year of the IMCA service nationally 5175 people who lacked capacity had the support of an IMCA, 681 were people in adult protection proceedings (DH 2008).

The role of the IMCA is described in the Act and in its Regulations (2006) and *Code of Practice* (Department for Constitutional Affairs 2007). Essentially the IMCA represents and supports the person who may lack capacity in relation to the particular decision and checks that the MCA is being followed. The IMCA also has a right to meet the person in private, access relevant medical and social records, seek a second medical opinion where appropriate and challenge the decision formally if necessary.

WHEN TO INSTRUCT AN IMCA IN ADULT PROTECTION

Regulations extended the role of the IMCA to include a discretionary power to involve an IMCA where the local authority is considering or has taken protective measures as part of adult protection proceedings. This is for has person allegedly abused or perpetrating abuse, where they may lack the capacity to agree to these protective measures. An IMCA may be involved in adult protection proceedings when there is a particular benefit to the person, regardless of family and friend involvement. However, if during adult protection proceedings, consideration is being given as to whether the person may need to be moved long term in their best interests, and there are no family or friends involved, the local authority has a legal duty to involve an IMCA.

The Code of Practice sets out an expectation for local authorities to establish a local policy to set out criteria for using the discretionary powers to appoint an IMCA. To ensure that the resource is targeted at those most in need, the Association of Directors of Adult Social Services (2007) have produced guidance which many local authorities are using. This guidance advises that an IMCA is used in adult protection proceedings when 'other arrangements are not robust enough to support the necessary decision-making for the individual' (p.4). For example the person does not already have an independent advocate, and one of the following applies:

1. Where there is a serious exposure to risk of death, serious physical injury or illness, serious deterioration in physical or mental health or serious emotional distress.

2. Where a life-changing decision is involved and consulting the family or family is compromised by the reasonable belief that they would not have the person's best interests at heart.

3. There is a conflict of views between the decision-makers regarding the best interests of the person.

(Association of Directors of Adult Social Services 2007, p.4)

The guidance also suggests that where the person's wishes and preferences would have a significant impact on the investigative process or where immediate actions need to be taken to safeguard the individual prior to further investigation taking place the IMCA should be involved at the strategy discussion/meeting stage of cases. It also suggests that at other times the IMCA may not be required to be involved until the case conference/safeguarding planning stage to provide input into the safeguarding plan (p.3).

It is the local authority's responsibility to decide whether it is appropriate to instruct an IMCA. The local authority therefore must establish whether the person lacks capacity to agree to protective measures and follow their local policy on when to refer.

WHAT WILL THE IMCA DO?

The IMCA should support and represent the person through the adult protection proceedings. The balance of support and representation will largely depend on the ability of the person to be involved, but also on the timescales and the situation. The IMCA will try to determine the person's wishes and preferences and ensure they are being taken into account. The IMCA should ensure that the decisions about protective measures have followed the MCA and are the least restrictive options possible. They should also raise relevant issues and questions. Particularly in safeguarding adult situations the IMCA may not have the time to do all the actions they would like to; part of the skill of an IMCA is being able to determine how best to support and represent the person in the time available. The IMCA will have to prioritise which actions they can achieve in the timeframe available.

The IMCA and the decision-maker should discuss the process and be clear about the expectations of IMCA involvement and where possible agree timeframes. The IMCA should be clear about what records they would like access to. This will usually include minutes of previous meetings, reviews, community care assessments, care plans and risk assessments. The IMCA will request the decision-maker informs any relatives of IMCA involvement and that safeguarding adults procedures have commenced. If relevant the IMCA will check if the police have been informed. The IMCA's work will largely be determined by the risk the person is in and the decisions and actions required to protect the person. The IMCA should support the decision-maker to ensure the protective measures and safeguarding plan proposed, respect the person's rights, minimise the risk of harm to the person as much as possible whilst being proportionate and less restrictive. The IMCA will do this by ensuring the person and their preferences remain central to discussions, by asking questions, and by ensuring all appropriate options have been explored. The IMCA will write a report but both decision-maker and IMCA should keep each other informed of developments and actions. The IMCA should be clear with the decision-maker before they write their report if they have concerns about the safeguarding plan or any decisions being made or actions not being taken. After the decision-maker has received the IMCA's report they should review the IMCA involvement and agree if the IMCA should attend further reviews.

The IMCA is not the decision-maker and is not there to fill in gaps in the local authority team. They are one part of the decision-making process and ensure the person remains central to all planning. The responsibility for the decision and the safety of the person remains with the local authority.

The IMCA's role is to be there for the person. However, an important additional outcome is that on many occasions, particularly in complex and controversial issues or where relatives are not acting in the person's best interests, decision-makers have often felt that it was helpful to have an independent view which concurred with their proposed actions. This has at times meant that safeguarding plans were put in place more quickly than they would normally have been.

ADVOCACY PARTNERS' EXPERIENCES SO FAR

In 11 months of Advocacy Partners' IMCA service, 13 per cent of the eligible referrals were for an IMCA in adult protection proceedings. In over half of Advocacy Partners' adult protection referrals the alleged perpetrators were relatives. The average time for an IMCA to complete the role within adult protection proceedings to date is 13 hours. However, this is likely to increase as many of the most complex and timely adult protection referrals are still open. Of the adult protection decision-makers who evaluated Advocacy Partners' IMCA service, 100 per cent said that the IMCA had ascertained the wishes/preferences of the client, enabled the client to be more involved, provided useful information and made a difference to the outcome.

Table 9.1 Breakdown of Eligible IMCA (referrals to Advocacy Partners)	
Decision	*Number of eligible referrals from 1/4/07–31/3/08*
Serious medical treatment	85
Accommodation	377
Care review	21
Adult protection	39
Adult protection/accommodation	37
Total	559

Some decision-maker comments

'I found the IMCA really helpful and responsive to our tight timeframe.'

'I was very impressed with the IMCA as an advocate for Malgosia. She was competent and able to act quickly and gain his trust so as to get his views, which produced a good outcome for Malgosia.'

'It was very useful to have an independent person work with the service user under the Safeguarding Vulnerable Adults policy. I have found the IMCA to be very professional, recognising and understanding the risks and the difficulties the decision-maker is often faced with, whilst keeping the service user central.'

(Gorczynska 2008b)

Boundaries of role

The role of the IMCA can be more complex and wider in safeguarding adult referrals, as referrals can stretch into many areas of the person's life, and therefore involve many decisions. This results in the boundaries of the role of an IMCA being currently less clear in adult protection. There are often other issues in the person's life that require an advocate and the decision-maker involved would like the IMCA's involvement because there is no other advocacy available to provide that support. At times the IMCA may be the person who discovers other issues in the person's life that require advocacy support. Decision-makers may have an expectation that the IMCA will be able to have a far larger role. Due to the time constraints and the nature of the role, the IMCA and decision-maker need to be clear from the beginning the boundaries of the IMCA role and when it finishes. Establishing when the IMCA's role is completed is a challenge because the outcome is not always as clearly defined in as an accommodation or treatment decisions and may require continuing monitoring (Gorczynska and Thompson 2007b).

Time

The University of Cambridge's evaluation of the pilots found that the average time taken for an IMCA to complete working within serious medical treatment decisions, long-term accommodation changes and care reviews was around eight hours (Redley *et al.* 2006). This research was completed before the role of the IMCA was expanded to include adult protection proceedings. The University of Cambridge's more recent research on time spent by IMCAs on adult protection referrals was 13 hours (Redley *et al.* 2008). Therefore the extent of the time needed for safeguarding adult referrals has not yet been evaluated. Representing and supporting a person in safeguarding adult proceedings can often require eight hours in the meetings attended alone particularly if a long-term move is being considered. Often both the decision-maker and the IMCA will feel that satisfactory representation and support in the situation does require more than eight hours. IMCA funding contracts and service specifications need to take this into account.

Talking to the alleged perpetrator

Safeguarding adult proceedings may involve relatives as alleged perpetrators. These relatives may have information about the person's preferences that may be important for the IMCA to establish. The IMCA therefore may need to contact the perpetrator, they must however be careful not to get involved in investigating nor breaching confidentiality and must be clear with the perpetrator about their role. If the police are involved the IMCA should discuss with them the nature of any investigations taking place before speaking to the person or the alleged perpetrator. The decision as to whether to contact the alleged perpetrator must be taken on an individual basis and include the involvement of the adult protection chair person. Sometimes the decision-maker may not have informed the relatives that an IMCA has been instructed nor that safeguarding adults proceedings about them are being instigated. This can have impact on the IMCA's role as relatives may react negatively and restrict access to the person.

Access to IMCA report

The IMCA's report is for the local authority/NHS decision-maker. However, on occasions relatives might request access to the report. Advocacy Partners engagement protocols with commissioners set out that the report is written for the decision-maker and that any additional requests for the report will be directed to the decision-maker to decide. IMCA services must ensure that whilst their reports remain independent, person-centred and factual they are mindful that relatives may be given access to the report. It can also be a challenge to ensure the reports reflect all factors when relatives refuse to engage with the IMCA.

Access to the person

It can be difficult to establish a person's wishes and preferences due to the referral happening a day or two before the meeting, the person being in a frightened and distressed state or the family refusing access. It is always prefer-able for the IMCA to have the opportunity to spend time with the person they are representing and therefore it is important that there is awareness around local authority staff of their power to refer to an IMCA. However, where it is not possible to meet the person, due to time or access issues, there is still a valuable role for the IMCA in asking questions and ensuring that the person's rights are respected, their known preferences and wishes are taken into account, the safeguarding plan is least restrictive and the MCA is being used. The IMCA will also ensure the potential for the person to be involved at a later date is explored.

The process

The knowledge of local Safeguarding Adults policies and the Department of Health's guidance *No Secrets* (2000) varies across London boroughs. This can result in situations taking a long time to be resolved and adult protection policies, particularly the timeframes, not being adhered to. Additionally, the IMCA then needs to advocate for the correct process to be followed. Adult protection proceedings can be further impeded by confusion about who is the decision-maker particularly when several boroughs are involved; for example, where the person is living in one borough but is funded by another. At times it has been difficult to get access to minutes of previous meetings and to be accepted as part of the decision-making process.

There can be difficulties for local authorities to establish the person's capacity to consent to protective measures, that have not been decided on. There have also been situations where lack of medical records, difficulty in accessing the person or lack of time due to the person being at serious risk have meant doing a capacity test before instructing an IMCA is problematic.

Effective use of the *Mental Capacity Act 2005*

As the MCA is relatively new not all local authority staff have had training on the MCA and may not yet have a clear understanding of the Act as the IMCAs have. IMCAs particularly work to ensure that protective measures are decided using the best interests checklist in the MCA, and in particular that these measures are the least restrictive option. Local authorities have experienced delays in getting legal advice to support them, meaning that IMCAs may be in the position of needing to raise awareness about the Act and its frameworks including the new Court of Protection and the new criminal offence of wilful treatment and neglect. This can also mean that the IMCA may need to spend time supporting other professionals to understand the potential the MCA has to protect vulnerable people in adult protection proceedings. Particular chal-lenges are often around local authorities feeling powerless to remove people at risk, who cannot consent, from their homes, or taking decisions which go against the wishes of relatives not acting in the person's best interests. There can also be difficulties in getting the police to remain involved. It is important therefore to have a forum to feed back to the local authority separately from client issues about where processes are not working.

MAKING A DIFFERENCE

The first year of providing the new IMCA service has given us a wealth of experiences, including extensive learning about supporting and representing clients in adult protection proceedings. Adult protection coordinators interviewed for the University of Cambridge's research were unanimous in their belief that involving an IMCA in adult protection proceedings benefited the person being allegedly abused, most specifically because of the independence of the IMCA (Redley *et al.* 2008). The following quotes are from Advocacy Partners dedicated and skilled IMCA team.

Being an IMCA

'Working as an IMCA with people in adult protection means I have ensured the person has a better chance of having their rights respected and that the process is centred around their needs rather than the easiest option.'

'As an IMCA in adult protection proceedings I have amplified the voices and choices of those who are unable to say as much as they would like, it is a valuable, privileged and intricate role to play. Knowing that the activity and report of IMCA will provide extra safeguards, and enable social workers and other professionals to perform a more comprehensive service in adult protection, is a reassurance for the most vulnerable.'

'I made a difference by recommending supervised access to protect an elderly mother from her son and supporting the professionals to appreciate this was necessary. Until this point the Adult Protection meetings had been unwilling to go this far, despite the son having caused his mother physical harm.'

'I ensured my client's strong views about staying in the family home were fully taken into account, making it possible for them to stay at home with their neglectful parent, by ensuring the local authority explored the option of increasing all the other services that supported her.'

'I was told the police did not want to be involved in a situation with an elderly woman who had been sexually abused. The police were very confused about the act, and it was about ensuring their support and protection and following up, despite the fact that there was slim chance of a conviction coming out of it.'

'As an IMCA I focus everyone's thoughts on the real person at the centre of investigations, widen the social worker's view of the person's lifestyle, situation and support them to concentrate on quality of life outcomes for that individual.'

'Several times in financial abuse situations I have ensured that my client has been able to maintain contact with perpetrator as that person is very important to them but contact needs to be maintained in a controlled and safe way.'

'I think the main difference I made as an IMCA was to push the process along and ensure that the social worker continued to take action and that the process was "monitored". The process often "stalled" and only once I requested actions were they done. This was in part due to the social worker's their competing priorities and time restraints and lack of clarity as to what action to take.'

'As an advocate I was not always invited to adult protection meetings, being an IMCA means I have access to these meetings and professionals look to you to explain how the MCA impacts on proceedings. Usually as an IMCA I am positively treated by social care professionals as they see the value of the IMCA to the clients. Social workers may feel unable to "rock the boat" and are happy that we ask difficult questions that people may not want to discuss, they value our independence.'

'Without IMCA involvement the police would never have been involved in this situation.'

'I enabled both social services and the family to hear what my client wanted.'

'Safeguards were put in place much quicker than they would have been after my initial visit to a client.'

'I ensured my client's views/wishes were heard, rather than the issue just being an argument between local authority, family and staff at residential home.'

(Gorczynska 2008b)

CASE STUDIES

The following case studies are examples of how some IMCAs have worked in adult protection proceedings.

CASE STUDY 9.1

Yanni, who was in his seventies and had dementia, was living at home with his daughter who was the main carer. She was not giving her father sufficient nutrition nor his diabetes medication and would not allow carers into the house for support do this either.

The IMCA met with Yanni with a translator; the daughter did not want to meet the IMCA. The IMCA also met with and spoke to the decision-maker who was the care manager, as well as the community psychiatric nurse, care manager, district nurse and GP involved in Yanni's care. The IMCA also read relevant reports and minutes. The IMCA then wrote a report and gave actions to consider, including recommending that the decision-maker explained to the daughter the medical and legal implications of not providing care. The IMCA report also recommended that appropriate religious leaders met the daughter to explain about fasting for elderly and sick people. The IMCA supported the social worker to understand how the MCA was relevant and showed them the relevant parts of the Code of Practice.

The outcome was that the daughter allowed nurses into provide support to Yanni and to monitor the situation and Yanni's health improved.

CASE STUDY 9.2

Irena, who was in her eighties and had dementia, had been moved from her home where one of her two sons cared for her after she alleged to day centre staff that he verbally abused her. The referral was to ascertain what Irena wanted and to reach a decision about whether she would stay in the residential service or return home. The IMCA met with Irena three times, spoke with the alleged perpetrator, spoke with day centre staff, met and spoke with adult services, read relevant records and documents, spoke with residential service staff, attended meetings and wrote a report.

Irena was obviously scared of her son but did not have a good relationship with social services either. Irena wanted to remain in the service but the most important thing to her was that her son could continue to visit her. Her sons felt that she wanted to go home but once they read the IMCA report and understood that the IMCA was independent from the local authority, they accepted what their mother had said and she stayed at the service with frequent visits from her family. The local authority disregarded the value of the Irena's property to enable one son to continue living there so he could visit his mother.

CASE STUDY 9.3

Owen is a man with autism in his early thirties who lives in a house with five others. The funding authority (out of area) made an adult protection alert as allegations of abuse had been made concerning another resident verbally and occasionally physically attacking/abusing Owen. I met with Owen and observed him in his home undertaking everyday activities and in the company of the other resident (the alleged perpetrator). I spoke with staff who felt that they were finding it difficult to safeguard Owen as he became frustrated when in the house for too long and this would make his behaviour of moving items to different places more pronounced which would in turn aggravate the other resident.

Staff at the home, however, were very good at dealing with incidents and had called the police in to make it clear to the perpetrator that she should not act in this way. They also had a very good recording system for ensuring that they tracked the incidents and found different ways to manage the situation. The funding authority had not visited and believed that Owen was inappropriately placed at that home. Staff felt that Owen would encounter these problems in any shared home and that it was better for him to stay where he was supported by people who knew him well. The funding authority felt they were asked to pay 'danger money' to protect Owen by giving more one-to-one time. Staff said that Owen's one-to-one time had been reduced and that this extra time in the house caused him to become frustrated which exacerbated his behaviours. Upon receiving the IMCA report the funding authority reinstated the one-to-one time for two afternoons a week and there appear to have been no further issues since this time.

RECOMMENDATIONS

The role of the IMCA is new and further research and evaluation is required to inform continuing good practice. To further develop the role of the IMCA in safeguarding adult procedures the Department of Health and the Social Care Institute for Excellence (SCIE) has recently commissioned the following work as part of a programme of work on implementing the *Mental Capacity Act 2005*:

1. The involvement of IMCAs in adult protection procedures in England April 2007 to 31 March 2008 (University of Cambridge).

2. 'Mental Capacity Act and Safeguarding Vulnerable Adults' – a two-day training workshop (The Ann Craft Trust).

3. Guidance on IMCA in adult protection proceedings (Advocacy Partners).

The work is a positive step towards ensuring the role of the IMCA and the MCA are as effective as possible within safeguarding adults procedures. It is hoped that local authorities will sign up to using the guidance and the training.

There is currently a wide variation nationally in referral rates. The number of referrals to IMCA services for long-term moves and serious medical treatment will affect the IMCA service's ability to accept the discretionary referrals for adult protection. Local implementation networks (LINs) and commissioners should consider the demand locally, to inform whether resources need to be extended either to IMCA services or to other local advocacy organisations to ensure an advocate is available to vulnerable adults within safeguarding adult proceedings.

Advocacy Partners has found it helpful to develop engagement protocols with commissioners, setting out expectations and agreed methods of working. Additionally, IMCAs and decision-makers should discuss and agree how to work effectively in each situation.

Local authorities need to ensure that where an IMCA is involved and there are relatives involved that the decision-maker informs the relatives of the decision to involve an IMCA. Advocacy Partners has produced an IMCA frequently asked questions leaflet, aimed at supporting relatives, friends and carers to support understanding about the role of the IMCA.

Local adult protection training and local adult protection policies should be reviewed to include the MCA and IMCA. The local adult protection training and local adult protection policies should refer to the local policies on when to refer to an IMCA and the new guidance on the role of the IMCA in adult protection proceedings.

CONCLUSION

IMCAs are only available to a limited number of people facing specific decisions and so are ideally commissioned as part of a wider advocacy strategy. Some of the people who were referred to the IMCA service did not meet the criteria for an IMCA, although they had a clear need for advocacy (Gorczynska 2007a). Therefore wider advocacy provision will help streamline the provision of IMCAs and ensure that more vulnerable people have an advocate available to them.

The IMCA is a specific and specialised type of advocacy. There are similarities and differences to other forms of independent advocacy. The work of the IMCA is decision-led but it is also person focused. The experiences of IMCAs show that greater awareness of the *Mental Capacity Act*, and clarification around the role of the IMCA in the guidelines being developed, could further extend the IMCA services ability to ensure they continue to develop as a vital safeguard. IMCAs ensure the person remains at the centre of the process and has the potential to become a key element in how society shows its respect for and concern about the autonomy, rights and protection of some of its most vulnerable citizens.

STATUTES

The Mental Capacity Act 2005. London: The Stationery Office.

REGULATIONS

The Mental Capacity Act 2005 (Independent Mental Capacity Advocates) (Expansion of Role) Regulations 2006. London: The Stationery Office.

The Mental Capacity Act 2005 (Independent Mental Capacity Advocates) (General) Regulations 2006. London: The Stationery Office.

REFERENCES

Association of Directors of Adult Social Services. (2007) *Practice Guidance: Criteria for the use of IMCAs in safeguarding adults cases*. London: ADASS.

Department for Constitutional Affairs. (2007) *Mental Capacity Act 2005 Code of Practice*. London: The Stationary Office.

Department of Health. (2000) *No Secrets: Guidance on Implementing Multi-agency Policies and Procedures to Protect Vulnerable Adults from Abuse*. London: DH.

Department of Health. (2008) *The First Annual Report Of The Independent Mental Capacity Advocacy Service. Year 1. April 2007 – March 2008*. London: DH

Gorczynska, T. (2007a) 'The First Legal Right to Advocacy'. *Working with Older People 11*, 1, 17–20.

Gorczynska T (2008a) *Advocacy Partners IMCA Report 2008*. London: Advocacy Partners

Gorczynska, T. (2008b) *Guidance on the IMCA in Adult Protection Proceedings*. London: Advocacy Partners.[1]

Gorczynska, T & Thompson, D. (2007b) 'The Role of the Independent Mental Capacity Advocate in Adult Protection'. *The Journal of Adult Protection*. Volume 9: Issue 4: pp. 38-45. Currently missing in Refs on proofs. Relates to page p164 on proofs – Section re Boundaries of role

Redley M, Luke L, Keeley H, Clare I & Holland A. (2006) *Evaluation of the Pilot Independent Mental Capacity Advocate (IMCA) Service*. Cambridge: University of Cambridge

CONTACT DETAILS

Advocacy Partners

McMillan House

54 Cheam Common Rd

Worcester Park

Surrey KT4 8RH

Tel: 020 8330 6644

Fax: 020 8330 6622

E-mail: info@advocacypartners.org

Website: www.advocacypartners.org

1   This work has been commissioned by the Department of Health and Social Care Institute for Excellence as part of a programme of work on implementing the *Mental Capacity Act 2005*. The views expressed are those of the authors alone.

CHAPTER 10

THE COMMISSION FOR SOCIAL CARE INSPECTION'S LEGAL POWERS: WHAT IT CAN AND CANNOT DO

ADRIAN HUGHES

INTRODUCTION

In 1999 the then Secretary for Health, Frank Dobson, said that current regulatory powers gave regulators only the choice between 'a nuclear weapon and a feather duster'[1] – they could make requests to the change practices, or in the most serious cases close a service down, but had no powers in between. Since then the regulation of social care in England transferred to the Commission for Social Care Inspection (CSCI) in 2004. With the move, there has been a substantial change to legislation and guidance, which has resulted in the regulator having a broader range of powers to respond to poor practice and specifically the abuse of vulnerable adults. The aim of this chapter is to clarify the legal powers the Commission has and can use in responding to abuse in social care settings. It should eliminate the myth that the Commission can close down services immediately and explain the range of powers, how they are used and the safeguards which are in place.

THE LEGAL FRAMEWORK: COMMISSION FOR SOCIAL CARE INSPECTION (CSCI)

The Commission for Social Care Inspection (the Commission) was launched in April 2004 as the single, independent inspectorate for all adult social care services in England. It was established by the *Health and Social Care (Community Health and Standards) Act 2003*. The establishment of the Commission brings together the inspection, regulation and review of all social care services into one organisation. This results in a more effective organisation,

---

1   Select Committee on Health Minutes of Evidence, Examination of Witnesses (Questions 905–919) 13 May 1999.

which has an independent overview of the complete social care industry including the commissioning, purchasing and delivery of services.

The vision and values of the Commission are to promote improvements in social care for the benefit of people who use care services and to make social care better for people.[2]

There are four key aims which guide the work of the Commission:

- Put the people who use social care first.

- Improve services and stamp out bad practice.

- Be an expert voice on social care.

- Practice what we preach in our own organisation.

KEY LEGISLATION

The primary legislation which underpins the work of the Commission is the *Care Standards Act 2000*. This Act sets out remit for the work of the Commission and the way in which it discharges its functions. In addition to the regulation of care services, the Commission is also responsible for the performance assessment of councils with a social services responsibility and for the publication of an annual 'State of Social Care' report. An overarching general duty of the Commission is to encourage improvement in the quality of registered social care services. To support the work of the Commission there is a suite of regulations which cover specific services together with service specific National Minimum Standards.

Since the responsibility for regulating services for children transferred to Ofsted in April 2007 the Commission now regulates the following services as presented in Table 10.1, which summarises information from the *Care Standards Act*, Regulations and National Minimum Standards (NMS).

The primary legislation and the regulations give the Commission four main roles in relation to care services: to register, to inspect and report, to encourage improvement, and if necessary to use enforcement powers to encourage improvement and/or cancel registration. The Commission is not a complaints investigation body and no provision in the legislation is made for this. The Commission encourages people who use services to raise concerns directly with those providing the service but recognises that this is not always possible or easy. The Commission therefore will use information about complaints to ensure that the persons registered are discharging their responsibilities.

---

2   The Commission for Social Care Inspection regulates care services in England. The regulation of care services in Wales is covered by Care and Social Services Inspectorate Wales (CSSIW), www.csiw.wales.gov.uk/index.asp, and for Scotland the Scottish Commission for the Regulation of Care, www.carecommission.com.

Table 10.1 Services requiring registration – Care Standards Act 2000

Service type	Definition	Regulations	National Minimum Standards
Care home	**Section 3 (1) p.3:** An establishment is a care home if it provides accommodation, together with nursing or personal care, for any of the following persons: (a) persons who are or have been ill (b) persons who have or have had a mental disorder (c) persons who are disabled or infirm (d) persons who are or have been dependent on alcohol or drugs.	The Care Homes Regulations 2001 – SI No. 3965 (these have been amended several times since publication)	Care Homes for Older People National Minimum Standards (Department of Health (2001b)) and Care Homes for Adults (18–65) National Minimum Standards (Department of Health (2001a))
Domiciliary care agency	**Section 4 (3) p.4:** An undertaking which consists of or includes arranging the provision of personal care in their own homes for persons who by reason of illness, infirmity or disability are unable to provide it for themselves without assistance.	The Domiciliary Care Agencies Regulations 2002 – SI No. 3214 (these have been amended several times since publication)	Domiciliary Care National Minimum Standards (Department of Health (2001c))

Table 10.1 Services requiring registration – Care Standards Act 2000 cont.

Service type	Definition	Regulations	National Minimum Standards
Nurses agency regulations	**Section 4 (5) p.4:** An employment agency or employment business, being (in either case) a business which consists of or includes supplying, or providing services for the purpose of supplying, registered nurses, registered midwives or registered health visitors.	Nurses Agencies Regulations 2002 – SI No. 3212	Nurses Agencies National Minimum Standards (Department of Health (2001d))
Adult placement scheme	**The Adult Placement Schemes (England) Regulations 2004 Regulation 2 p.3:** A scheme under which an individual agrees with the person carrying on the scheme to provide care or support (which may include accommodation) to an adult who is in need of it.	The Adult Placement Schemes (England) Regulations 2004 – SI No. 2071	National Minimum Standards for Adult Placement Schemes (Department of Health (2004))

REGISTRATION

Before providing a service as set out in Table 10.1 the person providing the service and the manager, if required, must be registered with the Commission. Registration is a process which confirms that a person is suitable to provide the service. During registration the applicant will have proved that they have in place essential safeguards which will assure that those who use the service are protected. This will include checks on the individual and the way in which they intend to run the service to ensure good outcomes for those using the service.

GOOD PRACTICE POINT

If a service is provided and registration is not in place, not only is the person providing the service committing an offence but essential safeguards are not in place for those using the service. For example, the provider may not have insurance in place, there may be no external scrutiny of the service and there is no redress for users if things go wrong.

Once the Commission is satisfied of the fitness of the applicant registration is granted and a licence to operate, a certificate, is issued. Registration is a key process in safeguarding vulnerable adults as it seeks to ensure that those who are registered are fit to do so. In practice this means they understand the care sector and have in place staff, services and facilities to ensure that people who use services are not exposed to harm. It is recognised that abuse can occur in any care service, and acceptance of this is no reflection on the service itself, but is a responsible and necessary approach to the care of vulnerable adults. There is provision in the legislation to refuse registration.

GOOD PRACTICE POINT

Practitioners should support people to use services which are registered with the CSCI. If they want to check if a service has been granted registration they should check on the CSCI website www.csci.org.uk

CERTIFICATE OF REGISTRATON

The certificate of registration is a legal document and must be displayed in a prominent place; failure to do so is an offence and the Commission may initiate prosecution proceedings. The certificate is important, as it sets out key information for users and their carers, purchasers of services and those seeking placements or services. The certificate also details, if required, the number of people who can use the service along with broad descriptors of needs. The *National Care Standards Commission (Registration) Regulations 2001* provide for specific service categories and service user categories. The former describe the type of service and the latter the specific user needs such as older people, people with learning disabilities, mental health needs and dementia. The Commission may only use the categories set out in the legislation.

GOOD PRACTICE POINT

Practitioners should check the certificate of registration to see if registration conditions describe the needs of users they are supporting. It is the legal responsibility of a registered person to operate in line with the certificate but social care practitioners could inadvertently be supporting providers to operate outside their registration.

POST-REGISTRATION

Once registered the duty is on all providers and managers to run a service in such a way so as to protect those using the service. The service should operate in line with NMS and the Statement of Purpose. This gives those who use services and practitioners a reference point if a service is below an acceptable level.

Within the standards and regulations, there are only a few specific references to protection, safeguarding and abuse. It is clear that explicit reference to abuse and safeguarding is light within the legislation and guidance. However, it is implicit that the standards are all geared to seeing abuse or the risk of abuse being from a number of sources including the day-to-day running of the service and the interactions with staff, other people using the services and the environment in which they live. This means that the provider in reading all standards should be aware that the outcome for people from each is to keep them safe and free from harm.

INSPECTION

The regulation of services by the Commission is undertaken within the broad framework of *Inspecting for Better Lives* (Commission for Social Care Inspection 2006). This is based on targeting poor services and focusing on outcomes for those who use the service. Services are rated by the Commission on a four-point quality rating scale ranging from zero to three stars. This rating will influence the frequency and type of inspection. Following registration services will not have a quality rating until the first inspection, usually within six months of registration. Inspection involves considering information about a service from a range of sources including those who use the service and making a judgement about the outcomes. The Commission's response to allegations of abuse is set out in the agreed protocol with the Association of Directors of Adult Social Services and Association of Chief Police Officers (2007). The information from such allegations will be added to the overall intelligence the Commission has about every service.

The Commission maintains a record for each service and all information received about a service is considered and an analysis of this is added to the record. Building up intelligence about a service enables the Commission to determine what targeted intervention it will have with each service. Greater weight is attached to certain key outcomes areas including health and personal care, management and complaints and protection.

GOOD PRACTICE POINT

Social care practitioners should give information to the Commission about their experience and that of their clients. This will assist with an accurate assessment of services and reflect the experience of those who use services.

There is concern that the Commission may not visit services and the quality of the service will deteriorate. This notion is based on the premise that the Commission is responsible for the quality of individual services. This is not the case and one of the principles of *Inspecting for Better Lives* is that care service providers, not inspectors, are responsible for the quality of the services they provide. Care providers must be honest in how they judge their own performance so that they gain the trust and confidence of the public. This idea was supported by the Department of Health at paragraph 26 (p.7) of its consultation document *Proposed Changes to the Regulatory Framework for Adult Social Care Services*:

The proposed inclusion of annual quality assurance assessments and improvement plans within the statutory framework also reflect an important step forward, in that they reflect the proposition that the quality of a social care service is the responsibility of its provider, not its regulator. This is essential in a proportionate regime. It is the Commission's responsibility to sample, test and validate the provider's performance and quality of delivery through their knowledge of a service, their understanding of the experience of those who use it, and proportionate on-site inspection. (Department of Health 2005, paragraph 26, p.7)

Table 10.2 Inspection types	
Type	*What's included*
Key	A detailed review of how well a service is operating. Information provided by the registered person and/or manager together with all information received since the last inspection is considered. The inspection includes seeking the views of people who use the service. An assessment is made as to how well the service is meeting the National Minimum Standards. The inspection will recognise good practice and any improvement since the last inspection; if necessary it will make requirements to improve outcomes for people who use the service. The provider and/or manager must comply with requirements and there are penalties for failing to do so. This type of inspection always includes a visit to the premises in which or from which the service is provided. The inspection will result in an overall judgement of the service based on a 'star rating' of zero to three stars. The key inspection is the only way in which the Commission alters the overall quality rating of a service. Following the inspection a report of the findings is published and available from the Commission website or the publishers.
Random	Short inspection which focuses on specific aspects of the running of the service or to check on improvements that should have been made. Like key inspections they can result in requirements being made and the findings are set out in a report.
Annual Service Review	Does not include a visit to the service but is based on an analysis of all information the Commission has about a service. These are only available to services which are rated as good or excellent. Following the Annual Service Review the Commission may undertake a key or random inspection if information comes to its attention which indicates that good outcomes for people who use the service are not being consistently delivered.

The key issue here is for the Commission to be in a position in which it can use its powers independently or in partnership with other agencies to intervene if the outcomes for people who use services are poor. Inspection itself is the tool to identify or confirm the poor practice, gather the evidence and determine what action it will take. The inspection may temporarily stop the abuse and give the provider a warning but in itself, it will not cause sustained improvement.

However, what the inspection will do is place on public record via the publication of the inspection report how the Commission rates the service, what it found and what action the provider must take to improve. This is a powerful tool, which can be used by those using services, those supporting them, commissioners, contractors and practitioners to make informed decisions as to whether to use or continue to use a service.

CANCELLATION OF REGISTRATION

If a provider is failing consistently to provide good outcomes for the people who use the service and is placing them at risk of harm the Commission may take action to propose to cancel the registration. This is the ultimate action the Commission can propose to take and in respect of residential services means that people using the service have to move or change provider. For non-residential services, there is still disruption for people as they have to have a new care provider and both parties have to establish new relationships. The decision to cancel registration is never taken lightly and has to be balanced with stopping harm to people using the service and delivering the Commission's role in stamping out poor practice. The legislation provides for two courses of action, the ordinary procedure and emergency or urgent action. Urgent action is when the Commission is of the view that there is serious immediate risk to a person's life, health or well-being. The case can be brought before the magistrate with or without the registered person's knowledge and if it appears to the justice that, unless the order is made, there will be a serious risk to a person's life, health or well-being then an order is made requiring the immediate closure of the service. This is a significant step and requires close work with other agencies, especially social services departments and primary care trusts. In the event of the order being made the registered person would have a right of appeal to the Care Standards Tribunal.

The ordinary procedure requires the Commission to serve a notice of proposal to cancel registration together with the bundle of evidence to support the action. The registered person has 28 days in which to make representation to the Commission. Like the statutory notice, representation is in writing and is considered by a regional director who is not directly involved with the matter or with the person serving the notice. The regional director has two options –

to uphold the notice or agree the representation. If the notice is upheld the provider may make an appeal to the Care Standards Tribunal within 28 days from the date on which the regional director made the decision. Failure to lodge an appeal by the required date means that the notice takes immediate effect and the provider should make plans to cease to operate the service – move people out or sell the service – or risk prosecution. The Commission would link with the local social services department so that disruption to people especially in residential settings is minimised.

If the provider lodges an appeal the proposal of the Commission does not take effect until the Tribunal has arrived at a judgement. This can take some months and it is not unusual for the period from the original proposal being served to the Tribunal decision being in excess of six months. Commissioners are working with the Department of Health to see if additional powers can be given to the Commission to improve safeguards to those using services.

Forthcoming tribunal hearings are listed on the Care Standards Tribunal website and are open to the public and decisions are available from the website soon after the hearing has been concluded.

GOOD PRACTICE POINT

The Care Standards Tribunal is an independent body and more information about it can be found at www.carestandardstribunal.gov.uk including its decisions and pending appeals. The decisions of the Tribunal are beginning to provide a reference point of what is seen as acceptable when providing services.

STATUTORY POWERS

The Commission has a range of statutory powers, set out in the Act or Regulations which can be used at different stages. They can be used individually or together and if necessary the ultimate sanction of proposing to cancel the registration of a provider can be pursued on its own when there is risk to the health and well-being of those using the service.

The use of enforcement powers is not sequential and each action can be applied at different stages. Unless the situation is very serious in terms of immediate harm to those using the service the first stage of enforcement usually starts with making a requirement following an inspection. This would be set out either in the inspection report or in an 'immediate requirement notification and letter'. Requirements are based on the Act or the relevant regulations and set out what the provider must do and why, i.e. what will be the benefit for people using the service, and the timescale for compliance. It is the provider's responsibility to comply with requirements and to confirm to the Commission that they have done so. Failure to comply with a requirement may lead to the serving of a statutory notice. These are covered by the relevant regulations and set out again what the provider has failed to do, what they must do together with the timescale for compliance and the consequence of non-compliance, which is prosecution or the issuing of a caution. The notice will also inform the provider of the right to make written representation and the process for dealing with this is the same as above.

The Commission will take steps to monitor the service to determine if the compliance has been secured. If so the matter is not pursued further although the need to impose improvement is recorded and forms part of the intelligence the Commission has about the service. This information has less weight over time, providing there is no further repeat of non-compliance. In the event of the notice not securing the required improvement then the Commission may initiate prosecution proceedings. This would be pursued through the Magistrate's Courts and, if successful, the registered person would be guilty of an offence and may be fined. As an alternative to a prosecution the Commission can issue a formal caution, this requires the person to accept that they are guilty of non-compliance and has the same effect as a prosecution without the fine. In the event of a repeat offence, the registered person would be prosecuted for the new offence and the offence to which the caution related.

If a service is rated as providing poor outcomes for the people using it the legislation requires the registered person to submit an improvement plan to the Commission. The plan should be detailed and set out what action will be taken, by when and by whom to address any shortfalls identified. The Commission would monitor compliance with the plan and if necessary would serve statutory notices to secure compliance and improvement. If improvement is not secured the Commission may use additional powers such as cancellation as set out above.

The Commission has the scope to amend the conditions attached to registration by agreement with the provider or by imposition. An example of this could be about the number of people living in a care home. A service is registered to accommodate up to 30 older people some of whom may require care because of dementia. There are problems with the quality of the service; social services may have put a block on placements. This would still allow the provider to admit those who are privately funded. The Commission could seek to agree that no new admissions are made or no new admissions of those with dementia as this is the area which is causing the most challenge to the service. If the provider accepts this an amended certificate of registration would be issued. If agreement could not be agreed, the Commission can serve a notice of proposal to impose conditions. The registered person has the same rights to make representation and, if required, lodge an appeal with the Care Standards.

OFFENCES

Statutory powers in summary set out the action the Commission may take when an offence or breach of regulation has occurred. Offences are failures to comply with specific sections of the primary legislation – *Care Standards Act 2000* (CSA) – or specific regulations. The offences covered by the Act include:

- Section 24 – Failure to comply with conditions.
- Section 25 – Contravention of regulations.
- Section 26 – False descriptions of establishments and agencies.
- Section 27 – False statements in applications.
- Section 28 – Failure to display certificate of registration.
- Section 30 – Offences by bodies corporate.

These are offences against the primary legislation and the remedy is for the Commission to initiate prosecution proceedings.

As a general rule the social care practitioner would not concern themselves with these offences. The offences which will be of more interest to practitioners are concerned with the way in which services operate and these will be breaches of the service specific regulations. These are more likely to have a detrimental impact on the people using the service and are often observable by practitioners. However, it is important to stress that the offences under this legislation do not seek to cover offences in other legislation such as theft, offences against the person. The redress should be via existing legislation and most likely by other agencies especially the police. Those who use care services are citizens and therefore should be supported to have equal access to law.

The service specific regulations are set out with the clear expectation that those registered comply with them all, but an offence is only committed when specific regulations are breached. These are broadly similar for all types of regulated services. The regulations are clear as to the expectation and failure to comply is likely to be to the detriment of people using the service. Examples of these are set out in Table 10.3.

The Commission can take action in respect of all these offences with the primary aim of encouraging the provider to deal with the issues. If improvement is not made or the detriment is significant to those using the service then action against the provider as set out above would be taken.

Table 10.3 Offences	
Areas covered by regulations	*Possible outcome/detriment of failure to comply*
Providing a statement of purpose and service user guide	Users are not clear about what is on offer and cannot challenge if the service falls below their expectation.
Statement of charges and fees	Users unable to know what is included in the costs, when they are reviewed and what contribution, if any, they are expected to make.
Notifing the commission of offences by registered person	Commission unable to make a judgement about the ongoing fitness of the registered person.
Health and welfare including care plans, medication, access to services	Needs not met, access to primary care services curtailed. Poor administration of medication, poor care plans leading to inappropriate provision of care.
Quality of environment	Could result in poor care – failure to provide aid/adaptations, not promoting independence, failure to address dignity issues.
Staffing – safeguards, induction, training supervision, conduct	Users exposed to harm by staff who are not suitable or not equipped to provide good quality care.
Complaints procedures	Results in users being passive recipients of care rather than consumers of care.
Records	Inappropriate services being delivered, inconsistent and unreliable care provided. Difficult to hold providers to account.
Improvement plans and Quality Review	Providers not addressing issues of concern and demonstrating continuous improvement and development.
Notification of events within the service	Commission is unable to make assessment of how the service manages or responds to events with the service. Denies those using the service ongoing external scrutiny.

PROTECTION OF VULNERABLE ADULTS SCHEME

Over recent years the government has made a commitment to ensure that vulnerable adults have access to the greatest protection possible from harm. This is achieved in part by raising standards of care via the National Service Frameworks, regulating providers of care in a more thorough and consistent way, and introducing National Minimum Standards for regulated care services. In addition to this the Protection of Vulnerable Adults Scheme (POVA) was introduced in July 2004 (Department of Health 2004). In short the scheme will ensure that those who are deemed as not fit to be working with vulnerable adults because they have abused, neglected or otherwise harmed vulnerable adults in their care or placed vulnerable adults in their care at risk of harm will be barred from taking up such posts again.

The scheme is enshrined in law under Part 7 of the *Care Standards Act 2000*. The legislation places a duty on those who employ staff to refer individuals as set out above for inclusion on the POVA list. Anyone seeking to employ staff to work with vulnerable adults has a duty to check the POVA list before permitting an individual to take up post. POVA checks are requested as part of disclosures from the Criminal Records Bureau[3] (CRB). In the first phase of implementation it only applied to registered care homes but over time it has been extended to other settings such as registered domiciliary care agencies. In 2006, following further extension of the scheme, a practical guide was produced: *Protection of Vulnerable Adults Scheme in England and Wales for Adult Placement Schemes, Domiciliary Care Agencies and Care Homes* (Department of Health 2004 and 2006). This remains a key document for providers of care and sets out responsibilities and encourages providers to rethink about how they recruit staff.

The Commission is clear that the primary duty rests with the registered person to refer staff and therefore it is anticipated that the Commission will not exercise its 'default power' to refer. A failure of a registered person to refer a person to POVA may be evidence of a lack of fitness on the part of that provider. However, there will be occasions when the actions of a registered person warrant referral to the POVA scheme and there is no employer to make that referral. In those cases the Commission is likely to make the referral and would work with other agencies to ensure that this is progressed. As part of the registration process checks are made against the POVA list via the CRB disclosure process.

The POVA scheme has been successful but it is clear that there have been some shortfalls in particular how it is applied across all agencies providing

---

3   The Criminal Records Bureau is an executive agency of the Home Office set up
     to help organisations make safer recruitment decisions. For further information
     see www.crb.gov.uk.

services for vulnerable people. In addition, the inquiry by Sir Richard Bichard into the deaths of Holly Wells and Jessica Chapman in Soham in 2003 highlighted that insufficient action was being taken to prevent unsuitable people from gaining access to work with children and vulnerable adults. The *Bichard Inquiry Report* (House of Commons 2004) made a number of recommendations all of which were accepted by the Government, including a proposal to set up a registration scheme for everyone who works with children and vulnerable adults. The *Safeguarding Vulnerable Groups Act 2006* established the Vetting and Barring Scheme which replaces the POVA scheme and list, along with the equivalent scheme for children, POCA. The scheme will apply to health and social care services in the statutory, voluntary and independent sectors.

The following case study sets out how the Commission works with other agencies when abuse of vulnerable adults in a regulated service is raised.

CASE STUDY 10.1

Primrose Lodge is registered to accommodate up to 25 older people with dementia. The provider and manager have been registered for two years. There have been regular inspections of the service and other than requirements being made following inspections no other concerns have been raised. The home usually has a few vacancies but the manager has always insisted that this is because they are discerning about whom they admit. They want to ensure that the needs of a new service user do not compromise the service for those already living there.

Following a visit to see her aunt, Agnes Myrtle, whom she has not seen for a number of years, Rene Atkins reported to the Commission that she is concerned about money being taken from her aunt's bank account. When she raised the matter with the manager she was evasive and hinted that the money was being used as a contribution to care costs.

The Commission referred the matter to the local social services department and encouraged Rene to do likewise as she would have detailed information. Social services convened a strategy meeting and the Commission was invited to attend. As the concern was about the registered person the Commission attended the meeting. Had the issue been about one of the staff in the home and the registered person was dealing with the matter appropriately then it is likely that the Commission would not attend the meeting. The strategy meeting was attended by representatives of the Commission, social services contracting section, care managers, the police and Rene Atkins. The registered persons were not invited to the meeting.

The decision of the meeting was the police would interview the manager to ascertain her view on the money taken from the account. Following the interview, the police determined that they would not be able to pursue any action, as the manager was the appointee. She had paid the money into the home's account as a contribution to care costs and there was no evidence that the money had been fraudulently withdrawn from the account. The manager immediately resigned from her position and notified the Commission.

Social services worked with the service and made arrangements for external appointees for all users of the service. The department remained dissatisfied with the actions of the manager but agreed that the primary role was to protect the people living there.

The Commission considered all matters and following an internal review determined that the transfer of the user's money from a private account to the home's account amounted to an unacceptable breach of trust.

The provider would not accept that the money was inappropriately used. A social services department had been paying for the care and this additional amount transferred amounted to the home being paid twice for the same care. Scrutiny of the home's account showed that transfer of the money always coincided with a significant purchase. For example, a new assisted bath, replacement of carpets to the entrance hall, stairs and landing. The provider was willing to repay the money to Agnes's account but only on the condition that the Safeguarding Board would formally record that this was not seen as tantamount to admitting wrongdoing.

Following all considerations the Commission decided to propose to cancel the registration, on the grounds that the provider was not fit to be concerned with the running of a care home. The provider should have monitored the running of the home including safeguarding matters and had failed to do so. The response from the provider was based solely on the actions of social services i.e. external appointees for all users. Following service of the notice the provider made arrangements to sell the home and therefore was not in a position to make an appeal to the Care Standards Tribunal. As the provider did not have an employer, the Commission made a referral to POVA.

CONCLUSION

The role of the Commission for Social Care Inspection provides the statutory framework to ensure that only those who are fit to be registered are licensed to provide care services. The Commission as a regulatory body has a programme of assessing and inspecting care services. However, in a modern regulatory framework based on a proportionate approach the Commission relies on a wider source of information about care services. There is an expectation that those charged with commissioning and purchasing services take a lead in protecting users from harm and abuse. The Commission works in partnership with other agencies in safeguarding adults in regulated services. In the agreed protocol, the Commission stresses its commitment to working with other agencies to ensure that people within regulated services are appropriately safeguarded. However, it goes on to explain that its function in response to safeguarding adults concerns is primarily as a regulator, contributing its knowledge of the service, regulations and standards to the multi-agency assessment.

STATUTES

Care Standards Act 2000. London: The Stationery Office.

Health and Social Care (Community Health and Standards) Act 2003. London: The Stationery Office.

The Safeguarding Vulnerable Groups Act 2006. London: The Stationery Office.

REGULATIONS

The Adult Placement Schemes (England) Regulations 2004 Statutory Instrument 2071. London: The Stationery Office.

The Care Homes Regulations 2001 Statutory Instrument 3965. London: The Stationery Office.

The Care Standards Act 2000 (Extension of the Application of Part 2 to Adult Placement Schemes) (England) Regulations 2004 Statutory Instrument 1972. London: The Stationery Office.

The Domiciliary Care Agencies Regulations 2002 – Statutory Instrument 3214. London: The Stationery Office.

The National Care Standards Commission (Registration) Regulations 2001. London: The Stationery Office.

Nurses Agencies Regulations – Statutory Instrument 3212. London: The Stationery Office.

REFERENCES

Commission for Social Care Inspection (2006) Inspecting For Better Lives. London: CSCI.

Commission for Social Care Inspection, Association of Directors of Social Services and the Association of Chief Police Officers (2007) Safeguarding Adults Protocol and Guidance. London: CSCI.

Department of Health (2001a) *Care Homes for Adults (18–65) National Minimum Standards*. London: DH.

Department of Health (2001b) *Care Homes for Older People National Minimum Standards*. London: DH.

Department of Health (2001c) *Domiciliary Care National Minimum Standards*. London: DH.

Department of Health (2001d) *Nurses Agencies National Minimum Standards*. London: DH.

Department of Health (2004) *National Minimum Standards for Adult Placement Schemes*. London: DH.

Department of Health (2005) *Proposed Changes to the Regulatory Framework for Adult Social Care Services*. London: DH.

Department of Health (2004 and 2006) *Protection of Vulnerable Adults Scheme in England and Wales for Adult Placement Schemes, Domiciliary Care Agencies and Care Homes: A Practical Guide*. London: DH.

House of Commons (2004) *The Bichard Inquiry Report*. June. The Stationery Office.

CHAPTER 11

MY USE OF THE LAW IN PROTECTING VULNERABLE ADULTS: FROM POLICE OFFICER TO CHIEF EXECUTIVE OF A CARE PROVIDER

STEVE KIRKPATRICK

I first encountered the legal issues and complexities around investigating the abuse of vulnerable adults in 1991 whilst in a new post as detective inspector of a market town within the Thames Valley Police area. One of our local social workers responsible for older people was concerned over a number of reports he had received which indicated that older people within a residential home were being bullied and assaulted by the manager of the home. These allegations were coming from ex-staff and ranged from the manager forcing older people to have baths they did not want to have to the more serious offence of common assault by slapping them across the face. I appointed a detective sergeant to work together with the social worker.

The frustrations with the law encountered with this case were:

- The only way to record a victim or a witness statement at this time was by way of interview and to record it on a Criminal Justice Act Statement form which the person then read through and signed as being a true record.

- As a result of making this witness statement the vulnerable adult would be required to provide their evidence-in-chief live in the witness box. This was entirely inappropriate and impractical, especially in relation to a vulnerable older person whose memory would not have been so clear as to when they made the statement.

- Video interviewing was not accepted in law until 2002 although it had been the practice to video record interviews of children where it was suspected that they might have been abused. These videos were not accepted in a court at this time so the video interviewing of vulnerable older people was considered a non-starter.

- No alleged incident had been witnessed by more than one member of staff. Two witnesses were required in practice for a chance of a criminal prosecution. The law then and now requires all allegations to be corroborated by something independent or by a third person.

- The allegations were historical. Some residents of the home who had been the victims of an assault had since died from natural causes.

- The offences amounted to a common assault contrary to Section 39 of the *Criminal Justice Act 1988* which were only prosecuted in the criminal court in 1991 if they were considered aggravated and in case had a statute of limitation of proceedings of six months. Aggravated assaults were prosecuted in extremely rare cases involving children and women in domestic cases. In all my 15 years' service up until then I had only pursued one case of 'indictable common assault' and this was where a wife had been raped by her husband.

- All older people who were interviewed could not recollect any incidents of concern involving them as individuals nor others.

- Those who had voiced their concerns were ex-staff and it could be so easily alleged by the suspect that they had an 'axe to grind'.

- The suspect had an impeccable character and denied everything when interviewed.

There was therefore no evidence in this case although the joint investigating officers firmly believed that the allegations were genuine. So dealing with and debriefing the investigators was complex but I could not see how things would have been any better if we had an offence of assault which could be prosecuted in the courts. However, even if this were the case and even if video interviewing had been recognised in law in 1991 we would not have been any further forward in bringing this case to the court because there was no corroboration of anything suspected. A common thread in so many allegations I dealt with.

During this time I also dealt with the rape of a vulnerable adult with learning disabilities in a residential care home where the attacker had entered her ground floor room via an open window and brutally raped her. I remember encountering the same frustrations with the inability to properly record her account or even obtain a proper description from her. She was interviewed by officers from the then Women's Specialist Unit and a statement was obtained which I was able to read. As the senior investigating officer (SIO) it would have been so much better for me if I had had a working copy of a video interview with the victim as I would have been able to have a clearer understanding of what she was able to say and how she said it. Many years later I was to notice the difference it made to me as SIO to be able to watch the video interviews for myself.

The good news in this case was that the corroboration was provided by a DNA sample which the offender had left on the victim and he was eventually convicted of rape.

Throughout 1991 there was a rise in the number of what the police called 'distraction' burglaries of older people in the police area where I worked. These were despicable crimes preying on the weaknesses and the vulnerability of older people. Often or not the offenders would knock on the door of the older person's home on the pretext of wanting to read their electricity meter or asking the way to somewhere, whilst their accomplice would enter the house through the back door and steal cash or small antiques or jewellery from the home. Sometimes the older person would see the accomplice who would run past them and knock them to the ground. At times the older person would be injured, but always extremely frightened and traumatised. On one occasion a woman in her nineties was tied up and gagged with her own underwear taken from her bedroom. If she had not somehow managed to crawl out of her house, down her path and into her neighbour's driveway where she was discovered, she would have probably died.

The frustrations of dealing with these cases were in the fact that the evidence often relied upon the older person being able to attend an identification parade, to recognise and to pick out the person they saw from the members of the parade. As the police normally had a number of likely suspects, it took a great amount of time to arrest them and then try to set up individual and separate identification parades. Within 12 years this was to change for the better.

In April 1992 I commenced my new post as detective inspector in charge of the Family Protection Unit at Reading and went straight into the role of being jointly responsible for running joint agency courses in Berkshire and joint training on the new *Memorandum of Good Practice* for the video interviewing of child witnesses who were victims of abuse (Home Office and Department of Health 1992). At this time all Thames Valley Police Family Protection Unit Staff attended the Joint Investigation Course. Sometimes other staff attended and I had attended such a course prior to being transferred. Social workers from all over Berkshire also attended these courses. The ratio of social workers to the few police officers was always quite disproportionate and difficult to balance.

Some of the dilemmas and issues here involved would be pertinent to the kind of issues which would be faced later when the video interviewing of vulnerable adults became acceptable in law:

- The training of staff had to involve them being fully conversant with the points to prove with regard to the criminal law offences whilst ensuring that they always maintained an impartial and child/young person-centred approach.

- Social workers had never received training on the criminal law so were disadvantaged in this respect.

- Police officers received training on all aspects of the law during their ten-week initial training. Family Protection Unit officers also attended a two-week sexual offences course normally prior to being posted to the Family Protection Unit.

- Social workers however were streets ahead of the police in being child friendly and being focused on the needs of the victim.

- There were only 12 police officers designated to undertake video interviews in Berkshire whilst there were nearly 50 social workers designated to undertake video interviewing.

- Police were therefore going to initially have more experience in video interviewing than their social worker colleagues.

- The lead interviewer normally fell to the police in the majority of cases due to the lack of confidence amongst social workers because they were to undertake in practice so few video interviews.

- As the legislation was new, it was untested to begin with, and it was not known whether the videos would be allowed to be used as evidence-in-chief by the judges as it was ultimately up to them to decide.

- There was much anxiety with practitioners that they could 'ruin' a video interview by a wrongly conducted interview and consequently ruin a case. In one case at the Reading Crown Court I was forced to recommend that a child abuse case was not proceeded with because the social worker had not complied with the *Memorandum of Good Practice* and I did not want to put the child and family through a court ordeal and an inevitable collapse of the case.

- Video interviewing was quite intrusive and there was a feeling that they should only be conducted if absolutely necessary.

- It was highlighted that storage of video cassettes would be a problem in the years to come. This was before CD-ROMs and hard drive storage.

- There was a need for the continual assessment of the video interviews by a line manager not only so that a decision could be made about prosecution but also to provide staff with valuable critiques of their interviewing skills and style. This was crucial to improve the overall quality of the video interviews going before the court and to present uncontaminated best evidence to the juries thereby often preventing the necessity of the child or young person having to give evidence-in-chief. In some cases a properly conducted video interview produced overwhelming powerful evidence and a guilty plea by the offender preventing the need for the victim to give evidence at all.

I was also privileged to be part of the working group set up to write the inter-agency procedures on the protection of vulnerable adults. The document produced was held to be quite pioneering and innovative at the time by other professionals in other areas. When the procedures were adopted across Berkshire it was decided that the investigation of the abuse of vulnerable adults would be investigated by either general policing or by the criminal investigation department. However, one thing I insisted upon was that the detective inspector, or my detective sergeants, on the Family Protection Unit would act as a filter of all cases reported so that we could offer on the spot advice and also monitor the cases progress during the investigations. I also on occasions would attend a strategy meeting to discuss the ways forward.

Amazingly the majority of the cases referred to me during 1993–98 were not suitable for police investigation. They invariably revolved around two vulnerable adults having 'consensual' sexual activity or intercourse with each other and the query was whether this was a police matter. These cases were not suitable for investigation because the two adults involved were taking part willingly and with consent. In my discussions with the professional who was reporting the matter I explored whether any one or more of the following factors existed:

- In the view of the professionals involved were they able to consent to the sexual activity?

- Was there any sign or indication of distress from either of the parties involved?

- Was there a clear aggressor?

- Was there any violence used or did either of the parties have injuries which were caused immediately before or during the activity?

- Was there any forced entry of anyone's room or space?

All this acted as a much needed springboard to when attention needed to be focused on the use of video interviewing of vulnerable witnesses and victims; something that was not accepted in the courts until 2002.

In 1993 I was approached by one of my senior colleagues for advice concerning the way forward regarding the police investigation into suspected sexual and physical abuse committed at Longcare residential home in Slough.[1] I recommended to my colleague that:

- All vulnerable adults should be video interviewed, even though the video evidence could not be accepted in court at that time.

- To use personnel from the Family Protection Unit who had been video interview trained so that the best impartial evidence could be obtained from the victims and so that the victims could be properly supported through any court process.

- That the video interview would be a transparent record to show the way the interviews had been conducted. This would preserve the integrity of the interviews.

- That the video interview would reveal exactly the way the victim said something and the context in which it was meant.

- That a witness statement should be produced from the transcript of the video interview; the video lending support to the statement if there were any later challenge at court.

The investigation went ahead with the victims being video interviewed and the use of specially trained police officers from the Family Protection Unit.

It had always been a weakness with the video interviewing of children or vulnerable adults that they relied upon the subject being able to communicate to some degree and certainly to be able to provide the account of what happened to them in a free narrative, uninterrupted by the interviewer. Unfortunately, this did not really cater for anyone with learning disabilities who was unable to speak and relying upon signs or 'tools' in order to communicate. We were always open to the use of experts to interview in this way but I never saw an example of this in my entire service; a great shame. This problem was exacerbated by the requirement in legislation that the victim should not be interviewed unless available to be cross-examined otherwise the video evidence would not be accepted by the courts (s32A of the *Criminal Justice Act 1988* as amended by s54 of *Criminal Justice Act 1991*). This requirement prevented those who were non-verbal or difficult to understand being interviewed in the first place.

Whilst on the Family Protection Unit I always advocated that the unit was best placed to deal with adult protection and vulnerable adult abuse, and would be more conversant with the aspects and knowledge of the criminal law

---

1   Longcare was a private company owning two care homes for adults with learning disabilities. For full inquiry see Burgner (1998); for further information refer to Pring (2003).

and procedure needed for dealing with vulnerable adults, and that if need be it would be best to increase the numbers of staff on the unit to cater for it. The video interviewing of children, vulnerable adults and vulnerable witnesses requires the same training approach and the same methodology of the continual assessment and professional development of the interviewer. In my view the Family Protection Unit were best placed to undertake this. Also, the detective inspectors and detective sergeants on the unit had the experience and ongoing knowledge of working with the multi-agencies to provide sound advice when deciding whether a case was suitable for police investigation or not. Sadly in the years which followed I saw the Family Protection Unit shed its dealing with vulnerable adult work, change its name to the Sexual Crimes Unit and have no increase in personnel.

However, since my retirement the Thames Valley Police now have the Public Protection Unit which has brought all of this under the one umbrella. The Public Protection Units are responsible for adult protection. Their role in part is to liaise with their local authority counterparts, monitor investigations and provide advice to police officers and staff. I understand that a standard operating procedure is currently being developed.

The Home Office Code of Practice *Achieving Best Evidence in Criminal Proceedings: Guidance for Vulnerable or Intimidated Witnesses, Including Children* was published in 2002 and has recently been revised (Criminal Justice System 2007; Home Office 2002). This document built on the previous *Memorandum of Good Practice*. Much of what had been learned in dealing with the video interviewing of children could be used in the video interviewing of vulnerable adults victims and witnesses. I first was able to make use of the new guidelines when they were in draft form but by the time the case came to court they had been fully implemented. This was a case I began working on before the draft codes were published and concluded with a conviction at the Crown Court at the end of 2004. It was the worst possible case of the abuse of a vulnerable adult – the murder of Kenny,[2] aged in his early thirties. He had been stabbed to death in his home. Kenny was someone who invited lots of people into his home. Most of them were good natured and good friends. Others took the opportunity to prey on his vulnerability, borrowing money which was never repaid and making fun of his ways. On three occasions he was beaten up, once requiring hospital treatment.

This was a difficult and quite lengthy investigation; particularly as there appeared to be no information coming from the community as to who could be responsible.

2   All the names of people involved in this case have been changed to maintain anonymity.

One of Kenny's friends was a young man, Matthew, aged 17 years, who had mild learning disabilities. He may or may not have had invaluable information to provide so I decided almost from the outset of dealing with him that I would appoint two skilled detective constables to carry out and supervise all his interviews ensuring consistency of approach and adherence to the new codes then contained in *Action for Justice* which were still in draft form.

The two officers struck up a good rapport and relationship with him always ensuring the presence of a family member and taking pains to inform his mother and father of the process and even assisting where they could with life's daily stresses and strains. I decided that I would personally train in one of the video interviewing techniques should it ever be necessary to video interview this vulnerable witness. Consequently as soon as it became apparent to the detectives that Matthew might have some relevant evidence to provide regarding the murder they decided not to ask him any further questions but arranged to conduct a video interview. Due to the new codes it was now possible to video interview a vulnerable witness, not as a victim but as a witness. This was important because by the time the case came to trial, Matthew would be 19 years of age and prior to the codes he would have had to give his evidence-in-chief from the witness box in full open court.

I appointed a lead interviewer who was a police officer who had been video interview trained but I also decided that it was important to have one of the detectives who had dealt with Matthew present from the start in the interview rather than on the live link. I considered that it was vital that if he decided that a question needed to be asked then he should ask it and that he should ask it in the way that it was best asked and not have it vetoed by the person conducting the interview; something I had seen occur on a number of occasions.

In interview Matthew named another young man, Peter, aged 18 years, who was the suspect in the investigation. Matthew told the interviewing officers that he and Peter had arrived at the flat of Kenny, they sat talking with him. Both Kenny and Peter were drinking quite heavily. Matthew said that Peter asked Kenny about a video he lent to him and was told that he had sold it. Peter then told Matthew to go and wait outside. Matthew said he waited outside and Peter came out after 10 to 15 minutes. They then drove back to Peter's home. Matthew said that Peter did not say anything to him about what happened but a few days later he became aware from reports in the media that Kenny had been murdered.

Matthew went on to say during his video interview that a couple of months after this Peter told him what had happened. He was at Peter's home when he turned round to one of his friends and said 'I'm going to tell him what happened.' Peter then told him what had happened. Matthew said, 'He just turned round to me and said, you can't tell anyone what I am going to tell you 'cos I would go away for a long time. He just turned round... "I killed Kenny and I didn't mean to" or something like that, and then turned round and said come on let's go for a drink.'

After the lead interviewer had finished asking the questions the other detective officer thought it important to ask some further questions about Matthew's lack of awareness of time, dates and dusk. The murder appears to have been committed at about dusk. Matthew did not have any awareness at all about these things.

After the interview there was a criticism made to me by the lead interviewer who thought the line of questioning was overbearing and unprofessional. I reviewed the video interview and saw the point being made but I had given the other detective permission to do this so it was hardly his fault. I did think, however, that there might be some challenge at court because of this and even considered the possibility that the video interview might be disallowed at the trial. However, this was not the case at all and Peter was convicted of murder and sentenced to a long term of imprisonment.

Legal issues and other issues pertinent to the court proceedings were:

- There was a re-trial due to circumstances not relating to Matthew. He therefore had to give his evidence twice. Matthew therefore underwent more fear and anxiety than he would otherwise have done but it did mean that he had the chance to 'rehearse' his evidence before the trial that mattered.

- At the first trial examination the defence argued that Matthew was not a vulnerable witness and so his video interview should not be played but that he should give his evidence live from the witness box. Fortunately I had written to Matthew's ex-head teacher of the special school he had attended who had replied with a letter outlining Matthew's special needs. The defence submission was not accepted and the video evidence was played to the court as Matthew's evidence-in-chief.

- The defence made no submission that the video evidence was improperly conducted or the interview overbearing.

- Matthew was extremely frightened about giving evidence. Witnesses had been threatened.

- The two detectives needed to provide ongoing support and advice not only to Matthew but also to his whole family as each had issues affecting them as a result of the court proceedings. Sadly I have since heard that this support ceased after the court case.

- On the first occasion Matthew was due to give evidence he was 'high' on what was believed to be drugs and was not fit to be available for cross-examination. He was sent home by the judge until the following day when he was better disposed to provide evidence under cross-examination.

- In the days leading up to Matthew giving evidence in the full trial, with the permission of prosecution counsel, I tasked the two detectives to stay with Matthew for the weekend before to ensure his safety and to ensure that he did not go off and abuse himself with drink and drugs.

- This worked to our advantage because on the day of the trial Matthew was completely composed and reasonably calm.

- Unexpectedly he also came across well under cross-examination; better than we had ever hoped for.

- The video evidence came across extremely well when played in the live court situation and there was no criticism of the way in which the interview was conducted.

- The detective officer's questioning was crucial in helping to present a young man who was credible, who was telling the truth, but due to his special needs was not aware at all about times of the day, days of the week, the difference between dusk and full darkness, special dates or birthdays, or how long Christmas was prior to when he was interviewed by police. This aspect appeared to be accepted by the jury who clearly believed his evidence when they returned their guilty finding.

In October 2003 I moved back to the market town where I started my role as detective inspector in January 1991, to serve the last 18 months of my service providing special support and consultancy advice to the police area. As part of this role I assisted with a new and exciting procedure called the Video Identification Parade Electronic Recording (VIPER) parades. This had only recently been implemented (31 July 2004) under code D of the *Police and Criminal Evidence Act 1984* and meant that witnesses no longer had to attend identification parades and face the suspect in a line up of 12 other member of the parade. This new procedure was pioneered by West Yorkshire police who still maintain a database of 20,000 volunteers who make up the other at least eight members of the VIPER 'parade'.[3]

Each of the subjects including the suspect are filmed from head and shoulder height, looking forward to begin with, then looking to the right for a few seconds, then back to the front for a few seconds. A film is then made of the parade members and the witness views the film on a laptop computer. The showing is arranged and conducted by a police officer or civilian with experience of identification issues. The suspect's solicitor is involved in picking the

3   See www.westyorkshire.police.uk/section-item.asp?sid=6iid=3799.

members of the parade from a database and is able to choose to have two or three different DVDs made. The solicitor can also be present during the showing of the VIPER DVD to the witness and the whole process can in turn be filmed in order to show fairness.

Some of the first VIPER parades I conducted were in relation to three separate 'distraction' thefts and burglaries of three very vulnerable older people. What a difference they made to the interests of justice and to the way of treating vulnerable adult victims! I recall them all quite vividly because it just made the process so user friendly for the victims involved.

The first showing I conducted (rather nervously I might add) was to a 95-year-old woman who lived near to Stoke Mandeville. I decided that I would not have her come all the way to the police station but that I would go to her home. I provided the opportunity for the solicitor to come with me but he declined. I visited her in her home just before Christmas 2003. She was quite sprightly and alert. She took great delight in telling me that she was having her children, her grandchildren and her great-grandchildren to stay for Christmas and that she was cooking Christmas dinner herself! She had been robbed of her jewellery by a man who had sneaked into her home a few months earlier and had had the misfortune to suddenly come across him in her lounge. The man had run off quickly and drove off in his car.

Although she was a little apprehensive in looking at the laptop containing a DVD of various faces, she was somewhat reassured that she would be looking at the faces of at least eight people who could not have been involved. She was much more relaxed than I had seen any witness and was quite intrigued that we were being filmed ourselves. Without any hesitation at all she identified the suspect.

Another case was of an 83-year-old man in Chesham who had been coerced by two men to have his roof mended and charged an exorbitant fee of several thousand pounds. When he did not pay the bill they took him to his bank and made him take the money out of the ATM outside. He did not make an identification because he found it so difficult to remember their faces.

The last one I conducted in regard to vulnerable adult victims was with a man, aged 90 years, in his home at Amersham. He and his wife had been distracted by one man whilst the other stole valuable silverware and loaded it into a car parked in the driveway. This man had confronted the thief but had been struck across the head with his own silver teapot. This was a difficult VIPER showing but once again the solicitor declined to attend. I was able to have a cup of coffee and a friendly chat before I moved into the more formal side. After I had shown the film at least twice the man said with some conviction, 'Definitely NOT there, Inspector!' I believed him, though the officer in the case did not.

One of my other special projects during this time was to act as 'scrutineer' of the recorded crime for the police area. I had to ensure that no crime file was filed until it had been properly dealt with either by court process, caution, 'detected no proceedings' or 'no further action'. I was pleased to see that common assault was now something that the police dealt with and the Crown Prosecution Service (CPS) proceeded with if there was enough evidence. Common assault had been declared a recordable crime in 1998 by the Home Office but was only really taken on board by the police service properly in 2002/2003. It coincided with the decision of the CPS to downgrade assaults occasioning actual bodily harm to common assault where the injury was only rather minor or superficial. Now all assaults, even where there were no injuries sustained, were recorded as a crime under the classification of 'Common Assault'. The downgraded assaults occasioning actual bodily harm were now also classified as 'Common Assault' rather than 'AOABH'. Consequently the police began to take action on common assaults where they would not have done so before otherwise they would be held to account. Unfortunately for the police the same rules of evidence still applied in that even common assaults would only be proceeded with if there was some kind of corroboration. In the majority of cases this was sadly lacking. So because the minor common assaults were now also being recorded it meant that there was a sharp increase in undetected crimes of assault. From 1998 there was a steady increase in the number of crimes of common assault. By 2002/03 they represented 23 per cent of all recorded crimes of 'offences against the person' (Simmons and Dodd 2003).

I reflected on whether this would now help the case of vulnerable adults who were badly treated by neglect or common assault but I was left with the same conclusions: we would be no further forward in progressing these in law unless there was corroboration. During my reflections I had to concede that I had changed my stance drastically on this. Once I would have advocated that the Crown Prosecution Service should always proceed where there was an allegation of assault with an injury or mark, even without corroboration. In the case of Kenny, above, I am ashamed to say that at first we thought that another man had committed the murder. We were absolutely convinced of this other man's guilt and I even presented my evidence to the Chief Crown Prosecutor with a view to him agreeing to charge him with murder. I even had the support of a detective superintendent. Fortunately for the police the Chief Crown Prosecutor had the experience and wisdom to disagree. It is an example of how we, the police, could be so absolutely convinced of something and be so totally wrong. So I have to say it is dangerous to think that it is alright to charge on the word of one witness alone!

I spent the last 12 months of my service setting up the newly established Crown Prosecution Service Charging Scheme Liaison Service at the same police station where I began my service as a detective inspector. During that time I had the privilege of seeing cases of almost every one of the 300 or so police officers in the local police area before they were brought to the Duty Crown Prosecutor. They only saw the CPS lawyer if I agreed that they should have an appointment and if I was satisfied that they had completed all their enquiries and were ready to seek advice about a charge. Another name for my role was 'gateway officer'. Many of the cases involved the abuse of vulnerable adults or the protection of vulnerable adults. The issues pertinent throughout were:

- Trying to encourage and convince my CPS colleagues of the need to view the video evidence in its entirety. Very occasionally one would criticise the evidence of the witness or victim but I took pains to explain why the video needed to be viewed in its full context so that the credibility of the victim/witness could be properly assessed; thereby, it is hoped, ensuring that the video would also be viewed in its entirety at court.

- The video interviews of vulnerable adults and witnesses conducted by general police officers were nowhere near to the standard of those I saw which were conducted by officers who were, or who had been, on the protection units, even though they had attended a video interview course.

- Those who were general patrol officers had never conducted video interviews before and although had been specially trained had not yet conducted the video interview of a vulnerable adult witness. This had now changed with the formation of the Public Protection Units.

I retired from the police in May 2005, after the completion of 30 years' service. In October 2006 the organisation I am currently working for were unexpectedly left without a chief executive officer and I was asked to step in to hold the reins until a new one could be appointed. The organisation is a non-profit making charitable organisation founded in the 1960s to provide care for older people. It is the provider responsible for a 32-bed residential care and dementia home, a domiciliary care service providing care for over 100 adults in the local community; it is also responsible for sheltered housing.

I had never considered that I would ever move into a role which involved the care of older people but in accepting the role my intention was to help out the organisation for a short term of six months to move them towards the appointment of a chief executive. I was also asked by the Board of Trustees to carry out a full management review of the organisation, to ensure that older people continued to receive the highest standard of care, and to ensure that staff still felt supported and continued to be developed in their roles during the interim period. Previous inspection reports described the two main services as 'adequate'.

The registered manager of the home had worked her way up through the organisation and now had over 20 years' experience of caring for older people. The manager of the domiciliary care services was new to the role of manager but had several years of working in care for older people and palliative care for adults. I sympathised with the manager of the home and guessed correctly that she must have been wondering what on earth the Board of Trustees were up to in appointing a retired police inspector, who had no experience working in care, as their chief executive officer.

One of my first steps was to empower her to use her experience, training and qualifications to do her job properly which I knew in turn would impact on the type of care the older people would receive. From the outset we worked at developing a good working relationship where we could speak openly to each other on any issue. We reminded ourselves that our aim was to provide the highest level of care we could to the service users, thereby preventing any possibility of abuse or neglect by any systems in place, or lack of them.

As we explored these issues together it was spelled out to us that there was a large question mark over the organisation in the eyes of social services and that there had not in the past been the level of cooperation from the organisation that there should have been. So one of the first things I had to consider to ensure that we built up trust was to investigate whether the cultural environment in which staff had worked had caused, in any way whatsoever, a reduction in the standard of care. It was as if I had to investigate whether there had been any emotional or psychological abuse of the residents by the previous management regime. As a person new to care and to the organisation I was in the privileged position of being able to interview as many staff as I could over the months that followed in order to get to know them and tease out any issues they may have had with the organisation. After many weeks of this I was able to satisfy myself that the service users had only ever received a high standard of care.

There are other general issues that we have to face, almost on a week-by-week basis. Is a staff member intimidating a service user by their manner? Is a staff member neglecting services users by not working hard enough, or providing them with enough time, or not speaking to a service user in a helpful and kind manner? If a staff member does not turn up to do someone's care in their own home is this neglect?

These are real dilemmas we now face each day. As always there are legal issues to consider. Not just with regard to the criminal law but also with regard to employment legislation and the ACAS guidelines of the Model Workplace (ACAS 2005). As well as the legal issues in all this we constantly need to ensure that we are loyal to our staff and only take action if we reasonably suspect that a service user is being or has been abused. There is also a tendency for someone like myself to be oversensitive and over-react and 'imagine' that abuse was there when it probably was not.

There is a legal duty placed upon us[4] that where there is a possibility of abuse that it is in the best interests of all care providers to consider the possibility properly, enquire into the circumstances and record thought processes and even our reasons as to why there was no abuse. For example, we would always properly consider and enquire deeper when it was learnt that residents sustained an injury of any kind from a fall or a minor knock or collision, developed a sore, or said they have been 'grabbed' by a carer or 'Would you like it if you were forced to get up in the early hours and forced to sit here?'.

When two older people fell on the ramps outside the home in a short space of time during cold weather, one seriously, although it was unclear whether the outdated and fairly steep ramps contributed to this or whether it was due to dizziness or giddiness or ice, it was still reported immediately to the Health and Safety Executive and the Commission for Social Care Inspection (CSCI). Regulation 37 of the *Care Homes Regulations 2001* requires the registered person(s) to notify the Commission for Social Care Inspection, without delay, of seven events or incidents. Two of them applied here:

- any serious injury to a service user

- any event in the care home which adversely affects the well-being or safety of any service user.

Also the Health and Safety legislation requires work-related incidents to be reported to the RIDDOR Incident Contact Centre. It lists nine occurrences which need to be reported, one of them being where injuries are caused to members of the public or people not at work where they are taken from the scene of an accident to hospital. We reported the incident by telephone in the first instance and then I completed an online form at the Health and Safety Executive website (www.hse.gov.uk/riddor).

If we did not act quickly in this way the omission on our part could be considered neglect and we might leave ourselves open to a tort claim due to gross negligence. Meanwhile we carried out a full risk assessment of our own and decided to install proper ramps which complied with the latest legislation and recommendations. The Health and Safety advice agreed with our assessment and because we had already commissioned their construction, were happy to leave it in our hands. A special non-slip service coating has been applied to the

---

4   We are required by law to safeguard people who use our service; this is embodied in the *Public Interest Disclosure Act 1998* requiring all employers to have whistleblowing policies. The National Minimum Standards also require us to have whistleblowing arrangements.

ramps and no falls have occurred since their installation. We even recovered the full costs for construction of the ramp by way of a special capital grant funded by the Department of Health to sponsor ways of improving the environment of the home for the benefit of the service users.

Soon after I started in my role it was discovered on the domiciliary care side that a member of staff had tried to pay two cheques into his bank account drawn on a service user's account. The managers and myself acted quickly in suspending the suspected staff member on full pay after first hearing if he had an explanation. He did not. We also imposed a condition that he was not to have any further contact with any service users until an investigation had been completed. The purpose of the suspension was to ensure that there was no possible further danger to the service user or to any other service users, and in the best interests of the member of staff so that a thorough enquiry could be made without any suggestion of interference by the member of staff. We also notified the police, CSCI and social services, and carried out our own speedy investigation with other services users with whom the employee had dealt.

It was then quickly established by the manager's enquiries and the cooperation of the service user's families that large sums of money had indeed been stolen from another service user's bank account via altering the amounts on cheques she had signed for payment of newsagent's bills. The offences which have been committed here were the theft of monies by deception and the forgery of the cheques by altering the amounts.

Finally, we constantly have to wrestle with whether we should acquiesce to criticisms from GPs that we are calling them on too many occasions. I do see their point that there will be times when no viral infections are found or things are of such a minor nature they would run their course and heal naturally. However, in my previous role, I would have been suspicious of any residential home that was not calling the GP enough times for residents' ailments. Could this be a form of neglect by omission?

CONCLUSION

I have now been in my new role for nearly 18 months and I have enjoyed every minute. What has amazed me is how easy it has been to transfer my investigative and managerial skills into my new challenge. In my past role as a senior investigating officer I learnt how to speedily research various aspects of the law, and new or pending legislation, and apply them to a particular task or strategy needed to work the investigation towards a successful conclusion. Also as a police manager I learnt how vital it was to not only motivate and encourage my staff effectively but also how important it was to air our issues and differences quickly and agree to move on; even if it was by way of compromise. Everything we did dealing with many high profile cases was constantly under public scrutiny and would be examined in minute detail later by the courts or inquiries. I think I can say that nothing has changed in my new role!

STATUTES

Criminal Justice Act 1988. London: HMSO

Criminal Justice Act 1991. London: HMSO

Police and Criminal Evidence Act 1984. London: HMSO

Public Interest Disclosure Act 1998. London: HMSO

REGULATIONS

The Care Homes Regulations 2001. Statutory Instrument 3965. London: The Stationery Office.

REFERENCES

ACAS (July 2005) *The ACAS Model Workplace.* London: ACAS.

Burgner, T. (1998) *Independent Longcare Inquiry.* Buckingham: Buckinghamshire County Council.

Criminal Justice System (2007) *Achieving Best Evidence in Criminal Proceedings: Guidance on Interviewing Victims and Witnesses, and Using Special Measures.* London: Criminal Justice System.

Home Office (2002) *Achieving Best Evidence in Criminal Proceedings: Guidance for Vulnerable or Intimidated Witnesses including Children.* London: Home Office Communication Directorate.

Home Office and Department of Health (1992) *Memorandum of Good Practice on Video Recorded Interviews with Child Witnesses for Criminal Proceedings.* London: DH.

Pring, J. (2003) *Silent Victims: The Continuing Failure to Protect Society's Most Vulnerable and The Longcare Scandal.* London: Gibson Square Books.

Simmons, J. and Dodd, T. (eds) (2003) *Crime in England and Wales 2002/2003.* London: Home Office Research, Development and Statistics Directorate.

CHAPTER 12

REFLECTIONS ON PRACTICE

JACKI PRITCHARD

Just because we increase the speed of information doesn't mean we can increase the speed of decisions. Pondering, reflecting and ruminating are undervalued skills in our culture

Dale Dauten

INTRODUCTION: ABUSE, HARM AND JUSTICE

I have always been a reflective practitioner and in my early days as a trainee social worker and years later as a manager I relied heavily on Janet Mattinson's book *The Reflection Process in Casework Supervision* (1975). It was a long time since I had read this book so last year I decided to try to find a copy of it (knowing it was out of print) to buy and managed to do so. It is still a wealth of knowledge and revisiting it made it even more important for me to include a chapter in this book which is a collection of reflective thoughts. I know I personally feel very strongly about using the legal framework when working with adult abuse cases, but I wanted to hear from other practitioners regarding what they think the key issues are at the present time regarding the law and safeguarding adults.

We constantly talk about inter-agency working, multidisciplinary teams and it all sounds great in theory. However, we all know that we often still fail to learn from the past (and inquiries) – that is, communication is often poor or non-existent. Some professionals can be very precious and fail to communicate with the people they should have regular contact with. When we talk about inter-agency working maybe we are not thinking broadly enough.

I said in the introduction to this book that I have been very fortunate in that I have had the opportunity to meet and work with some very dynamic people who are connected to the legal system in some way and feel just as passionately as I do about adult abuse. Feeling passionate about a subject is vital;

if a job or task is forced on someone they are unlikely to feel enthusiastic. I can remember in 1991 a solicitor approaching me to ask if I would have lunch with him to 'teach him' him about elder abuse because he had a client who had been financially abused admitted to the hospital where I was manager of the social work team. That solicitor has gone on to do great things nationally in relation to protecting adults who lack capacity. It was around the same time that I met Simon Leslie and Steve Kirkpatrick, who again were (and still are) full of drive and commitment; their interest was not a passing phase. Being vocal and a 'doer' is what is required when dealing with abuse and District Judge Marilyn Mornington certainly fits that requirement. I just wish more judges could become enlightened about the abuse of adults and actively involved.

I spend a lot of time reflecting on the use of jargon and terminology. It really concerns me how over the years we have drifted away from the regular use of the term 'adult abuse'. I have always maintained that abuse is abuse; we should not be afraid to use the word 'abuse'. We should definitely not hide behind other terms such as 'mistreatment' to make people feel more comfortable. Everyone in society needs to know that abuse of adults happens and it is a real social problem that needs to be addressed. Whilst we continue to use terms like 'protection of vulnerable adults' and 'safeguarding adults' rather than 'adult abuse', people may not realise what we are actually talking about and how serious it is. We have to give a clear message and explanation about how adults can be harmed and that everyone has the right to justice.

Nowadays I often feel like a dinosaur as I have been in the field of social care and working with abuse for so long. So when I was thinking about this chapter (rather than the book as a whole) I asked myself what have been some of the key examples of good practice relating to the law and adult abuse cases I have been directly involved with in recent years. I decided to limit myself to the work I do in Beyond Existing, an organisation I founded eight years ago which runs therapeutic support groups for men and women who have been abused either in childhood or adulthood. So here are some examples of best practice where professionals connected with the law have helped abused vulnerable adults (both young and old) in a very practical way:

- An older woman had been a victim of domestic violence all through her married her life. She eventually decided to leave after being starved and grossly neglected by her husband. The police officer who was involved in the investigation continued to help and support the woman for two years after the investigation had been completed. He visited her every Thursday afternoon 'just for a cup of tea', but that made her feel very 'safe'. He had been involved in the initial interviews and after the case conference was proactive in making sure the house she was moving to was secure; an alarm system which was linked to the local police station was installed and locks were put on all the windows and doors.

The same police officer at a different point in time used to casually drop in to see a younger woman with learning disabilities who was living with her husband; but always called when he knew the husband would be out. The husband claimed to be blind, but social workers who had been involved previously believed he was not. The woman, who regularly presented with injuries, knew that people were concerned she was being physically abused but she denied this. She understood why the police officer was visiting; she did admit to him that she was 'frightened' of her husband but kept denying the violence. The officer visited regularly for six months.

- Susan started attending a Beyond Existing Support Group after she had divorced her husband who had abused her. The husband still had a key to the marital home, but Susan was too frightened of him to ask for the key to be returned. He came in regularly and threatened her when she would not hand over money. The social worker was not addressing this problem. Susan was also being harassed by local children. With her permission we contacted a policeman who was involved in a special project whose main objective was to keep older people safe in the community. He visited within 24 hours of our referral; he discussed the situation with Susan, who agreed he could arrange for locks to be changed on all the doors; again this was done within a day. Susan had reported the damage to the council many times but they had failed to carry out the repairs. The policeman (using the special project's money) employed workmen to do the repairs which were completed within a week.

- Jim had a lot of health problems and was physically disabled. He had been physically abused by his wife, who was excessively violent, throughout their marriage. The really positive thing in this case was that from the beginning the police *did* take his allegations seriously; they never doubted the fact that a woman could abuse a man. After Jim had been interviewed under the adult protection procedures two police officers plus a social worker went out to arrest the wife. One of the police officers suffered injuries as a result of the wife attacking him when he tried to arrest her.

- Simone was 38 years old when she said she wanted to do something about the sexual abuse she had experienced from her father who was now dead. She was angry that no one had believed her when she was a child and she had never had the chance to tell the police what had happened to her. I contacted a policewoman I knew in the local police who dealt with child abuse cases and explained that Simone needed closure. The policewoman agreed to meet with Simone in the police station and formally take a written statement from her. Obviously everyone was aware that nothing could be done from a criminal justice point of view, but the policewoman enabled Simone to tell her story and to go through the exact procedures that should have happened years ago. The policewoman spent hours with Simone in the police station. Afterwards Simone said she felt she had 'put it on record'.

- Margot had mental health problems and had been repeatedly raped by her partner who was HIV positive. She was put on a witness protection programme. When her perpetrator died of AIDS she came back to the area where she had originally lived and started to go through the therapeutic healing process.

These are just a few of my reflections, I now want to explain what follows in the rest of the chapter. I have already said that I wanted to include reflective thoughts about the law and adult protection work from practitioners. So I approached a variety of people for whom I have great respect; that is people who I know are sound both from a theoretical base, but also they practise brilliantly in the jobs that they do. It was vital for me to include writings in this chapter from people who are 'doing the job' and who are not detached from practice and the real world. What was very interesting but also disappointing was that some organisations refused to let their workers write for the book; in some cases that was the final decision without any possibility of negotiation. Two other people have decided to contribute anonymously so they can be heard because they knew their organisations would not agree to let them write.

When I approached people I gave them a free hand to write in any format they wished. I just asked them to reflect on what they thought were key issues for them in their current job regarding the law and adult protection. I said I wanted them to reflect on their own roles and practice. What follows is a collection of reflections from colleagues doing very different jobs; all of whom feel passionately about getting justice for victims of adult abuse.

REFERENCE

Mattinson, J. (1975) *The Reflection Process in Casework Supervision*. London: Tavistock Institute of Marital Studies.

REFLECTION I

Reflector: Glyn Hughes

Job Title: Detective Constable, Lincolnshire Police

Subject: Is there an inevitable tension between the investigation of child abuse and adult abuse which is detrimental to both?

My rank is detective constable and my post since last March is as Public Protection Unit referral co-ordinator. I have been in the police for over 25 years and have worked for approximately the last ten years as an investigator of child abuse and adult abuse. As the current job title describes, with a colleague I receive/identify the bulk of referrals/incidents that require Public Protection Unit (PPU) involvement, do the initial strategy discussions and allocate to an officer on the ground. I am physically located within the Customer Service Centre of Lincolnshire County Council – the gateway for most professional and public referrals. For the year before I started this job I was the PPU trainer.

In my small force specialist investigators deal with both types of victims (child and adult) and this attracts comment that these disciplines are too disparate, and the spectrum of vulnerability too wide, to be always successfully investigated without dedicated staff for each. The cynic might say the victim unwittingly faces what is essentially a lottery of professional skill, experience and a 'jack of all trades' approach to investigation that does not maximise the chances of justice being done.

On the other side of the balance sheet I see colleagues who investigate all criminal matters, irrespective of the class and complexity of vulnerability, with absolute commitment and vim. The broad categories of abuse only recognise 'financial abuse' as unique to vulnerable adults and therefore the identification of offences and the 'points to prove', bar a handful of offences, are typically the same. Also, the procedural and legal processes of dealing with a suspect are identical, as are the rules of evidence and the application of forensic science. Communication issues around capturing evidence from a competent victim can often be successfully addressed by proper planning, sufficient time and the use of intermediaries, interpreters and technical aids. The same interviewer can be assisted to successfully obtain evidence from any qualifying vulnerable person. From what I have seen the case to justify some sort of cynical discrimination between a child and adult case is not made out.

I do see the professional and public recognition and appreciation of adult abuse becoming increasingly widespread, intelligent and insightful. A veil is being lifted; adult abuse as a phenomenon stands the chance of promotion to the premier league and complaints will grow exponentially. This will be notwithstanding the drama of demographic change. The ratio of child versus adult cases will change and the numbers will grow across the board. There is also pressure for legislation which, I think, will broadly mirror what we see in the context of child protection. Some sort of 'Adult Protection Act' to compel the police and other agencies seems inevitable and in my view will probably happen sooner rather than later. Then and now it is how we as a service are able and willing to dynamically resource our response to increasing demands to investigate adult abuse while maintaining the quality of our response to child protection. This will create the real tension and result in consequences that, unless dealt with properly, may not be so welcome.

REFLECTION II

Reflector: Alan Carter

Job Title: Vulnerable Adults Coordinator, North Wales Police

Subject: A view from Wales: communication, mental health issues and assessing capacity

I have been in the police service for almost 12 years. Prior to that I was a paramedic in Manchester for 16 years. I transferred from Greater Manchester Police to North Wales Western Division in 2002. After serving a couple of years on general police patrol duties at Caernarfon, I expressed an interest in family protection work and was successfully given an opportunity to work on the Western Family Protection Unit filling in for staff absence. Later I gained a full time post in the unit. The Family Protection Unit changed to Public Protection Unit (PPU) in 2007.

I was primarily involved in child protection but the occasional vulnerable adult referral made a change to the routine and it was a side of the role from which I received a lot of job satisfaction. I was also used for a couple of larger-scale Vulnerable Adult investigations concerning abuse in care homes; being involved in the interviewing of older abuse victims.

During my time on the unit, child protection guidelines were in place and established. However the vulnerable adults procedures were introduced later and when adopted came into their own. Dedicated Protection of Vulnerable Adults Coordinators (POVACs) were put in place on the Eastern and Central Divisions; and were up and running for two years before Western Public Protection Unit introduced the same post. I expressed an interest in the role and have been doing it ever since. I am grateful to my POVAC colleagues on Eastern and Central Divisions as they have supported me in the role and are a point of reference when needed for advice along with training courses (though few and far between have been useful).

Western Division covers a large area mainly rural and is naturally Welsh speaking. This has been a personal challenge for myself as a non-Welsh speaker; particularly in meetings with the social services department and correspondence from them as occasionally documents are shared without a translation. As colleagues in my network of partner agencies have got to know me I have been grateful to them for providing a translation or translator.

I have always had to hand a police colleague either in the department or elsewhere in the organisation as a reference to provide a translation from Welsh to English.

I must stress this has never been an obstacle in terms of obtaining an account from a victim/vulnerable person or delayed an investigation as on Western Division there are Welsh-speaking officers trained in *Achieving Best Evidence* (Home Office 2002) to be called upon from within the PPU or on Section. As my role is primarily Vulnerable Adults Coordinator I am only occasionally involved in investigations; the majority are reviewed and allocated to the divisional officers to deal with.

The most frequent challenge met by attending police officers as initial responders is that they are called on frequent occasions to a person deemed to be 'vulnerable' due to mental health issues. I must point out that officers are called upon in situations to make decisions based on limited facts and factors about an individual and it is the first responder who determines the 'vulnerable' status in order to make a referral (by the adopted Vulnerable Adult CID 16 email report).[1] If that person is not or has not been known to them previously it can be especially difficult to glean information.

From personal experience of working on patrol and as a paramedic it comes as no surprise that calls to attend to vulnerable people are not just limited to the normal working hours of social services and GP surgeries – when all the departments are at your fingertips to glean information and advice from. At three o'clock in the morning when an officer is called to speak to a lone person presenting with mental health issues at a remote residence that officer is left with a challenge of getting them support especially when there are no relatives or neighbours available, answering the phone, to hand or willing to get involved.

That unfortunate officer is left with the additional burden of determining whether the person is safe to be left to fend for themselves until the daylight hours. Are there needs at that time such that you can justify removing them from their domestic environment to the nearest accident and emergency department? The challenge has always been that person's mental capacity to understand and to consent to be subject of a referral onto another agency in order to receive further support that the police are not in a professional position to give.

---

1   This is an alert form which is shared between the police and social services.

When an officer makes a referral without true consent (i.e the vulnerable adult has not been able to consent due to their lack of mental capacity or the person gives consent at the time to the officer that a referral to a partner agency is going to be made), and when the partner agency representative makes contact the vulnerable adult denies they have given consent or have been told a referral was being made or they can't remember that they have given consent, then where does that leave the police agency? More importantly where does that leave the vulnerable adult? When a person has been identified as 'in need of support', the referred agency will not become involved until full and true consent has been obtained.

This has been a debate between the agencies particularly Health and Community Mental Health Teams and I am sure is not at all isolated to Manchester and North Wales. My concern is that to seek clarification over the issue of consent could incur unnecessary delay to the referral process and delays the vulnerable adult accessing the support. The *Mental Capacity Act* legislation is now in force and the powers this gives to emergency services attending to such individual more scope to deal with them particularly in a domestic setting.

I hope that this has lowered the height of the bar of this hurdle at least!

REFERENCE

Home Office (2002) *Achieving Best Evidence in Criminal Proceedings: Guidance for Vulnerable or Intimidated Witnesses including Children.* London: Home Office Communication Directorate.

REFLECTION III

Reflector: Anonymous

Job Title: Co-ordinator for the Protection of Vulnerable Adults

Subject: Vulnerable adult abuse: the legal framework

I am a professionally qualified social worker and during my career I have worked in the fields of older people, learning disability and mental health. I was an Approved Social Worker under the *Mental Health Act 1983* for ten years and for ten years subsequently, I managed a mental health operational assessment team (CMHT). I have been an Adult Protection Lead for three years.

My key reflections on abuse and the law are:

- The legal framework surrounding vulnerable adult abuse is complex and extensive. It covers a wide area of legislation.

- The legislation continues to develop and it is strongly recommended that key professionals are enabled to undertake sufficient good quality up to date training.

- Vulnerable adult protection legal procedures can appear daunting because there are over 20 areas of legislation which govern/underpin adult protection work and the involvement of the police will often be necessary.

- It is important to keep abreast of changes in the law and new legislation, so it is important that practitioners are enabled to participate in the overall adult protection infrastructure which should include legal services representatives in order to be well informed and knowledgeable and trained.

- When any area of law is considered the implications of the *Human Rights Act 1998* which came into force in October 2000 must be addressed.

- Vulnerable adults require support and counselling during the inevitable legal processes involved in stopping abuse and dealing effectively with crime. It is estimated that there are at least 8.5 million people who currently meet the definition of 'disabled person' under the *Disability Discrimination Act 1995*. It is acknowledged that the mental or physical abilities of a person will influence their experience of the criminal justice process. An overemphasis on disability and lack of consideration of ability and strengths can lead to potential witnesses being screened out, and an undue anxiety about the credibility of witnesses. This can result in a denial of justice to vulnerable adults. *Speaking Up for Justice* (Home Office 1998) made 78 recommendations designed to encourage and support vulnerable and/or intimidated witnesses through the stages of investigation, pre-trial, the trial, and beyond. *Action for Justice* (Home Office 1999) laid out an implementation programme for *Achieving Best Evidence* (Home Office 2002) as outlined above. The *Youth Justice and Criminal Evidence Act 1999*, *Disability Discrimination Act 1995* and *Human Rights Act 1998* all place a duty on criminal justice agencies to take account of the special needs of defence and prosecution witnesses.

- Professionals who have not undertaken statutory work and responsibilities prior to working in the field of adult protection sometimes struggle with the huge responsibility involved in invoking appropriate legislation.

- Key legislation includes the *Crime and Disorder Act 1998* (section 115) which provides professionals with the power (not a duty) to share information with other professionals within the local authority, NHS Trusts, the police service and the probation service.

- Major new legislation affecting adult protection work includes the *Domestic Violence, Crime and Victims Act 2004* which provides a new offence of familial homicide (section 5).

- The *Sexual Offences Act 2003* which was introduced to help jurors make fair and balanced decisions on the question of consent and also introduced new offences to improve the protection for vulnerable adults and children.

- The *Mental Capacity Act 2005* (MCA) and the *Deprivation of Liberties Safeguards Amendment*. The MCA creates a criminal offence of ill-treatment or neglect of a person who lacks capacity (section 44).

- The Protection of Vulnerable Adults (POVA) scheme as set out in the *Care Standards Act 2000* was implemented on a phased basis from July 2004 (Department of Health 2004, 2006). At the heart of the scheme is the POVA list. Through referrals to, and checks against the list, care workers who have harmed a vulnerable adult or have placed a vulnerable adult at risk of harm will be banned from working in a care position with vulnerable adults. As a result the POVA scheme has significantly enhanced the level of protection for vulnerable adults.

- The *Safeguarding Vulnerable Groups Act 2006* is a major element of a wide-ranging and ambitious programme of work established across government to address the systemic failures identified by the Bichard Inquiry (House of Commons 2004). It introduces the new Independent Safeguarding Authority[2] (ISA) Vetting and Barring Scheme. The scope of the new scheme will be required, for example, in a range of new sectors. In relation to vulnerable adults this is a significant step forward from the existing Protection of Vulnerable Adults (POVA) scheme which applies in regulated social care settings only.

- All professionals specialising in the field of adult protection raise the issue of a major lack of resources and multi-agency investment in adult protection work. This should not be an excuse for highly skilled and trained professionals to lose their sense of commitment to the task but it does pose a problem.

- With the new raft of legislation could come additional resources; for example coordinating managers to implement the MCA and Deprivation of Liberties Safeguards amendments across all sectors.

- In considering all the many aspects of law governing the adult protection agenda one has to think about the judgements demanded of professionals and *how* they reach them.

- The different agency perspectives are also a major issue in the field and *how* we work together effectively is crucial if we are to succeed in protecting vulnerable adults from abuse.

- Offences highlighted most frequently are physical abuse and financial/material abuse.

- Joint training in adult protection and the law has increasingly become a major objective for localities. It follows that training strategies and plans should adequately reflect this requirement.

---

2   For further information see the Independent Safeguarding Authority website: www.isa-gov.org.uk/

KEY STATUTES

Care Standards Act 2000. London: The Stationery Office.

Crime and Disorder Act 1998. London: The Stationery Office.

Disability Discrimination Act 1995. London: HMSO.

Domestic Violence, Crime and Victims Act 2004. London: The Stationery Office.

Human Rights Act 1998. London: HMSO.

Mental Health Act 1983. London: HMSO.

Mental Capacity Act 2005. London: The Stationery Office.

Sexual Offences Act 2003. London: The Stationery Office.

Safeguarding Vulnerable Groups Act 2006. London: The Stationery Office.

Youth Justice and Criminal Evidence Act 1999. London: The Stationery Office.

REFERENCES

Department of Health (2004 and 2006) *Protection of Vulnerable Adults Scheme in England and Wales for Adult Placement Schemes, Domiciliary Care Agencies and Care Homes: A Practical Guide.* London: DH.

Department of Health (2007) *Mental Capacity Act 2005. Deprivation of Liberties Safeguards. Briefing Sheet November 2007.* Gateway Reference 8965. London: DH. www.cambridgeshire.gov.uk/ NR/rdonlyres/86C37BEA-7A7C-4168-859B-D95E4888161D/0/DH_0807171.pdf, accessed 27 March 2008.

Home Office (1998) *Speaking Up For Justice: Report of the Interdepartmental Working Group on the Treatment of Vulnerable or Intimidated Witnesses in the Criminal Justice System.* London: Home Office.

Home Office (1999) *Action for Justice.* London: Home Office Communication Directorate.

Home Office (2002) *Achieving Best Evidence in Criminal Proceedings: Guidance for Vulnerable or Intimidated Witnesses including Children.* London: Home Office Communication Directorate.

House of Commons (2004) *The Bichard Inquiry Report.* June. London: The Stationery Office.

REFLECTION IV

Reflector: Peter Sadler

Job Title: Lincolnshire Safeguarding Vulnerable Adults Team Service Manager

Subject: The safeguarding team interface with the law and the legal framework

I am a service manager of the Lincolnshire Safeguarding Vulnerable Adults team, which operates within the requirements and process of the *Multi-Agency Safeguarding Vulnerable Adult Policy and Procedures* (Lincolnshire Adult Protection Committee 2007). In March 2008 Lincolnshire County Council separated the Safeguarding Coordinator post into two separate posts, one being responsible for the operational delivery of the Safeguarding team and the other to lead on the Safeguarding strategic agenda. I was asked to lead on the strategic agenda which includes supporting the development of a new Safeguarding Board for Lincolnshire, the creation of a raising awareness of abuse strategy and to lead on the quality monitoring of the safeguarding team/service.

The Safeguarding team, which comprises a Safeguarding Adults Coordinator, three liaison managers[3] and nine investigation officers, undertakes investigations into allegations of abuse and also assesses and manages risk through a coordinated multi-agency approach. The team undertakes its own investigations and also jointly investigates with other statutory organisations i.e. police, the Commission for Social Care Inspection, Health Care Commission and primary care trusts.

The work of the team has a close interface with the law and the legal framework; that is, both criminal law and civil law including adult social care and health law. When investigating, the liaison managers and investigation officers have to be mindful of the legal framework within which they are operating. At all times the work of the Safeguarding team has to evidence the legal framework in which they are operating to justify their actions and also be able to meet any challenge.

In Lincolnshire there has always been good communication between social services staff and the local authority solicitor,

---

3   This is the term used for operational team managers; the Safeguarding team is divided into three sub-teams to cover three geographical areas.

within the County Council legal department, who has been actively accessible and supportive by giving clear advice to both practitioners and managers. Before the Safeguarding team came into being in November 2007, review courses for liaison managers were run annually. In the previous 12 months two solicitors from the legal team had a half day's input into the manager's training programme. One of the solicitors had previously worked for the Crown Prosecution Service (CPS). I had highlighted that both managers and practitioners were unclear about what constituted an offence under criminal law, so the solicitor delivered a presentation on the criminal law in relation to adult protection work together with an explanation regarding the role of the CPS and the test of evidence to which the CPS work. The second solicitor presented other aspects of the law which were relevant to adult abuse cases and adult protection work e.g. health and safety law (emphasising the responsibility of managers to staff – sending them out into violent situations, stress at work, etc.), the *Mental Capacity Act 2005*.

As part of developing an understanding of the *Mental Capacity Act,* Lincolnshire County Council had commissioned a number of training events led by a solicitor who had expert knowledge regarding the Act and its implementation. The training events were targeted at operational managers and practitioners, so they could better support their colleagues.

The new Safeguarding team had a three-week induction training period before it 'went live'. Once again the legal department had an input, covering the criminal and civil legal frameworks. Also members of the team had training on interviewing from the police to enable them to work to the standards of *Achieving Best Evidence* (Criminal Justice System 2007; Home Office 2002). This training included developing skills in video interviewing.

The safeguarding arrangements in Lincolnshire are designed to promote close joint working between the Safeguarding team and the police. When there is a suspicion about or an allegation of abuse is made there is a discussion between the Safeguarding team and the police. The discussion takes place between the police and the liaison manager of the Safeguarding Team to decide whether the allegation should be investigated by the police within the criminal justice framework. There are some areas of alleged abuse that do not fall easily within criminal law; for example, certain types of emotional/psychological abuse; in cases of neglect where victims have capacity to make informed decisions; and also where a person with capacity decides not to make a statement/complaint to the police in any alleged criminal offence. These are the areas that the Safeguarding team investigates without the police. The team were trained and developed to undertake the investigation within the requirements of the Home Office and criminal justice framework guidance *Achieving Best Evidence*. I believe that the standards of *Achieving Best Evidence* should drive County-Council-led investigations but there is always the potential for such an investigation to turn into a criminal investigation when further evidence is established. If the initial investigation was not up to the criminal standard there is a possibility it could contaminate a criminal investigation.

The Safeguarding team also work within the framework of adult social care law including the *Mental Health Act 1983*, the *NHS and Community Care Act 1990* and the *Mental Capacity Act 2005*. The legislation allows the right of access if the requirements of the *Mental Health Act* are met and the rights of intervention if the requirements of the same Act or the *Mental Capacity Act* are met. There is also an interface with the *Care Standards Act 2000* and direct links to contract and contact law. The investigation officer has to have a wide range of knowledge of criminal law, civil law and law specifically relating to care standards and regulation as defined by the *Care Standards Act 2000* and contract law in relation to commissioned services.

Where investigations are conducted within the requirements of the multi agency Safeguarding Vulnerable Adult policy (which is agreed within the framework of the statutory guidance *No Secrets* (Department of Health 2000), the policy requires that investigations, whether criminal or County-Council-led, will be presented at a case conference.

The case conference is held within the framework of civil law, being led by the County Council. The test of evidence and proof used at the conference is 'balance of probability' a lesser test than the criminal test 'beyond all reasonable doubt'. In Lincolnshire there have been positive outcomes from the case conference system in that even when an investigation for alleged abuse has not been referred to a criminal court, a case conference has substantiated that abuse has occurred on the balance of probabilities. In the case of paid workers a referral has been made at case conference that the organisation which employs them should undertake a disciplinary enquiry, under the organisation's disciplinary procedures. This has led to employers dismissing a paid worker and making a successful referral on to the Protection of Vulnerable Adults List.

The Safeguarding team is now firmly established and there is an ongoing development within the team to increase knowledge and understanding of the legal framework. Liaison managers and investigation officers are always mindful they are working in a legal framework and need to evidence their work on this basis. A positive working relationship has been established between the team and police colleagues. The provision of a specialist police officer in the Lincolnshire County Council Customer Services Centre has proven to be invaluable.

The Safeguarding team has also developed a strong link to the specialist legal services of the County Council and seeks their advice and support on a regular basis. County Council solicitors will attend subsequent strategy meeting and case conferences.

In Lincolnshire we are also developing stronger links with the Crown Prosecution Service and the Chief Crown Prosecutor is a member of the new Safeguarding Adult Board.

Through these links the Safeguarding team will continue to develop knowledge and understanding within the framework of law.

STATUTES

Care Standards Act 2000. London: The Stationery Office.
Mental Capacity Act 2005. London: The Stationery Office.
Mental Health Act 1983. London: HMSO.
NHS and Community Care Act 1990. London: HMSO.

REFERENCES

Criminal Justice System (2007) *Achieving Best Evidence in Criminal Proceedings: Guidance on Interviewing Victims and Witnesses, and Using Special Measures.* London: Criminal Justice System.

Department of Health (2000) *No Secrets: Guidance on Developing and Implementing Multi-Agency Policies and Procedures to Protect Vulnerable Adults from Abuse.* London: DH.

Home Office (2002) *Achieving Best Evidence in Criminal Proceedings: Guidance for Vulnerable or Intimidated Witnesses including Children.* London: Home Office Communication Directorate.

Lincolnshire Adult Protection Committee (2007) *Lincoln Safeguarding Adults Committee Multi-Agency Policy and Proceedures for the Safeguarding of Vulnerable Adults in Lincolnshire.* October. Lincoln: Lincolnshire Adult Protection Committee.

REFLECTION V

Reflector: Anonymous

Job Title: Local Authority Lawyer

Subject: The lawyer and case conferences

I have nearly 20 years of post-qualification experience and I have had 16 years' experience in working in the field of child protection and adult care in both the public and private sector.

As a lawyer working for a local authority providing legal advice to adult care services, I am surprised to find that I am often over-looked when invitations for adult protection case conferences are circulated. It may well be that social workers do not see the need to issue an invitation to in-house legal services. However, in my opinion this is very remiss.

Lawyers can make a valuable contribution to the whole of the decision-making process. They can assist with the evaluation of the evidence provided in the investigator's report and ask probing questions with a view to eliciting further information for the confer-ence or seeking clarification on a point of issue. They can provide legal advice to the forum when required to do so and assist with the decision-making process.

In an adult protection case conference, the conference partici-pants have an important role to play. They have a duty to protect the vulnerable adult who has been the subject of the alleged abuse from future harm. However, they also have a duty to protect other potential victims from future harm. In performing this function, they are engaging the human rights of the alleged perpetrator. A finding of abuse could affect the individual's ability to work with vulnerable adults in the future. Therefore, the decision-making process must be robust and able to withstand scrutiny. In my expe-rience this has not always been the case.

When making decisions, participants should use the tools provided: the definition of abuse in the government guidance *No Secrets* (Department of Health 2000). They should refer to the explicit criteria of physical, sexual, emotional and psychological abuse and ensure that one or other of the criteria are met when making a finding. Participants should have sight of these criteria when making their decisions and make reference to the specific elements of the criteria throughout their discussions. These are the building blocks of the decision-making process in adult protection which should be used at all times.

Participants at an adult protection case conferences have a significant role to play. Their decisions will affect not only the lives of the vulnerable adult victims but also the lives of the alleged perpetrators of abuse. As such, all decisions need to be soundly based upon reliable evidence and it is the duty of the participants to evaluate the evidence to ensure that it is credible. If the participants consider that they require further information before they can make a finding they should request an adjournment of the case conference so that further investigation can take place and reconvene the case conference at a later date.

Vulnerable adults need protection from harm but this must not be at the expense of the human rights of the alleged perpetrator.

REFERENCE

Department of Health (2000) *No Secrets: Guidance on Developing and Implementing Multi-Agency Policies and Procedures to Protect Vulnerable Adults from Abuse*. London: DH.

REFLECTION VI

Reflectors: Mark Pathak and Geraldine Monaghan

Job Title: Social Worker and Manager, The Investigations Support Unit, Liverpool City Council

Subject: Ten years of 'Witness Support, Preparation and Profiling': The Investigations Unit, Liverpool City Council

Witness support, preparation and profiling (WSP&P) aims to promote equal access to justice for witnesses with learning disabilities and other Vulnerable Witnesses (s 16, *Youth Justice and Criminal Evidence Act 1999*). The support and preparation deals with the understanding, information and skills acquisition required of the witness, while avoiding any discussion of their evidence. The process leads to the production of a witness profile, which identifies the obstacles the witness will experience and the challenges they will present to the court, and then recommends ways of reducing these. It may recommend the use of Special Measures (ss 23–30, *Youth Justice and Criminal Evidence Act 1999*) or identify 'Additional Measures to Assist'. Special Measures have been used in a minority of cases we have dealt with (Silverman 2005a).

Our model focuses both on the individual and on the criminal justice system (CJS), promoting changes in both. So far 31 witness-complainants have been supported to give evidence in 28 trials in Liverpool. Current figures give an 85 per cent conviction rate for some of the most serious sexual offences heard in Liverpool Crown Court when the witness-complainant with learning disabilities has received WSP&P. The effectiveness of this model has been recognised by the present and former Directors of Public Prosecutions and also by the The Rt Hon. Lord Justice Judge, Deputy Chief Justice. As a consequence of their endorsement, the Crown Prosecution Service (CPS) has promoted the adoption of this service throughout England and Wales.

Ten years ago when we developed WSP&P, we had a blank canvas. Mark had specialised in field and residential social work with people with learning disabilities, especially working with those people whose challenging behaviour had a sexual focus, whilst Geraldine was a longstanding fieldwork manager (both child and adults) with experience of Court work. What we both shared was a commitment to the social work values of empowerment and inclusion, expressed through person-centred practice, systems theory, implementation of the Personal Developmental Model of Learning and the promotion of citizenship rights.

The WSP&P model was developed to meet the needs of one complainant with learning disabilities who would give evidence in four separate trials (Faiza 2006). It had to be individualised and specific and has remained so ever since. The model is adapted for each new witness; what may work with one witness may not work with another. While each witness has been unique, they have all become better informed, assertive and confident by the time of the trial and have been able to give Best Evidence. Because their abilities and needs have been different, the requests made and advice given to barristers and judges has also varied.

Ten years on we have positive working relationships with our fellow partners in the Merseyside criminal justice system – Merseyside Police, Merseyside CPS, the Bar and the Judiciary. This is reflected in the 'Tripartite Protocol' (Merseyside CPS, Merseyside Police and Liverpool City Council ISU 2000) endorsed by Liverpool Crown Court Vulnerable Witnesses Committee. This protocol is the basis of the enhanced service offered to all potential witnesses with a learning disability by all three agencies. Both WSP&P and the Tripartite Protocol have achieved national and international recognition from criminal justice agencies and also endorsement from learning disability services across the United Kingdom.

Much of what we have achieved has been because we have spent a great deal of time networking with our CJS partner agencies, demonstrating that we all share the same goal – a fair hearing for people with a learning disability (Monaghan and Pathak 2000). It was not uncommon in the early days for us to attend police team briefings at 8.30am, or meetings in chambers with barristers in the evenings. All in a day's work! None of it was wasted. Slowly, case by case, we were all able to recognise the value of strong, clear professional boundaries. Once other agencies understood what our model had to offer them, without it impinging on their responsibility or compromising the evidence, then we felt as if we were pushing at an open door.

Years later, not only do we not stand on each other's toes but we all know how to work together productively, without defensiveness or deference.

Interestingly, as we travel around the country explaining WSP&P and encouraging local initiatives and partnerships, we hear of problems encountered by all agencies – 'How do you manage to speak to the CPS lawyer?', 'How do you get the police to attend strategy meetings?', 'How do you get yourself invited to conferences in Chambers?', and to be fair – we also hear 'How do I contact the social worker?'. Different areas have different issues. What is clear is that there are still problems of communication and expectation between agencies, many of which require patience, persistence, and recognition of other agencies 'drivers' if they are to be improved.

The CJS has dramatically changed for people with a learning disability since our first trial in the late 1990s. Social care services have become better at supporting individuals to report crimes (*No Secrets*; Department of Health 2000), police training has improved (*Achieving Best Evidence*; Criminal Justice System 2007; Home Office 2002), the CPS are more aware (*No Witness, No Justice*[4]) and the Bar and Judiciary recognise witnesses with a learning disability as (potentially) credible. The *Youth Justice and Criminal Evidence Act* introduced Special Measures and the groundbreaking interview tool *Achieving Best Evidence* was implemented and has just been revised. Yet, in our opinion there is still an over-reliance on physical or process-focused adaptations. While Special Measures do 'level the playing field' for many witnesses, there is a significant place for a specific individualised service which requires interpersonal engagement in order to help 'this witness in this trial' (Judge 1998). It is often the direct advice to the barrister on how to recognise and handle the difficulties presented by the witness in court which is the most effective aspect of the profile.

Colleagues in the CJS have said that they are 'initiatived out' and that unless our partnership work, e.g. the Tripartite Protocol, achieves the objective of the latest initiative then good practice established will not necessary be sustained. There can be some confusion about what the latest initiative is and how it fits with others.

We also worry a little in case too much is expected of the recently launched Disability Hate Crime initiative in criminal proceedings. While it has the potential to assert and confirm society's respect for disabled people, it is an 'aggravating feature' of a crime, which will affect the sentence if the criminal offence is proven.

4   The 'No Witness, No Justice' project is introducing dedicated Witness Care Units across England and Wales, bringing police and the Crown Prosecution Service together for the first time to jointly meet the individual needs of victims and witnesses in criminal court cases.

This means that the recognition, reporting, investigation and pros-ecuting of crimes against disabled people are dependent on awareness, confidence in the criminal justice system and an informed, individualised sensitive response from all criminal justice agencies. The introduction of third-party reporting centres should have a significant impact in these areas. Remember, if we can't prosecute burglaries and assaults against disabled people then we can't prosecute 'hate crime'.

Whilst we may all think we have finally cracked it about how best to support people with learning disabilities to give Best Evidence in criminal and perhaps civil trials, there remains the ongoing issue of them being targeted. Clearly the future role and development of Adult Safeguarding remains critical in any joined-up model of inter-agency work practised to reduce this. We will be interested to see what the review of *No Secrets* reveals and hope it recognises that local variations in strategy and planning fre-quently mean that successful experience of the criminal justice system for witnesses, complainants, social care services and criminal justice partners depends very much on individual commit-ment and personal relationships in a professional context.

Other positive avenues also exist. The development of Personal Safety Initiatives and the increasing awareness of transport providers, for instance about personal safety, shows positive change. Local Crime and Disorder Reduction Partnerships provide a forum where the prevention of crimes against people with learning disabilities can be pursued.

But let's not forget what witnesses with a learning disability have said to us, at every opportunity, over the years: that despite developments in legislation and policy and an improved CJS awareness, giving evidence is a very scary and daunting experi-ence, one they are anxious about or even frightened of (as discussed on *You and Yours*, BBC Radio 4, by J. Kay on 5 June 2000 and P. White on 27 November 2003; see also Silverman 2005b). However, when witnesses experience the WSP&P model, they absorb information, develop an understanding of the criminal justice process and learn new skills and coping strategies. It has been inspiring to watch witnesses change from quiet apprehensive individuals, too scared to walk through the metal detector at the Crown Court, to people who insist on giving evidence in the courtroom in the presence of the judge. Giving evidence is a daunting prospect for us all, and perhaps this is inevitable. However, we believe that we have demonstrated that while 'what can't be cured must be endured', the anxiety and distress can be reduced by careful, individualised support and preparation, so that people with learning disabilities can get a fair hearing ('Michael' and Pathak 2007; Monaghan and Pathak forthcoming).

Perhaps the last 'reflection' should be left to the person who started it all off – 'Michael' who gave evidence in four trials regarding 29 counts of the most serious sexual assaults. Supported to write an article for The Ann Craft Trust he said:

> When I told Bev and Mark I thought I was in trouble. Bev was a po-licewoman. I didn't want to talk to them because walls have ears. I never told my mum because you see walls have ears. I did not think they would do anything because I opened up a can of worms and they all came out. I thought that outside people would be stopped from coming in. I thought that the staff would tell lies to Bev and Mark and nothing would happen. ('Michael' 2007, p.4)

Later he remembered:

> Mark told me slowly what would happen to me in the courtroom. It took a long time to do this. I was scared because the building was so big and it had 6 floors in it. I went to the court building every week to see the place. I went to watch a few trials with Mark and we would have lunch out. Mark wrote a report to the Judge-man about what I could do and what I need help with about being a witness. The Judge-man said 'hello' to me once when I was watching a trial. He was a nice man. If all Judges were like him it would be good for people with learning disabilities. When he had to shout at someone in the court-room I was scared. In the beginning I was nervous, but the more I went, the better I was at it. In the end I had four trials and I won three.
>
> We need people to help us not criticise us. I am glad I opened up a can of worms but it was sad that a lot of my friends from the olden days were abused. I have been to court four times and would do it again but only with support. Okay I did a good thing. I got them people convicted, but there is a lot more to come out. A lot more. ('Michael' and Pathak 2007, p.5)

REFERENCES

Criminal Justice System (2007) *Achieving Best Evidence in Criminal Proceedings: Guidance on Interviewing Victims and Witnesses, and Using Special Measures.* London: Criminal Justice System.

Department of Health (2000) *No Secrets: Guidance on Developing and Implementing Multi-Agency Policies and Procedures to Protect Vulnerable Adults from Abuse.* London: DH.

Faiza, F. (2006) 'Unequal Justice.' *Viewpoint*, November/December, 16–19.

Home Office (2002) *Achieving Best Evidence in Criminal Proceedings: Guidance for Vulnerable or Intimidated Witnesses including Children.* London: Home Office Communication Directorate.

Judge, Sir Igor (1998)'A view from the judiciary.' Speech at *A Fair Hearing: Justice for People with Learning Disabilities* conference, London, 12 February.

Merseyside CPS, Merseyside Police and Liverpool City Council ISU (2000) Protocol for Dealing With Cases Involving A Complainant/Witness/Defendant With A Learning Disability. (Internal document.)

'Michael' and Pathak. M. (2007) 'My life.' The Ann Craft Trust, *The ACT Bulletin*, Issue 61, October 2007, 3–8.

Monaghan, G. and Pathak, M. (2000) 'Silenced Witnesses.' *Community Care*, 27 April – 3 May, 20–21.

Silverman, J. (2005a) 'Not Every Vulnerable Witness Needs a TV Link.' *The Times*, 25 January, pp.8–9.

Silverman, J. (2005b) *Law in Action*. BBC Radio 4, 29 January.

REFLECTION VII

Reflector: Marilyn Mornington

Job Title: District Judge

Subject: Honour-based violence and forced marriage

We have in the UK and other first world countries, begun to recognise new forms of domestic violence – originating primarily in the developing world – having at their core the abuse of power and control (primarily through the abuse of patriarchy) and having the internationally accepted title of honour-based violence (HBV). These forms of abuse have been spread to, and are being increasingly carried out in, Western countries as a result of mass immigration. The recognition and firm response by legal/governmental agencies has come late – in part due to misguided political correctness and fear of being labelled as racist/Islamaphobic – to the detriment and in some cases the death of victims. The increasing education of and demands of women to make choices in their own lives – both here and in the developing world – have led, if anything, to an increase in HBV as cultural and familial expectations come into direct conflict with emancipation and individualisation.

These forms of abuse have existed in many parts of the world for hundreds if not thousands of years; they arise from a totally misguided understanding of individual and in particular family and community 'honour' or 'Izzat'. The honour of the family is seen to rest in the control of family members and in particular but not exclusively through the sexuality and marital choices of its women (although men are also victims to a far greater extent than in other forms of domestic violence; the recognised rate for forced marriage (FM) in the UK is 15 per cent of victims being male[5] but this is widely accepted to be an underestimate due to lower rates of reporting). Individual choice and human rights – such as the right to choose a spouse or to escape an abusive relationship – are subsumed and ignored. They are seen as a threat to the far more important perceived group 'honour' which must at all times be

---

5   For more information see www.mensadviceline.org.uk/HelpAdvice/
MaleVictimsofForcedMarriage/tabid/194/Default.aspx, accessed 30 July 2008,
and www.fco.gov.uk/en/fco-in-action/nationals/forced-marriage-unit, accessed
30 July 2008.

protected and avenged; even at the cost of rejection, violence towards and murder of previously loved family members.

The abuse is not only not condemned by the wider community (in the UK and abroad) but can be applauded – resulting in the protection of perpetrators (including by the police and courts in countries of origin) and the hounding down of victims – by vigilantes – paid and unpaid. In countries such as Pakistan/Iraq and Bangladesh in the unlikely event a prosecution takes place and a conviction ensues, sentence may be non-existent or vastly reduced due to the accepted mitigation of 'honour'. Many potential and actual victims and perpetrators in the UK misguidedly believe that a similar response from the police and courts will pertain here and act accordingly. In countries with high prevalence 'Izzat' governs every aspect and hour of life and the deeply ingrained attitudes of entire societies (top to bottom) have to be altered – a gargantuan task.

This type of abuse comes under the generic heading of HBV; it includes FM, female genital mutilation and killing in the name of 'honour'. They are forms of domestic violence and an abuse of the human rights. Victims can suffer many forms of physical and emotional damage including being held unlawfully captive, assaulted and repeatedly raped.

In recent years we in the UK have reached out into the communities where these practices take place and commenced a process of bringing perpetrators to justice, supporting victims and most importantly, through education in all its forms, seek to change hearts and minds.

Enormous advances have been made since 1997 in tackling the issue of domestic violence (DV) in England and Wales. A major factor in this has been the joined-up approach to good governance of the Inter-ministerial Domestic Violence Group. This has led to new legislation and good practice protocols and the dissemination throughout the UK of previously isolated areas of good practice and the development of a true multi-agency cross departmental strategy. HBV/FM is now at a place where DV was in 1997 – with isolated areas of good practice, protocols being developed in isolation and no national training/funding strategies. The joined up approach of the inter-ministerial group has a proven track record. The Family Justice Council[6] strongly recommends that a similar long-term Inter-Ministerial Group now be set up to coordinate and take forward a national strategy for HBV/FM.

6   See www.family-justice-council.org.uk

In 2000 following an extensive consultation, the working group on FM published *A Choice by Right* (Working Group on Forced Marriage 2000). The government has since produced guidelines for police, social services, education and health professionals on tackling FM. We have also commissioned international guidance for lawyers. However, there is still an issue which the Family Justice Council considers requires urgent attention of practitioners in many relevant fields still not being aware of the guides or of following them.

The Ministry of Justice sponsored a series of six nationwide multi-agency conferences between 2003 and 2004 on the issues affecting victims from the Asian community, with a government minister speaking at each. The strength of a joined-up response has been of particular value in this area, due to the sensitivity and barriers created by cultural, religious and race issues.

The Association of Chief Police Officers (ACPO) has set up a specialist 'honour'-based violence working group, which is developing a coordinated national police response, and sponsoring research into this increasingly recognised form of DV. The government, again through the Inter-Ministerial Group, is using its now established procedures for multi-agency engagement in seeking to develop an effective response, in particular utilising the auspices of the Women's National Commission, to consult and engage with otherwise hard to reach Asian women's organisations. Specialist black and minority ethnic (BME) refuges and outreach services are being set up nationally and in conjunction with Karma Nirvana/Derby University developed a government-sponsored mentoring scheme for victims of FM in 2006. Non-governmental organisations (NGOs) are swamped with referrals and have to turn many women away, particularly those with no recourse to public funds – their value needs to be recognised and they need proper long-term funding.

Understanding the value of an international approach, the British Council and the Foreign and Commonwealth Office have undertaken an extensive three-year programme to tackle honour crime in Sindh – including a world conference, education and media programmes. There is much to learn from this initiative for the UK. Sharing of knowledge/joint initiatives between countries affected by HBV is a vital tool – particularly with countries such as Pakistan from which many of our affected communities originate and with other EU countries such as Norway also facing these issues for the first time.

FM is not solely a 'Muslim' or 'South Asian' problem. The Forced Marriage Unit (FMU)[7] has dealt with cases from East Asia, Africa, the Middle East and Europe. Freely given consent is a pre-requisite of Christian, Jewish, Hindu, Muslim and Sikh marriages. It affects both young women and young men. New communities are coming to the UK daily. Bradford alone had 400 new Roma children enlist in its schools in 2007 – we need to reach out to these new communities proactively.

The Family Justice Council would recommend that the education series for schools and the DVD *Watch over Me*,[8] which was funded and developed by Cabinet Office/DFES (December 2004) be made part of a national programme for all schools; the DVD effectively dealing as it does with DV, FM, HBV, gun and knife crime, drugs, bullying etc.

The UK police initiatives have been led by the London Metropol-itan Police – and I wish to pay credit here to Commander Andy Baker, Brent Hyatt and Laura Richards of the Homicide Prevention Unit and to Nazir Afzal of the Crown Prosecution Service for their dedication to the victims of murder in the name of so-called honour. They have developed new and innovative ways of analysing, understanding, investigating and preventing HBV. Their work has informed police training and best practice nationally par-ticularly with regard to risk assessment and risk management. They have concluded that there is no typical case of HBV. Honour killings are 'atypical' and they fall within the 'umbrella' of honour crime and HBV. Many of these crimes are interlinked, being drivers for one another, and they are listed here:

- domestic violence
- forced marriage
- acid attacks
- dowry-related crime
- bride price
- female genital mutilation
- honour rape
- customs like 'swara'

---

7   The Forced Marriage Unit can be contacted by telephone on 020 7008 0151 or by e-mail: fmu@fco.gov.uk.
8   Visit www.missdorothy.com.

- female infanticide

- blood feuds.

Victims are often subject to psychological pressures that can lead to mental breakdown, self-harm and even suicide. We are not judging cultures, we are judging murderers/abusers and those who shield them from justice.

Most countries have signed up to human rights conventions and there has been a great deal of research and international cooperation on these issues, yet we seem powerless to date to effect change. We now understand the misguided concept of 'honour' that crime committed in its name is based in feudalism, lack of education and denial of the fundamental human rights of women. We acknowledge that it is forbidden by all of the major religions and in particular Islam. The Family Justice Council say that change will only come when there is determined, assertive, consistent action by governments, faith leaders, judiciary, police, the media and educationalists.

Governments need to enact and enforce legislation that outlaws all forms of honour crime. The *Forced Marriage (Civil Protection) Act 2007* will need to be monitored as to its effectiveness. It will require training for professionals, the availability of legal aid and national media campaigns so that the remedies and message of the Act are well known. The Family Justice Council is daily receiving reports that since the coming into force of the *Domestic Violence and Witnesses Act in July 2007* there has been a considerable fall-off in applications for injunctions – anecdotally because women do not wish to criminalise their partners. The Family Justice Council Domestic Violence Steering Group is urgently seeking further information/research in this issue and the reported failures of the police to act in breach cases. Women from communities governed by Izzat may well be particularly badly affected by this issue of criminalisation and a separate monitoring of the effects of the Act on them should be made.

Faith leaders are needed to educate their communities to understand that such crimes are abhorrent to God and all religions. Multi-faith DV guidance for faith leaders and communities has been developed by Northern Ireland. This should be taken forward and then extended to all other faiths as a matter of urgency. Such guides are important tools for inter alia practitioners and courts and will be vital in tackling HBV/FM.

Police need to develop and enforce best practice and training so that they protect the victims and not the perpetrators. Our police have been at the forefront of seeking to outlaw FM.

The judiciary/lawyers/other court practitioners in family/civil and criminal courts of all levels must be well trained to understand the causes and effects of honour-based crime. Protocols should be developed for dealing with these cases. Not only must they ensure that laws are enforced but also put in place measures so that the Courts are safe places which victims can access without suffering further at the hands of their oppressors. Special Measures for victims/witnesses accessing the Courts in these cases are of particular necessity.

Funding and the lack of it is a constant difficulty. NGOs are swamped and under-resourced, and receive only short-term funding making it very difficult for them to plan ahead. Many women continue to be turned away from refuges due to lack of space or them having 'no recourse to public funds'. However, many of the advances I have outlined above have come about due to changing attitudes and methods of practice and by inspired leadership from a very small number of men and women of good will and insight. Much can be achieved on small budgets, particularly if there is cooperation between agencies, countries and regions in seeking to find solutions suitable for culture and circumstances.

Consideration should be given to a national information programme including video loops in Courts, hospitals, GP surgeries, housing and social security offices and at airports. Training of airport staff including police and airline check-in staff to recognise/assist victims of FM being taken out of the country. This work has already been successfully done in the North by South Yorkshire Police Diversity Team. Development of a multi-agency risk assessment tool is needed to encompass FM/HBV and amendment of present DV protocols/strategies/training programmes to encompass these issues.

REFERENCE

Working Group on Forced Marriage (2000) *A Choice by Right*. June. London: Home Office.

RESOURCES

DVD: *Watch Over Me* (December 2004) – for more information see www.redbeemedia.com or www.missdorothy.com

USEFUL ORGANISATIONS

Forced Marriage Unit
London
Tel: 020 7008 0151
e-mail: fmu@fco.gov.uk

Karma Nirvana Refuge
Derby
Tel: 01332 604098

LIST OF CONTRIBUTORS

Alan Carter has 12 years' police service; first with Greater Manchester Police and then North Wales Police. He currently works in the Public Protection Unit, Western Division, North Wales Police as Protection of Vulnerable Adult Co-ordinator/Investigator. He was Family/Child Protection Officer from 2004 to 2007 in the Menai Bridge Family Protection Unit and Penrhyndeudraeth satellite Family Protection Unit, Western Division, North Wales Police. He had transferred to North Wales Police in July 2002 from Greater Manchester Police North Division. He had been Township Officer Prestwich Village (2000 to 2002) and General Patrol Officer Bury North Manchester, plus he had attachments to specialist units within Greater Manchester Police. He had joined Greater Manchester Police in January 1996 and was assigned to North Division during an initial two-year probationary period until confirmed in post. Between 1978 and 1996 Alan had been employed by the Greater Manchester Ambulance Service. He was a Leading Ambulance Paramedic Trainer and NHS Qualified Ambulance Training Officer (1989), Ladybridge Ambulance Regional Ambulance Training Centre, Bolton.

Teresa Gorczynska is Head of IMCA with Advocacy Partners, managing their IMCA services in ten local authorities. She has been providing non-instructed advocacy for over five years, including leading and delivering Advocacy Partners' IMCA pilot. She previously worked for Mencap in their national campaigns department, was a member of the steering group for the IMCA commissioning guidance and the Making Decisions Alliance, campaigning for the Mental Capacity Act. Teresa has a masters of law in human rights and an extensive and in-depth knowledge of the MCA and has advised and been consulted by several local authorities on their MCA policies. She has developed and presented materials on the Mental Capacity Act, IMCA, non-instructed advocacy and human rights and is regularly invited to speak and be a member of panel at MCA conferences. Teresa has published articles on IMCA, was one of the writers and trainers for the national IMCA training qualification and is currently writing the guidance on the role of IMCA in adult protection proceedings.

Rob Harris has been Director of Advocacy Experience since 2001 and has led the organisation through a period of significant growth. Prior to his current position Rob worked extensively in the advocacy sector in the areas of mental health, learning disabilities and older people, both as an advocate and a manager. His areas of special interest are in the delivery of high-quality advocacy and advocacy commissioning. Outside work Rob is a keen golfer, and an enthusiastic supporter of Manchester City Football Club, both of which he describes as frustrating hobbies! Rob lists his interests as modern architecture, professional boxing and comedy. He is married with two daughters who are currently being heavily influenced to play golf and support Manchester City.

David Hewitt is a solicitor and a partner in Weightmans Solicitors. He holds visiting fellowships at Northumbria University and Lincoln University and sits on the editorial board of the *Journal of Mental Health Law* (of which he is also an assistant editor). For nine years, David was a legal member of the Mental Health Act Commission and he now sits as a president of Mental Health Review Tribunals. He is the author of *The Nearest Relative Handbook* (Jessica Kingsley Publishers, 2007) and *A Tendency to Laugh and Sing: Some Notes on Mental Health Law* (Northumbria Law Press, 2008) as well as a number of book chapters and articles.

Adrian Hughes is a qualified social worker and is registered with the General Social Care Council. He has worked in social care settings for over 30 years and since 1993 has been involved in the regulation of care services. At the creation of the Commission for Social Care Inspection he was appointed as a business relationship manager in the south of England. He has worked as a provider and purchaser of care services and as a training officer working in both the public and independent sector. These roles have enabled him to value the unique contribution training has on quality and safe services for people whose circumstances sometimes increase their vulnerability.

Glyn Hughes has been a police officer for over 25 years – serving first with Essex Police and transferring to Lincolnshire Police in the late 1980s. For the last 11 or so years he has been an investigator of child and adult abuse, the Force's Public Protection Unit trainer, and most recently a central referral unit coordinator for abuse cases located with Lincolnshire County Council's Customer Service Centre.

Steve Kirkpatrick is the chief executive of a charitable care provider and associate member of the Chartered Management Institute. Prior to this Steve was a detective inspector in the Thames Valley Police, retiring after completing 30 years' service. Steve worked in partnership with the multi-agencies in major crime investigations, child and vulnerable adult abuse investigations, and in general child and adult protection work. He has also been involved in the local and national training of police, social services, education, health, crown prosecutors and other professionals and sat on the Berkshire working group that produced the inter-agency procedures and guidelines for adult protection in January 1997.

Simon Leslie is a solicitor with the Joint Legal Team in Berkshire. Based in Reading, the team provide legal advice and representation to children's and adult social care in a consortium of local authorities in Berkshire. Professional interests include mental health and mental capacity, consent to treatment, and information-sharing. Simon has taken a particular interest in the legal aspects of adult protection for a number of years and contributed a chapter to *Elder Abuse Work: Best Practice in Britain and Canada* (Jessica Kingsley Publishers 1999). Simon spends his leisure time ferrying two children to birthday parties and standing on rugby touch lines in the rain.

Penny Letts is a policy consultant and trainer, specialising in legal issues relating to mental health and capacity. She was Specialist Adviser to the Joint Parliamentary Scrutiny Committee on the Draft Mental Incapacity Bill; and prepared a major part of the Code of Practice on the Mental Capacity Act 2005. Penny was Policy Adviser on Mental Health and Disability at the Law Society, 1987–2001, and a Mental Health Act Commissioner, 1995–2004; she is currently a member of the Administrative Justice and Tribunals Council. Penny has published widely on mental health and capacity issues – she is a contributor to *Mental Capacity: The New Law* (Jordans, 2006) and the Law Society/BMA guidance on *Assessment of Mental Capacity* (BMJ Books, 2004).

Kathryn Mackay qualified in social work in 1984 and has worked both in England and Scotland. Most of her practice experience has been with local authorities in community care and mental health. She was a mental health officer (ASW equivalent) and community care team manager before joining the University of Stirling as a teaching fellow in social work in 1997 with responsibilities on community care courses as well as the qualifying programme. She became a lecturer in social work in 2004 to pursue research and writing as well as teaching in community care law, policy and practice.

Geraldine Monaghan is a qualified, GSCC registered social worker who has 30 years' experience working in local authority social work. She has worked extensively with children and families and latterly with vulnerable adults. She has a good deal of court experience and considerable experience of major joint (police/social services) investigations, where her role has been to manage the social work input. Geraldine is currently the Investigations Manager in the Investigations Support Unit (ISU), a small unit within Liverpool's Community Safety Service, which works closely with police and other partners to support investigations into the abuse of both vulnerable adults and children, when that abuse has forensic elements which lie outside mainstream safeguarding procedures. The unit provides witness support before and during any court proceedings arising from investigation. Geraldine, together with Mark Pathak, has developed the 'Liverpool Model of Witness Support, Preparation and Profiling'.

Marilyn Mornington LLB (HONS) SHEFF; FWAAS; FRSA. As well as working as a district judge in Barnsley, Marilyn is a member of ACPO Domestic Violence and Honour-Based Violence Steering Groups; member of the Family Justice Council and Chair of the Domestic Violence Working Group; Founder and Chair of the Inter-Jurisdictional Governmental Domestic Violence Initiative 'Raising the Standards'; and Patron of the Community District Nurses' Association. She is a lecturer and writer on family law and, in particular, domestic violence and elder abuse – nationally and internationally. During 2007 Marilyn lectured at the London School of Economics, the Commonwealth Institute, Sheffield University, Punjab Law School, and Cranfield Defence College.

Mark Pathak is a qualified, GSCC-registered social worker, who has worked in social care settings for people with learning disabilities for over 23 years in both England and the USA. He has specialised in the area of challenging behaviour, with particular regard to relationships. This includes work for Liverpool Health Authority, developing programmes to address challenging behaviours which had a significant sexual component. In 1996 he was seconded by Liverpool Social Services Directorate to assist a large-scale joint investigation (police and social services) into historical abuse in children's homes. Since 1998 Mark has worked within the Investigations Support Unit of Liverpool City Council where, along with Geraldine Monaghan, he developed the 'Liverpool Model of Witness Support, Preparation and Profiling'. Outside work he has been a trustee and then Director of People First (Merseyside), a self-advocacy group for adults with a learning disability, for over ten years.

Jacki Pritchard practises as an independent social worker and is registered with the General Social Care Council. She is director of the company Jacki Pritchard Ltd which provides training, consultancy and research in social care and also produces training materials. Jacki specialises in working directly with victims of abuse and was the founder of the organisation Beyond Existing, Support Groups for Adults Who Have Been Abused. She is currently working on the research project 'The Abuse of Vulnerable Adults: Services for Victims of Abuse' and is also the Independent Chairperson for the Lincolnshire Safeguarding Adults Board. Jacki has written widely on the subject of adult protection and been Series Editor of the Good Practice Series, Jessica Kingsley Publishers, for the past 15 years.

Peter Sadler qualified as a registered nurse in the field of learning disability in November 1982. He has worked both within National Health and social services settings, working with vulnerable adults in residential services, day services and community support services. Peter has a wide range of experience within operational management, strategic planning and development. He has been interested in the adult protection/safeguarding agenda from the early 1990s and has been directly involved in the safeguarding agenda within Lincolnshire and regional forums since 2001, when he was the first project manager supporting the Lincolnshire Adult Protection Committee in developing Lincolnshire's first multi-agency policy post *No Secrets*. Peter presents at workshops and conferences within Lincolnshire and also enjoys leading training and development workshops.

Kathryn Stone is Chief Executive of Voice UK, a national charity promoting justice for vulnerable adults. Kathryn is a registered social worker and has experience of child protection, mental health social work and training. She was formerly Head of Inspection for two London boroughs and a metropolitan borough council. Kathryn is a member of the Bar Council Liaison Group for Victims, and the Home Office Ministerial Victims' Advisory Panel. Her interests in this context are violence against women and sex crime. She is also part of Do The Right Thing – an organisation promoting innovation (such as the use of the creative arts) in working with victims, survivors and child witnesses of domestic violence. Kathryn also chairs the CPS Direct Hate Crime Scrutiny Panel and is a member of the Home Office Race For Justice Hate Crime steering group.

SUBJECT INDEX

AUTHOR INDEX

Lightning Source UK Ltd.
Milton Keynes UK
UKOW041954240612

195002UK00001B/3/P